VISUAL QUICKSTART GUIDE

CUBASE SX 2

FOR WINDOWS AND MACINTOSH

Thad Brown

Peachpit Press

Visual QuickStart Guide
Cubase SX 2 for Windows and Macintosh
Thad Brown

Peachpit Press
1249 Eighth Street
Berkeley, CA 94710
510/524-2178
800/283-9444
510/524-2221 (fax)

Find us on the World Wide Web at: http://www.peachpit.com
To report errors, please send a note to errata@peachpit.com
Peachpit Press is a division of Pearson Education

Copyright © 2004 by Thad Brown

Editor: Cary Norsworthy
Production Editor: Lisa Brazieal
Copyeditor: Judy Ziajka
Compositor: Christi Payne
Indexer: Joy Dean Lee
Proofreader: Leona Benten
Cover design: The Visual Group
Cover production: George Mattingly / GMD

Notice of rights
All rights reserved. No part of this book may be reproduced or transmitted in any form by any means, electronic, mechanical, photocopying, recording, or otherwise, without the prior written permission of the publisher. For information on getting permission for reprints and excerpts, contact permissions@peachpit.com.

Notice of liability
The information in this book is distributed on an "As Is" basis, without warranty. While every precaution has been taken in the preparation of the book, neither the author nor Peachpit Press, shall have any liability to any person or entity with respect to any loss or damage caused or alleged to be caused directly or indirectly by the instructions contained in this book or by the computer software and hardware products described in it.

For information on music rights to the companion song in Appendix B, contact john@magnatune.com or see their web site: www.magnatune.com.

Trademarks
Visual QuickStart Guide is a registered trademark of Peachpit Press, a division of Pearson Education. Throughout this book, trademarks are used. Rather than put a trademark symbol in every occurrence of a trademarked name, we state that we are using the names in an editorial fashion only and to the benefit of the trademark owner with no intention of infringement of the trademark.

ISBN 0-321-24643-8

9 8 7 6 5 4 3 2 1

Printed and bound in the United States of America

Dedication

For my parents, who from my earliest memories taught me to love words and music in equal measure.

Acknowledgements

Good editors are as hard to find as good drummers, and for this book I was lucky enough to work, yet again, with Cary Norsworthy. If this book helps you, particularly if you are new to computer music, you should thank Cary. Thanks also to David Leishman for technical advice, and Judy Ziajka for working over my copy.

Rusty Cutchin was my editor at Home Recording Magazine, and while that magazine has folded, I owe special appreciation to Rusty for the work he gave me putting HR on newsstands. Vielen Dank to Stephan M. Sprenger and the rest of crazy Germans at Prosoniq who taught me volumes about software and development. Thanks also to Mary Tyler for getting new music to my ears, year after year, disc after disc. Levin Pfeufer earns special appreciation for the multiple, shape-shifting roles he played helping me with this book. He not only did the groovy illustrations, he also taught me survival InDesign skills and kept me fully loaded with dancehall mixes from the Canal Street Selector. Big up Lev!

As an American, I am almost genetically predisposed against state-owned media. Over the past year, this disposition has been sorely tested by the BBC digital radio station 1xtra. It's shameful that the corporate media in my country provides less variety and lower-quality music than does UK state owned media. I spent many of the hours revising this book for Cubase SX 2 listening to www.bbc.co.uk/1xtra, and I would like to give personal thanks Robbo Ranx, DJ Flight, Silver Star, L Double, Punjabi Hit Squad, Aaron Ross, Bailey, Femme Fatale, and Heartless Crew for keeping me company.

TABLE OF CONTENTS

Chapter 9: Advanced Audio Editing 185

Chapter 10: Editing MIDI 215

INSTALLING & CONFIGURING CUBASE SX 2

As recently as a few years ago, only very brave and very experienced people dared attempt to set up a computer as a serious music-recording platform. Beginners spent days or weeks slogging to get hardware and software to work together, while power users spent incredible amounts of time tweaking their computer configurations to squeeze a tiny bit of extra performance from their machines.

While it's certainly easier to set up a digital recording studio now than it was a few years ago, smart Cubase users will still want to learn more about how the program is installed and configured. In this chapter, you will discover how to install the Cubase SX 2 hardware and software, learn a bit about tweaks and tricks you can use to get solid audio performance, find out about the types of audio cards and MIDI interfaces that Cubase supports, and learn about monitoring as you record.

Most parts of this book apply equally to most users, because Cubase works about the same for everyone. However, hardware and software setup and configuration involve many variables, and specific details will differ from user to user. This is one of the unfortunate realities of getting multiple pieces of fairly complex audio hardware working together.

Installing Cubase SX 2

The Cubase SX 2 box contains the basic documentation, the installation CDs, a USB hardware copy-protection dongle, and various other pieces of paper relating to product registration, special offers, and sound files (**Figure 1.1**).

The USB hardware dongle prevents unauthorized use of the Cubase program. Over the years, software companies have used various tools to prevent software piracy. The USB dongle (like all anti-piracy tools) has its strengths and weaknesses. The good news about the dongle is that you can move it easily from machine to machine, so if you have both laptop and desktop systems, you can install Cubase SX 2 on all your machines and just plug the dongle into the one you are using at the moment to authorize it. The bad news, of course, is that if you lose or break the dongle, you can't run the program until you buy another from Steinberg, and it could cost you up to $200.

On both the PC and Mac versions of Cubase SX, you should run the installer on the CD-ROM without the dongle attached. However, once the program is installed on your hard drive, it won't run unless you have the USB dongle attached, and it will prompt you to attach the dongle if you've forgotten.

Once you've installed Cubase, you can access updates from Steinberg. As of this writing, Steinberg has released downloadable updates for both the Mac and PC versions of Cubase SX 2. To access updates, you can go to www.steinberg.net or use the help menu from within Cubase. Selecting the option in **Figure 1.2** will open your Web browser and take you to the download page on the Steinberg Web site.

Figure 1.1 In addition to the software CD and documentation, the Cubase box contains a USB dongle. The program will not work without it.

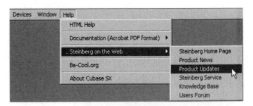

Figure 1.2 This menu provides a quick and easy way to get Cubase information and help, and it includes a direct link to the Product Updates Web page.

A Note about Updates

Before you install an update, always read the Read Me files and check the Cubase user forums at http://forum.cubase.net in case there are issues with the updates. For example, as of this writing, Mac users should drag their original copy of the Magneto plug-in out of their plug-ins folder before installing the 2.01 update, or else the plug-in will be overwritten by a newer version that doesn't work. After installing the update, drag the old copy of the Magneto plug-in back into the plug-ins folder.

What Goes Where?

If you accept the default installation options and you're using a PC, Cubase will be installed in C:\Program Files\Steinberg\Cubase SX, and this is where you will find most of the Cubase-related files you will ever need to see. If you want, you can install Cubase in a different directory, but I strongly recommend sticking to the defaults. This may reduce the risk of problems if you use Cubase in conjunction with other applications.

If you use a Mac, some of the files are scattered on your system, but the main application will be stored in ~/Library/Preferences/Cubase SX. (A quick search on "Cubase" will reveal other file locations.) I recommend adding the Cubase application to the Dock by dragging it there.

PC users have an additional file-location option. Because you may have many applications using many different audio plug-ins and software instruments, to keep your files organized, you can set one folder as the place where all of these plug-ins reside and where multiple applications can access them. (On the Mac, third-party plug-ins are located in Users/(username)/Library/Audio/Plug-Ins/VST, or in Drive/Library/Audio/Plug-Ins/VST.)

To select a shared plug-ins folder on a PC:

1. From the Devices menu, select Plug-in Information (**Figure 1.3**).

   At the top of the window that opens, the file path appears in the Shared VST Plug-ins Folder field.

2. Click the Change button to the right of the path name (**Figure 1.4**).

3. When the Select Directory file navigation box opens, select the folder you want to use for common plug-ins (**Figure 1.5**).

4. Click OK in the dialog box to save your settings and close the dialog box. Close the Plug-in Information panel as well.

Figure 1.3 Click to open the panel to configure and manage Cubase plug-ins.

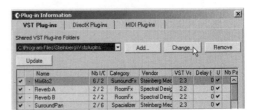

Figure 1.4 Click the Change button to set a new plug-ins folder.

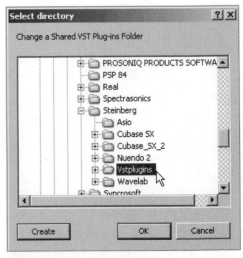

Figure 1.5 Selecting a folder for shared plug-ins.

Audio Versus MIDI

Recorded audio and MIDI are fundamentally different. Each is the best option in particular situations, and neither is universally better.

The goal of recorded audio is to capture and store a sound for future playback with as much fidelity to the original sound as possible. Over the years, audio has been recorded on wax discs, magnetic tape, cassettes, hard-disk recorders, digital tape decks, and computers. When live music is digitized, the analog sound path includes a microphone or line-level sound generator (voice or acoustic or electric instrument); it also can include an external sound modifier (such as a hardware reverb unit), and it generally is routed through a mixer. The sound can be converted to digital data either inside or outside the computer and then stored as bits on your hard drive.

Whatever the source, the whole point of an audio recording is to store the sound and play it back so that it sounds as much like the original as possible. Audio recordings by nature capture the tempo, duration, pitch, and timbre of whatever is being recorded. After the audio is converted to digital, it is comparatively difficult to change any of these values in a significant way after a recording is finished.

MIDI, in contrast, does not record acoustic events, but instead records data and instructions from a musical performance, most often from a keyboard. This data is not limited to a particular instrument, sound, tempo, or duration. When a sequencer like Cubase records MIDI data, it actually records something like this: "at bar 34, beat 2, play an A# that lasts until bar 34, beat 3." Normal MIDI recording also records the velocity of MIDI notes (how hard the key is struck), how much pressure is applied to a key as it is held down (the aftertouch), and how quickly the note is released.

Because MIDI records data, it provides a level of flexibility that recorded audio does not have. For example, if you record the audio output of a synthesizer playing a piano sound and store that in Cubase, you will pretty much have to use that sound as it is recorded. However, if instead you record only the MIDI information generated by your performance in Cubase, you can then send this MIDI data to any other MIDI device and select any patch you want to trigger the sound of a clavinet, organ, drums, flute, or whatever you dream up.

Because MIDI is recorded purely in reference to tempo and is easily transposed, a MIDI recording will automatically and transparently follow changes to the tempo and key of a project. After recording your MIDI performance, you can seamlessly change its characteristics; if you decide that the track sounds better five beats per minute faster or that a singer needs an arrangement that's three semitones lower, you can speed up the track or transpose it via a few clicks, with no loss in sound quality.

Neither MIDI nor recorded audio is "better," and both are used in almost every kind of music production. The smart musician uses each in its place, and a big part of what makes Cubase SX 2 so powerful is that it has extremely advanced audio recording and editing capabilities in the same window as a top-quality MIDI sequencer. Everything's there, and you should use as much of it as you need.

Recording Essentials

Cubase SX 2 enables you to perform the entire process of music production with a computer—you can record, play, mix, process, add effects, and master audio in pretty much any way you can imagine. However, you will almost certainly need more than just the application and a computer to make music. Here is a list of equipment you may need for your Cubase studio:

Figure 1.6 Some of the equipment you will likely use with your computer and Cubase.

♦ **Sound card** or **audio interface:** To record audio, you need a way to get it into the computer. Most, but not all, PCs ship with some kind of SoundBlaster-style sound card, and most, but not all, Macs have at least 1/8-inch minijacks for audio output (and usually for input).The new Power Mac G5s and many PCs also offer digital inputs and outputs that employ S/PDIF using optical cable and TOSLINK connectors. Digital inputs and outputs can be very useful if you happen to have access to a good external digital-to-analog converter and need only stereo recording and playback. If you plan to record or monitor more than stereo tracks, though, you almost certainly will want to upgrade to a higher-quality audio interface. The upgrade may be an internal PCI card or an external converter that routes data to a FireWire or USB port on the computer (**Figure 1.6**).

♦ **MIDI interface:** If you plan to do any work with external synthesizers, samplers, or controllers, or if you plan to record MIDI data to Cubase, you will need an interface to connect your MIDI hardware to your computer. Most MIDI interfaces these days use USB for the connection.

◆ **Monitoring setup:** Audio people refer to listening to a track or a mix as *monitoring*, so speakers are referred to as monitors. Most monitoring is done with near-field monitors: two speakers located a few feet away and pointed right at the spot where you sit when you mix. Headphones are not great for monitoring mixes, but they are indispensable for use in recording live musicians, enabling the performers to hear individualized mixes of the arrangement.

◆ **External mixer:** An external mixer will be handy if you plan to work with a large number of microphones or electric instruments or with external synths and samplers, all playing at the same time, or if you just want some extra inputs and convenience. Even small 12-input models that cost only a few hundred dollars can help a lot.

Of course, if you intend to record live instruments or hardware synths and samplers, you will need microphones, cables, and microphone preamps. There are many books written specifically about those topics, along with newsgroups and Web sites bursting with people ready to share their opinions and experiences.

RECORDING ESSENTIALS

Audio Interfaces and Drivers

Both Macs and PCs have system-level drivers for audio cards. They work fairly well for most people, but they don't always meet the needs of high-end users. If you are using Cubase SX 2, you're probably a high-end user, and you will want to get a card with an ASIO driver for use with Cubase. You can use only three kinds of sound-card drivers with Cubase, and if at all possible, you should use the ASIO driver for your card.

◆ **ASIO** stands for Audio Stream In/Out, and it's the driver model created by Steinberg many years ago. At that time, system-level audio drivers were severely limited in the number of channels of audio they could play and record simultaneously, and they were also limited in the sound quality of those channels.

◆ **DirectSound**, or **WDM**, is the most recent type of driver created by Microsoft for Windows multimedia. WDM drivers are quite good these days (earlier versions of DirectSound drivers were sometimes a horror show), but Cubase still works best with ASIO drivers, and you should use them if possible.

◆ **Core Audio** is the new system-level audio and multimedia specification for Mac OS X. More and more manufacturers are providing Core Audio drivers for their audio interfaces. When you select an ASIO driver in the Cubase control panels for audio cards, Cubase actually "talks" to the hardware via Core Audio. Because of this, any audio interface with Core Audio drivers should work correctly with Cubase SX 2.

Figure 1.7 You open the Windows System control panel by double-clicking this icon.

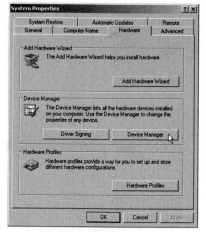

Figure 1.8 Opening the Device Manager from the Hardware tab.

Figure 1.9 The Device Manager has a list of all installed hardware, including audio and MIDI interfaces.

Checking the Windows XP Sound Card

After you have physically installed your sound card, but before you set it up for use in Cubase, you should check that it's installed properly so that Windows sees it. The easiest way to do this is through the Device Manager.

To confirm a working sound card in Windows XP:

1. From the Start menu, select Settings > Control Panel.

2. Double-click System (**Figure 1.7**) to open the System Properties panel.

3. Click the Hardware tab to display it.

4. In the Device Manager section of the Hardware tab, click the Device Manager button (**Figure 1.8**).

5. Click the small + symbol next to Sound, Video and Game Controllers to expand the list.

   Your sound card should be listed here (**Figure 1.9**). If it is not, or if it is covered with a red X, then there is a problem with the installation, and you should check the documentation that came with your sound card or try reinstalling it.

✔ Tips

- If you are using a PCMCIA card on a laptop, you may need to look under that item in Device Manager.

- If you are using a FireWire or USB interface, you may need to look in those sections of the Device Manager.

CHECKING THE WINDOWS XP SOUND CARD

What Makes a Good Sound Card?

Having the right sound card for your needs can make your recording and mixing experience a delight, and the wrong one can pretty much ensure that you'll hate turning on your music computer. You need to answer three questions before you choose a sound card.

First, how many inputs and outputs do you need? Note that the question is not how many could you possibly ever use if your band gets a major label record deal. If that happens, you can buy another sound card. In day-to-day use, though, how many inputs and outputs (usually called I/O) will you really need? If you are recording full bands, 8 inputs is the absolute minimum, and realistically you should shoot for at least 16. If you mostly sequence and overdub on your own, 4 or 8 I/Os may be plenty. If you are a DJ or samplehead, 4 I/Os, or even a stereo setup, may be enough.

The second question you need to ask is whether you should get a PCI card or a USB or FireWire audio interface. PCI cards have long been the high-end approach to audio interfaces. The PCI bus in a computer can handle many tracks of audio and MIDI, and the PCI specification has been around forever. The downside of PCI cards is that they are comparatively hard to install (you'll have to open the computer case) and inconvenient to move to another computer. In addition, some newer Macs have moved to a slightly different version of the PCI card spec, and older PCI cards will not work in them. Check whether your Mac uses PCI-X (the newer PCI cards) before buying a PCI audio interface.

USB (which stands for universal serial bus) audio interfaces are plugged into the USB ports that come on every computer built in the past few years. USB hardware is very convenient; it's easy to use and easy to move to another computer. You can even hot plug (plug the interface in with the computer already on) a USB audio interface. The problem with the original USB spec (usually called USB 1.1) is that because of the low bandwidth of the bus itself, you will almost always be limited to stereo input and output plus MIDI. That may be enough for you, and if it is, then you can buy a nice USB interface for very little money. Newer USB audio interfaces using the USB 2 specification are many times faster than USB 1.1 interfaces. In fact, they are close in performance to FireWire interfaces. You may find that a USB 2.0 audio interface can do enough for you to make it a viable choice.

FireWire is, in many ways, similar to USB; you can hot plug FireWire audio interfaces, and they are very convenient and easy to work with. FireWire, though, has a huge bandwidth advantage over USB 1.1 and can manage many more tracks at very low latencies. FireWire has worked well on Macs for awhile, and Windows XP has high-quality support built in for FireWire devices. FireWire audio, though, has lagged a bit on Windows machines because of drivers. Two companies with significant experience in the PC audio interface world, MIDI-MAN and Ego Systems, will probably have made FireWire a more viable option for the PC by the time you read this.

You also need to find out whether the sound card that fits your needs will work reliably with your computer. The sad fact is that not every computer works with every sound card, and the doubly sad fact is that the only way to really find out what works with what is to do research,

Checking the Mac OS X Sound Card

You can easily check Mac OS X to verify that your sound card is properly installed and that the operating system has loaded the proper drivers to use it. Your exact setup will not likely be like mine, but it should be fairly close. The following example will work if your audio interface has a control panel in the Mac OS X System Preferences panel; not all will, and if your card does not, there are two places to look. First, check the documentation that came with the audio interface for further information related to the location of the device's control panel. Second, use the OS X Audio MIDI Setup utility, which is described in relation to MIDI interfaces a few pages ahead in this chapter in the section "Checking the Mac OS X MIDI Interface." You can use the Audio MIDI Setup utility to view and configure both audio and MIDI hardware.

What Makes a Good Sound Card?

talk about your hardware setups and find out whether other people with a computer setup like yours have been happy using the sound card you are thinking of using. (Steinberg hosts a site for users to share their experiences—both good and bad—at www.steinberg.net/en/ps/support/forums. Use the Search function to find posts or threads on the cards you're interested in checking out.) Many hardware manufacturers also host mailing lists or newsgroups related to their hardware. I use an RME sound card, and the RME newsgroup has helped me keep my system working well.

The third question to consider is whether you have any specific and unique needs. Do you need digital I/O? Do you need microphone preamps or some kind of on-board synthesis or sampling capability? Do you collaborate with someone else who has a particular system that would be good for you to mirror? No two computer audio users are alike, and your setup may have a few quirks that influence your choice of sound card.

Once you've answered these three questions, you'll know the key options to look for in a sound card. Before you buy, check a variety of local dealers and online music retailers' sites to find the specs of cards that will fit your needs. It's also a good idea to check the return and exchange policies of the vendor from whom you buy your gear.

To confirm a working sound card in Mac OS X:

1. In the dock, click the System Preferences icon (**Figure 1.10**).

2. In the System Preferences panel that opens, look for the control panel for your sound card (**Figure 1.11**). There's a good chance it will be in the Other section at the bottom of the panel, as in Figure 1.10, which shows the USB audio interface.

3. Click the icon for your sound card to open its control panel (**Figure 1.12**). Try changing any parameter to be sure that the operating system and the hardware are communicating.

✔ Tip

■ You can also check the Sound preferences pane in System Preferences. Your sound card should be available for general system audio use.

Figure 1.10 Click to open the Mac OS System Preferences in the Dock.

Figure 1.11 Some of the preferences, including a USB audio interface (at the bottom of the window).

Figure 1.12 The OS X control panel for one audio interface.

Figure 1.13 Every digital audio system, including a computer, needs some time to perform analog-to-digital and digital-to-analog conversion.

What's a Millisecond?

It's possible to be *too* concerned about latency. The generally quoted speed of sound is 1,100 feet per second. That number changes with temperature, humidity, and altitude, but it's the standard reference. With 1,000 milliseconds in a second, this means that sound travels pretty close to one foot every millisecond. In other words, if you move your speakers a foot away from the listening position, you introduce about a millisecond of latency into your system.

This is not to say that latency doesn't matter; it does, and for some people, it's a crucial factor. If you plan to record with software synths and samplers, for instance, you need to be much more concerned about the latency between what you play and what you hear. DJs and sampleheads probably don't need to worry much at all, because they are accustomed to working with external mixing, cueing, and monitoring. If you are having problems with sound card latency, read the sections in this chapter about external monitoring, or consider investing in a new sound card.

Latency Defined

If you have done any work with audio on computers before, you have probably heard the term *latency*. If you haven't heard it yet, you'll be hearing it often now. A dictionary definition of latency is "the time that elapses between a stimulus and the response to it." In the computer world, latency generally refers to the time that elapses between the request for an action and the completion of the action.

For computer audio users, though, latency is used to refer specifically to sound card latency: the time the sound card takes to convert what you're recording into digital data and move the data to your hard drive, or the time needed to convert the stored data back to analog audio for output (**Figure 1.13**). Audio latency is of critical importance. If you are playing along with previously recorded material and there's a half-second lag between what you hear playing back and what you are recording, your new material will not play back in time with the old.

Latency is affected by a huge number of factors, including the speed of the computer, the quality of its chipset, the limitations of the sound card or hardware, and the amount of time a signal takes to pass among these components. But the most important factor in achieving low-latency, high-reliability audio recording is a good software driver for your sound card.

Setting Latency

Naturally, you want the lowest latency settings possible for your sound card. The only way to find the best settings is trial and error: setting the latency value lower and lower until the computer introduces clicks and pops and dropouts or excessive static into the audio. Keep in mind that there is also an insurmountable trade-off between lower latency and higher CPU use. These days, you can usually use the most aggressive latency settings because CPUs are so powerful, but if you seem to be surprisingly short on CPU bandwidth, consider bumping up your latency setting by a few milliseconds.

To set the latency for your sound card:

1. From the Devices menu in Cubase, select Device Setup.

2. In the panel that opens, select VST Multitrack (**Figure 1.14**).

3. Click the Control Panel button (**Figure 1.15**).

    The window for configuring your sound card settings opens (**Figure 1.16**).

4. Set the sound card latency in the sound card control panel and click OK to close the panel.

5. Click OK in the Cubase Device Setup panel to commit the changes to your Cubase setup.

✔ Tip

■ Not every audio interface will respond correctly and open from the VST Multitrack section of the Device Setup panel. You may have to exit Cubase and configure the card with its own control panel. If the steps described here don't work, check the documentation that came with your sound card.

Figure 1.14 Selecting VST Multitrack in the Devices panel.

Figure 1.15 Click to open the control panel for the currently selected audio interface.

Figure 1.16 The control panel is set to 3 milliseconds of latency. The control panel for your card will probably be different, but it should have options for setting latency.

Figure 1.17 The Hardware tab of the Sounds and Audio Devices Properties panel.

Figure 1.18 To check system-level MIDI, select the sound card or interface and click Properties.

Checking the Windows XP MIDI Interface

A few pages back, you learned how to be sure that your sound card is working under Windows and that it is available for use with Cubase SX 2. Similarly, with MIDI interfaces, you want to be sure the interface is installed and available in Windows before you configure it in Cubase.

To confirm a working MIDI interface in Windows XP:

1. From the Start menu, select Settings > Control Panel.

2. In the control panel, double-click Sounds and Audio Devices.

3. In the Sounds and Audio Devices Properties panel, click the Hardware tab to display it (**Figure 1.17**).

4. In the list of installed hardware, you should see the MIDI interface, or the name of your sound card. Select it and then click Properties (**Figure 1.18**).

5. In the panel that opens, click the Properties tab.

continues on next page

6. Click the small plus (+) sign to the left of the MIDI Devices and Instruments option to expand the list and see the installed MIDI interfaces (**Figure 1.19**).

7. If your MIDI interface is listed here, click Cancel to close the Properties window and then click Cancel to close the Sounds and Audio Devices Properties panel. All is well.

✔ Tip

■ If your MIDI interface is not visible in these panels, something is wrong at the system level. Try reinstalling the interface or check the documentation that came with the interface to see what you may need to do to get everything working correctly.

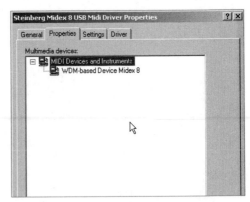

Figure 1.19 This list shows active, working MIDI interfaces.

Figure 1.20 The Audio MIDI Setup utility is in the Utilities folder of the OS X Applications folder.

Figure 1.21 The MIDI Devices tab shows all installed MIDI interfaces—in this case, a Steinberg MidEx8.

Checking the Mac OS X MIDI Interface

Every MIDI device you use on a Mac needs to be recognized at the system level, so you should check that the operating system sees the hardware before you try to use it in Cubase. To do this, you use the very convenient Mac OS X Audio MIDI Setup utility.

To confirm a working MIDI interface in Mac OS X:

1. Open the Mac OS X Finder and click Applications on the top toolbar.

2. Double-click the Utilities folder to open it.

3. Double-click the icon for the Audio MIDI Setup utility (**Figure 1.20**).

4. In the Audio MIDI Setup window, click the MIDI Devices tab (**Figure 1.21**).

   All installed MIDI devices will be visible in this window. If your MIDI interface is not shown here, you need to consult its documentation regarding installation procedures and check the company's Web site to make sure you have the correct driver installed.

✔ Tip

■ When you have a moment, check out the other options (for both audio and MIDI hardware) that can be configured with the Audio MIDI Setup utility. You will find this utility very useful in your music production work on your Mac.

What Is Monitoring?

In the world of audio, *monitoring* is the term used to describe various ways to hear recorded and live sounds. When musicians talk with recording engineers about monitoring, they generally mean being able to hear a mix of a previously recorded song so they can play along with it. On stage, monitors are the speakers sitting on the floor in front the band. Singers often have a mix with lots of their own vocals in those monitors so they can hear themselves above the rest of the band.

When recording in a studio, roughly similar setups apply. The musicians usually monitor through headphones to hear themselves without creating extra noise in the recording space. The person in charge of the mixing board and who runs the recording session monitors through speakers in the control room (**Figure 1.22**).

When you start recording with Cubase, you will also need some means of monitoring. If you record other musicians, you may need headphone amplifiers and an outboard mixer (**Figure 1.23**). If you record only yourself playing instruments or singing, you may need only headphones (**Figure 1.24**). No matter what method you use, though, you will have to make some decisions about monitoring, and they all involve problems with latency. Monitoring is complicated because every digital system has latency, which means that some traditional monitoring systems may not work well.

The following few pages provide examples of three ways to monitor: through Cubase, through an external mixer, and using ASIO direct monitoring. Each example assumes that you are playing a bass line to go with a drum loop. To simplify matters, these examples also assume that you're using a sound card for your sound conversion.

Figure 1.22 You can monitor with headphones, speakers, or both depending on the situation.

Figure 1.23 External monitoring avoids latency problems but involves more effort in routing audio. You probably will use some kind of external monitoring most of the time.

Figure 1.24 Monitoring through Cubase is simple and convenient but may create problems if your audio interface has high latency.

Monitoring Through Cubase SX 2

The simplest way to monitor is through Cubase, but it's the method with the most potential latency problems. For example, as your drum loop plays, you play along on your bass. The signal goes from the bass through a preamp to shape the tone and raise the level, and then it goes to the sound card on your computer. The sound card converts the analog signal to digital data, and Cubase records what you play. Cubase also plays back what you are playing through the main outputs so you can hear it.

Let's say the lowest latency at which your sound card will work reliably is 18 milliseconds. This means that when you pluck the bass string, it takes 18 milliseconds for the sound card to get the digital signal into Cubase, and then 18 more milliseconds to get the sound back to the outputs from which you are monitoring it. In other words, you will hear yourself playing the bass 36 milliseconds later than if you were just playing live through an amplifier. That might not seem like much, but in practice it's way too high for a good performance, because the two sounds will play back at slightly different times.

What this means is that you should monitor this way only if you have a very high-quality sound card that operates at very low latency (less than 10 milliseconds). As this is written, the very best sound cards can operate with latency as low as 1.5 milliseconds.

Monitoring Using an External Mixer

One of the more common ways to get around the latency problem is to use an external hardware mixer to route and monitor signals. In the scenario in the preceding section, outputs from Cubase and the computer or sound card would be plugged into the hardware mixer and would play back the drum loop. Your bass would be plugged into a preamp to boost the level and shape the tone, and it would also be plugged into the mixer. As you play along with the drum loop, the bass would be routed to one of the inputs of your sound card, which would convert the audio signal to digital data for Cubase to record. You would monitor the bass only with the hardware mixer while Cubase records it.

The advantage here is that there is no latency at all. The downside is that you can't hear any Cubase EQ or effects on the track you're recording, and it takes a little more effort to set things up. However, in general, I recommend that people use external monitoring if at all possible.

External monitoring is also often accomplished using the software mixer that comes with your sound card. Capabilities will vary from system to system and card to card, but look at the documentation that came with your sound card. You may have a software mixer with a control panel that lets you route inputs on your sound card directly to another output for monitoring while Cubase records the track.

The setup for external monitoring can take a bit of effort, but zero-latency monitoring makes it worth the trouble. I use a combination of an external mixer and the very full-featured software mixer that came with my sound card.

Figure 1.25 Click the check box to turn ASIO Direct Monitoring on or off.

Monitoring Using ASIO Direct Monitoring

Cubase includes an enhanced external monitoring function called ASIO direct monitoring. In practice, it offers the same features as a sound card control panel for routing sound card inputs to outputs for monitoring purposes, but it is integrated into Cubase.

Not all ASIO cards support ASIO direct monitoring, and those that do provide varying degrees of control. Some simply route hardware inputs to another output, while others include options for volume and pan to give you more choices for monitoring. The only way to be sure what you can do with ASIO direct monitoring is to try it.

To use ASIO direct monitoring:

1. From the Devices menu, select Device Setup.

2. In the Device Setup panel that opens, select VST Multitrack.

3. With VST Multitrack displayed at the right of the panel, click Direct Monitoring to activate it.

   A check mark appears in the Direct Monitoring check box when this option is on (**Figure 1.25**). If this option is dimmed, your sound card does not support ASIO direct monitoring

4. Click OK to exit the Device Setup panel.

   The features offered by your sound card in direct monitoring mode will vary depending on the card. Check the documentation that came with the card to get more information about these options.

Your Setup

Getting all of your hardware and software components talking to each other is usually the most difficult and frustrating part of making music with computers. Every setup is different, so every troubleshooting situation is different. If you're having problems, the first place to look is the documentation that came with your hardware, to ensure that you've hooked up all your cables and set all your switches correctly. Then check the system-level setup on your computer. If your audio interface isn't working in Cubase, try just playing back a CD through your interface. If you can't get MIDI input, import a MIDI file into Cubase and try playing it to determine whether you're getting MIDI output. You can also use the tutorial files that come with the application to test these systems.

You'll find a lot more information about selecting inputs and outputs and getting sound and MIDI in and out of Cubase in Chapter 4, "Recording Audio," and Chapter 5, "Recording MIDI." And don't forget those Cubase-related Web sites; if you have a question, they may have the specific answer you need. For starters, check out the Steinberg Cubase forum on the Web at http://forum.cubase.net.

Known Mac Glitch

Some Mac users have experienced difficulty getting audio out of Cubase SX 2 when they've installed it on a system running OS 10.3 (Panther). This affects those who use the internal Mac audio hardware and who aren't using an audio interface. If this is happening to you, try opening the Device Setup dialog box and select VST Multitrack from the Devices list. Then, under the Setup tab in this dialog box, click on the ASIO Driver field. By default, it should say "Built-in Audio," which is correct. However, sometimes this option needs to be reselected. When you click on the ASIO Driver field, a dialog box will pop up that asks "Do you want to switch the ASIO driver?" Select Switch. Then reselect Built-in Audio. This could save you from hours of frustration.

Hardware Suggestions

I am always wary of giving broad endorsement to any particular make or model of audio and MIDI hardware for two reasons. First, no two systems are the same, and no two users are the same; a breakbeat mixer user on an Athlon box running XP has different hardware needs than an OS X user recording a live jazz trio. The second reason I am wary is that hardware and software change so quickly. At the same time, I want to offer something about the topic, so here are a few suggestions as this book goes to press.

For audio interfaces, I use, adore, and pay full price for equipment from RME Audio (www.rme-audio.com). The company writes fantastic drivers, makes innovative hardware, and does a great job with support. RME products are also pretty expensive, but in this case, they're more expensive for a reason. RME also has Mac OS X drivers for most of its sound cards, though I haven't used them much personally.

For PC users, I also recommend Aardvark sound cards (www.aardvark-pro.com), and if you're tracking a lot of instruments, I recommend the Q10 in particular. It has great-sounding built-in microphone preamps and is a great choice for people recording their own bands. Aardvark is working on Mac OS X drivers, but their availability, quality, and stability are as yet impossible to test.

Both PC and Mac users should also look at the excellent, low-cost audio interfaces from MIDIMAN (www.midiman.com), which makes PCI, FireWire, and USB interfaces with drivers for both Macs and PCs.

Cubase SX 2 on both Macs and PCs supports system-level multichannel MIDI interfaces, so in theory, any interface with correctly installed drivers will work. If you are serious about MIDI, though, I recommend one of the MidEx MIDI interfaces from Steinberg. These use proprietary Steinberg technology to get around many of the timing problems that can crop up when using MIDI. If you don't want a MidEx, Mark of the Unicorn makes excellent MIDI interfaces for Macs, and MIDIMAN makes cross-platform MIDI hardware as well.

TOURING THE CUBASE SX 2 INTERFACE

2

Cubase SX 2 offers many ways to record, view, edit, and mix audio and MIDI. The interface gives Cubase a sleek, polished, user-configurable way to work with all parts of a music project (**Figure 2.1**). Learning how to exploit all of these windows and views will give you incredible power over your music and creativity. If you are completely new to Cubase, the variety can be a bit overwhelming at first, but everything is organized in a logical way, and in only a little time you will be working quickly and capably with it.

Figure 2.1 The Cubase SX 2 interface.

Cubase concentrates power in its main Project window, which can be used for deep audio editing, lots of MIDI editing, automation editing, and full editing of mixer settings for any one selected track. It is possible to create an entire song without ever leaving the Project window. The smart user, however, will learn where the other windows offer better or more convenient ways to edit and mix audio. As a general rule, the other editors, such as the MIDI Key editor, the Mixer, and the Audio Sample editor, are more specialized views that include more exact and finely grained tools for modifying audio and MIDI files.

In addition to the Project window, major innovations over Cubase SX's predecessor, Cubase VST, include new buttons that let you more easily accomplish many of the jobs and actions that were menu items in Cubase VST. With these useful buttons, you can use the program for hours without even looking at a menu. In addition, most Cubase SX windows include powerful contextual menus so that whenever a button won't do the job, one of these menus usually will. You access contextual menus by right-clicking (Windows) or Control-clicking (Mac OS). You can also right-click if you have a two-button mouse connected to your Mac. To see how much can be done with these menus, check out the contextual menu for an audio part in the Project window shown in **Figure 2.2**.

In this chapter, you will learn about the Project window and the other windows used in Cubase SX 2. You will also find important shortcuts and tricks to give you more control over your views and the way that you edit in Cubase. Cubase allows you to make choices about how you use the program, and this chapter will give you the skills you need to best set up and use the program to create your own music.

Figure 2.2 The contextual menu opens when you right-click an audio part in the Project window. Mac users with one-button mice might need to access some of these functions from the main menu.

Contextual Menus on the Mac

Many of the contextual menus that are accessed with a right click on a two-button mouse can also be accessed using Control-click on the Mac with a one-button mouse. However, that's not the case when you select a part in the timeline. As of this writing, Mac users running OS 10.3 (Panther) can't access the contextual menu on selected parts unless they have a two-button mouse. Otherwise, you'll have to look for the comparable menu selections in Cubase's main menu.

The Transport Bar

The Transport bar (**Figure 2.3**) lets you control playback, recording, and fast forwarding and rewinding for your project—but it also does much more than this. You will find the Transport bar mentioned in many places in this book precisely because it can be used to do so much.

Performance meter: This is a miniature version of the VST performance meter available from the Devices menu. The left bar shows processor load, and the right bar shows disk use.

Record mode selector: You can use the selector to control the way that MIDI data is recorded.

Left and right locator settings: You can set the left and right locators for looping and punch recording of audio and MIDI here or in the Project window Timeline.

Pre-roll and post-roll settings: When you click the Record button, Cubase can start playback before the current position to allow musicians to get a feel for the place in the song. You set the duration of this pre-roll, and the post-roll after recording stops, here.

Jog/Shuttle wheel: Click the outer wheel and drag to the left or right to move the cursor backward or forward in time. The farther you drag the shuttle wheel from its center position, the faster the project rewinds or fast forwards. Click the inner wheel and drag it in circles to continuously move through the project. The +/– buttons move the cursor very slightly backward and forward.

Dual time display: This displays the current playback position in several time formats.

Tempo and Sync mode buttons: These buttons control a few slightly related parameters. If you select the Click button, Cubase will generate an audio click as a tempo reference. If you select Master, the program can get tempo information from an internal tempo track, and if you select Sync, the program will synchronize to an external timecode.

Tempo and meter settings: These controls show the current tempo and meter for a project. You can edit them manually here in the Transport bar by double-clicking and entering new values.

continues on next page

Figure 2.3 The Transport bar

THE TRANSPORT BAR

MIDI activity indicators: The red In light indicates incoming MIDI data, and the green Out light shows that MIDI data is being sent out. These indicators are invaluable when troubleshooting MIDI problems.

Transport controls: These standard buttons control playback, recording, stopping, and fast winding of audio. The smaller buttons with a single arrow and a bracket are shortcuts to the very beginning or end of the project.

Loop, Autopunch, and Autoquantize buttons: These buttons let you configure Cubase to loop, automatically start or stop recording, and quantize incoming MIDI data if necessary.

Audio activity indicators: These bars display the first input and first output busses.

✔ Tip

■ The Transport bar is the easiest place to configure the way that Cubase displays time. Cubase can show time in bars+beats, various frame rates (also known as timecode, for working with video), seconds, and samples. Click to the right of the time display to open a menu and choose the way that time is displayed in Cubase (**Figure 2.4**). This setting also changes the default time display for the main project window ruler.

Figure 2.4 This menu sets the way that Cubase shows time throughout a project.

The Project Window

The Project window (**Figure 2.5**) is where you will spend the most time when using Cubase, because the complete view offered in this window makes it the best place to work. The Project window almost warrants its own book, but you will get a good start at understanding this critical part of Cubase in the next few pages. Each part of the Project window is described briefly here and then in greater detail on the following pages. Still, you should mark Chapter 5, "The Project Window," of the *Cubase SX Operation Manual* for reading at a later time.

Toolbar: You can use this collection of buttons to show and hide parts of the Project window and change the tools used to edit in the Event display. The toolbar also includes buttons for basic transport control and automation setup.

Overview line: The Overview line shows a minimal view of all events in a project and can be used for rough navigation within it.

Info line: When a MIDI or audio event is selected in the Event display, its properties are displayed here. Often parameters for an event can be edited here as well.

Ruler: The ruler is a graphical timeline reference for the Event display. The ruler can display time in multiple formats and also shows the left and right locators. Cubase can display multiple rulers if you wish.

continues on next page

Figure 2.5 The Cubase SX 2 Project window.

THE PROJECT WINDOW

Track inspector: The Track inspector displays parameters for the track selected in the track list. It organizes an incredible amount of information about audio and MIDI tracks in an easily accessible place. You can use it to show and change record and playback settings for audio tracks, as well as insert effects, send effects, and EQ settings. It can display a full channel strip, which includes buttons for changing settings and opening edit windows.

Track list: The track list shows every track in a project. Many track-specific parameters in the Track inspector and Mixer can be set here as well. The track list also shows and hides automation for audio tracks and MIDI continuous controller (CC) data for MIDI tracks.

Event display: All audio and MIDI events in a project appear in the Event display, along with any recorded automation and CC data for that track. Events can be edited directly in the Project window, which is structured like a timeline, or in specialized editor windows.

Snap and Grid settings: Located at the right end of the toolbar, the Snap and Grid settings are so important to Cubase SX 2 that they are discussed separately in this chapter.

The Project Window Toolbar

The Cubase SX 2 toolbar (**Figure 2.6**) serves multiple, sometimes seemingly unrelated, purposes. The toolbar consists of four general groups of settings. Much more about these buttons is included in other parts of this book and in the operation manual that comes with the program.

View Filter section: These buttons are used to show and hide the main windows in a project. You can display or hide the Inspector, Event Infoline, and Overview here. You can also use these buttons to open two commonly used windows: the Mixer and the Pool.

Automation mode: This menu determines how Cubase records and plays automation. Much about automation is covered later in this book.

Mini Transport bar: Record, Play, Stop, and Loop can all be controlled with these buttons. Often these controls are sufficient, so that you can hide the Transport bar.

Project Window tools: These buttons control cursor and editing actions. These tools change their functions and act differently depending on whether an audio or MIDI event is active, and they are covered extensively in the audio and MIDI editing sections of this book. Here is a list of the most common functions of the Project Window tools:

- ◆ **Object Selection,** or **Arrow tool:** These tools are most often used to select and resize events parts. Clicking and holding in this tool opens a contextual menu with options that determine the actions Cubase takes when resizing an event.

- ◆ **Range tool:** Use this tool to select all tracks or parts across a particular range of a project. This tool can be very useful when you are making larger edits or moving something like the entire chorus to a different part of the song.

- ◆ **Scissors tool:** Use this tool to cut events at a grid line that you specify.

continues on next page

Show/Hide Overview   Automation mode   Mini Transport bar   Project window controls   Autoscroll   Snap

Activate   Track Mixer   Object Selection tool   Play/Scrub tool
Show Inspector   Open Pool   Range tool   Draw tool
Show Event Infoline   Show Overview   Scissors tool   Time Warp tool
Glue tool   Mute tool
Eraser tool   Zoom tool

Figure 2.6 The Cubase SX 2 toolbar

◆ **Glue tool:** This tool fuses two parts or events into one new part or event.

◆ **Eraser tool:** Use the Eraser to remove parts and events in the Project window. Essentially a shortcut to selecting something and then pressing the Delete or Backspace key, the Eraser also can be used to remove specific notes or data in other editors.

◆ **Zoom tool:** Use this tool to zoom in to view a smaller amount of the Project window in more detail. You can also select the Zoom tool and drag a box over the area of a project you wish to view. This zooms both the vertical and horizontal areas selected to take up the full Project window space. You can also reduce an area by holding down the Option key while holding the tool over it.

◆ **Mute tool:** Click a part or an event with the Mute tool to prevent it from playing back.

◆ **Time Warp tool:** This tool lets you graphically edit changes to the tempo of a project in the Project window.

◆ **Draw tool:** The Draw tool is used extensively in other editors such as the Audio Sample editor and the Key editor, but also is used in the Project window. Most commonly in the Project window, you use the Draw tool to manually draw automation and MIDI CC data.

◆ **Scrub tool:** In the days when analog tape dominated recording, tape was "scrubbed" slowly back and forth over tape heads to find exact places to make edits. Selecting the Scrub tool allows you to digitally scrub over any part or event, and it even mimics the sound of tape being dragged slowly or quickly over tape heads.

Figure 2.7 The main section of a Track inspector for an audio track.

Figure 2.8 The same Track inspector with the Channel tab selected, showing the full channel for that audio track.

Figure 2.9 A Track inspector for a MIDI track.

The Project Window Track Inspector

The Track inspector is one of the most powerful features in Cubase SX 2. The Track inspector shows practically every parameter for a single track in a project, and it's where you select your input and output settings for each track. The track that is shown in the Track inspector window is determined by the track that is selected in the track list, and parameters vary depending on whether an audio track or a MIDI track is selected.

The Track inspector (**Figure 2.7**) shows many of the important audio track settings available in other menus and windows, as well as some settings available only in the Track inspector. The main tab of the Track inspector provides buttons for the most common settings, such as solo, mute, record-enable, pan, and hardware routing. If one of the other tabs is selected, the inspector displays a completely different set of parameters for the same track. For example, if the Channel tab is selected (**Figure 2.8**), the full channel strip from the Mixer window is displayed. Other tabs show insert effects, send effects, and EQ settings for the track.

The main tab in the Track inspector for a MIDI track (**Figure 2.9**) shows commonly used MIDI parameters. Selecting one of the other tabs displays additional track parameters, MIDI insert effects, MIDI send effects, or a MIDI channel strip.

✔ Tip

- Track types not covered here, such as Group tracks, Folder tracks, and Video tracks, also have their own Track inspector windows.

The Project Window Track List

The track list is a list of every track in a project, regardless of whether it contains any events to play back. The listing of a MIDI track on the track list will look different from the listing for an audio track.

The listing for an audio track (**Figure 2.10**) shows the track name, record-enable and monitor settings, track solo/mute, and whether automation will be written or read for that track. It also includes buttons to indicate whether send and insert effects are activated or bypassed. The listing for an audio track also shows buttons for additional track parameters and a small signal-level meter.

The listing for a MIDI track (**Figure 2.11**) shows many similar parameters, such as the track name, solo/mute and automation status, and record-enable and monitor settings. Some MIDI-only parameters, such as input and output channels, are also displayed.

To get a larger or smaller view of the track information, you can change its size in the track list.

To change the visual size of a track in the track list:

1. Move the mouse pointer to the vertical or horizontal edge of a track.

2. When the pointer changes to a double arrow, drag the edge of the track list (**Figure 2.12**).

3. When the track information is the size you want, release the mouse.

Figure 2.10 An entry in the track list for an audio track.

Figure 2.11 The track list settings for a MIDI track.

Figure 2.12 Resizing the track information in the track list.

✔ Tip

- To resize all track views simultaneously, hold down the Ctrl key (Windows) or the Command key (Mac OS) as you move the mouse pointer to the track edges and proceed as if resizing a single track. All tracks in the track list will be resized together.

Figure 2.13 The ruler in the Project window.

Figure 2.14 A MIDI track after it has been zoomed by clicking and dragging the ruler.

The Project Window Ruler

The Project window ruler provides a quick and easy way to keep track of your current location in a project and to set the loop and range selection.

Under normal circumstances, the ruler shows time according to the global setting for the project. (To change the time display setting to bars+beats, a video and film frame rate, minutes:seconds, or samples, see "The Transport Bar" earlier in this chapter.) **Figure 2.13** shows the ruler set to bars+beats, the most commonly used time display for music; about 10 bars from measure 16 to measure 26 are visible.

Also visible on the ruler are the left and right locators, shown as inward-facing triangles and the lighter color line that connects the locators. The locators are used to set punch points and loop points, which are used to automate some actions in Cubase. You'll read more about these in the chapters on recording audio and MIDI. In the example, the locators are set to 8 beats, from the beginning of bar 17 to the end of bar 25.

Finally, the ruler offers one of the most useful features in Cubase: the ability to move and zoom the Event display with the mouse, which is the easiest way to view events and edits in detail.

To zoom the Event display:

1. Click the ruler. Anywhere will work, but try to click near where you want to zoom in.

2. *Do one of the following:*

    ▲ Drag down toward the bottom of the screen. The display will zoom in (**Figure 2.14**).

    ▲ Drag to the right or left to move forward or backward in time.

    ▲ Drag up or down to increase or decrease the zoom level.

The Project Window Event Display

The Event display (**Figure 2.15**) shows all of the events in a project. Many people think of events as parts of clips or regions, but Cubase uses slightly different terminology. In Cubase, an event is not necessarily just a piece of audio or MIDI data (though those are the most common kinds of events), but events can be automation data, video data, or MIDI continuous controller (CC) information.

You will perform much of your audio and MIDI editing and processing directly in the Event display. In addition, you will use most of the tools you select from the toolbar to make changes in events in the Event display. For example, if you select the Mute tool from the toolbar, clicking an event will mute that event (**Figure 2.16**) and dim it in the Event display to indicate that it is muted. You will learn much more about the Event display in the parts of this book that cover audio and MIDI editing.

Figure 2.15 The Event display, showing both audio and MIDI tracks.

Figure 2.16 The audio track in the middle of the event list has been clicked with the Mute tool. It's dimmed and will not play back with the project.

The Project Window Info Line

One of the most underused parts of Cubase is the Info line. The Info line shows volume, length, and other information about whatever is selected in the Event display. Whenever you select a new event in the Event display, the Info line shows information about it.

A great feature of the Info line is that you can actually change parameters for events directly on it. For example, when an audio event is selected in the Event display (**Figure 2.17**), the Info line shows parameters important for an audio event, such as the name, start and end times, length, and so on. Double-clicking one of the parameters allows you to edit the setting directly. **Figure 2.18** shows the name of a file after it has been changed. Cubase usually has more than one place to make these sorts of changes, but the Info line is powerful because it collects so much of the information for a particular event in one place.

Of course, the parameters displayed on the Info line will change when a MIDI event is selected (**Figure 2.19**).

Figure 2.17 The Info line showing information for an audio event.

Figure 2.18 Making a manual edit on audio event data in the Info display, in this case changing the name.

Figure 2.19 The Info line for a MIDI event.

The Project Window Snap Settings

Among the most important points to learn about Cubase are the theory and practice of Snap. What Snap does is quite simple: with Snap activated, when you move, resize, change, or otherwise edit an item, the item snaps to the nearest value you've specified in the Grid menu. If Snap is on and set to Bar, for example, an object in the Project window can be moved only to the nearest bar. If Snap is on and set to Beat, then an object can be moved only to the nearest beat.

Snap makes it easy to perform actions such as the following:

◆ Drop an audio event at a particular bar location.

◆ Create tempo-synchronized automation information with the Pencil tool.

◆ Snip a long audio file into multiple pieces, each precisely two bars long.

◆ Place a trigger for a sample at a particular frame when editing sound for video.

These are only a few things that Snap can do, but they show how important Snap can be in almost any situation in your work in Cubase SX 2.

The Snap settings (**Figure 2.20**) are located on the toolbar, on the far right side. Snap can be turned on and off via the Snap button. When Snap is on, the settings to the right of the Snap button determine Snap behavior.

The first drop-down menu for Snap settings (**Figure 2.21**) determines the mode Snap uses when you perform events and edits that can be snapped, as follows:

Snap On/Off button   Snap mode   Grid mode   Quantize setting

Figure 2.20 Snap is activated and configured here.

Figure 2.21 The Snap mode menu.

Grid: When Grid is selected, Cubase draws an invisible grid in the project, and Snap uses this grid to guide snapped actions. More settings for the Grid appear on the next two Snap drop-down menus.

Events: When Events mode is selected, instead of a grid, the beginning and end of each event in the Event display is the guide for snapped actions. With Snap in this mode, when you move an event, it will snap to the beginning and end of each other event in the project. This mode can be very useful for editing projects with looser tempo, where a grid is too exact to work with the feel of the music.

Shuffle: When Shuffle is selected, Snap forces events to trade places when they are moved, but maintains a cohesive track.

Magnetic Cursor: The Magnetic Cursor setting turns the cursor (the line that moves from left to right showing the current playback position) into the snap guide. This enables you to snap actions to places that are easy to find manually but may not be on a predictable beat or time line.

Grid + Cursor: This mode combines Grid mode with Magnetic Cursor—the two most convenient Snap settings for music creation, both active at the same time.

Events + Cursor: This mode combines the Events and Magnetic Cursor modes.

Events + Grid + Cursor: This mode combines Events, Grid, and Magnetic Cursor modes.

continues on next page

THE PROJECT WINDOW SNAP SETTINGS

The Grid mode setting determines how the grid interacts with Snap when you make a change in a project that can be snapped. When the project is set to use Bar or Beat (**Figure 2.22**), the grid can be set so that events snap to each bar or each beat or to the Use Quantize setting. If a project uses another time format, the grid can be set so that events snap to seconds, milliseconds, frames, or samples.

If Use Quantize is selected in the Grid mode menu, the last menu in the Snap settings (**Figure 2.23**), usually called the Quantize menu, determines the grid. The Quantize setting is explained in detail in this book in Chapter 10, "Editing MIDI." The Use Quantize option here allows you to set the grid so that snapped actions can use very complex rhythmic-based time divisions.

Figure 2.22 The Grid mode menu is used to configure the type and granularity of the grid used for snapping.

Figure 2.23 Complex tempo and meter divisions are available on the Quantize menu.

The Audio Sample Editor

You can use the Audio Sample editor in Cubase to perform the most exacting audio editing and processing that the application offers. Double-click an audio event in the Project window to open the Audio Sample editor (**Figure 2.24**).

Many of the toolbar buttons and pointer tools in the Audio Sample editor are similar to those found in the Project window. The Audio Sample editor is a very powerful component of Cubase and is covered in detail in Chapter 9, "Advanced Audio Editing."

Toolbar   Info line   Thumbnail display   Waveform display   Ruler

Figure 2.24 The Audio Sample editor.

The MIDI Key Editor

Cubase includes a full set of specialized MIDI editors. The Key editor has much more flexibility for editing MIDI than the Project window—you can add or delete individual notes, for example—but is more intuitive than the List and Logical editors that you also can use to edit MIDI. Chances are you'll do most of your MIDI editing in the MIDI Key editor (**Figure 2.25**). The MIDI Key editor uses a piano roll metaphor to represent data. The piano keyboard at the far left of the window represents a vertical pitch orientation, with low notes toward the bottom of the window, and high notes toward the top. The Note display scrolls from right to left as time passes.

The bottom section of the MIDI Key editor is the Controller display, where you can view and edit MIDI continuous controller (CC) data.

Figure 2.25 The MIDI Key editor.

Figure 2.26 The Drum editor, used for programming drum parts.

Figure 2.27 The List editor, which provides the deepest control of individual MIDI events.

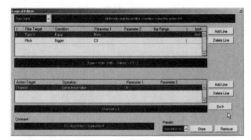

Figure 2.28 The Logical editor; it has been said nobody knows Cubase until he or she knows the Logical editor.

Other MIDI Editors

The Key editor is the most commonly used MIDI editor in Cubase, but there are other, somewhat specialized MIDI editors as well. Sometimes the Drum editor (**Figure 2.26**), List editor (**Figure 2.27**), or Logical editor (**Figure 2.28**) is the best tool for the job.

Drum editor: The Drum editor is a specialized editor for quickly entering percussion parts and creating grooves. The Drum editor was one of the features that made Cubase a hit (way back in the Atari days), and it still offers a great way to program beats.

List editor: The List editor contains a list of every single event in a project. The List editor is not as intuitive or graphical as the Key editor, but it offers complete, exact, super-accurate control over all MIDI data.

Logical editor: The Logical editor lets you modify data in a completely nongraphical way, by building conditional rules and applying them to MIDI data. The Logical editor is probably the least intuitive editor in Cubase SX, but it is extremely powerful if you take the time to learn it.

✔ Tip

■ If you used an earlier version of Cubase, you may be wondering where the Controller editor went. Long a Mac-only feature of Cubase, Windows users finally got the Controller editor when version 5 was released. The Controller editor is gone now, though, replaced by vastly expanded MIDI CC and automation editing capabilities in the Project window and the previously included CC editing tools such as the CC section in the MIDI Key editor.

OTHER MIDI EDITORS

The Pool

The Pool (**Figure 2.29**) provides a complete listing of all audio and video files contained in a project, as well as a convenient location to add audio and video files to a project without bringing them into the Project window. When Cubase starts a project, it insists that a working folder be designated for the audio, MIDI, fade, and other files created during the course of a project. The Pool is a specialized view of the audio and video files in a project.

Using the Pool, you can:

◆ Add audio files and video files to a project.

◆ Sort files according to time, duration, record date, and many other parameters.

◆ Search for audio and video files by name.

◆ Audition files before adding them to a project.

◆ Create archive and master files for a project, in which all files referenced in a project are collected in one place. This makes moving projects from computer to computer, as well as backing up projects, much easier.

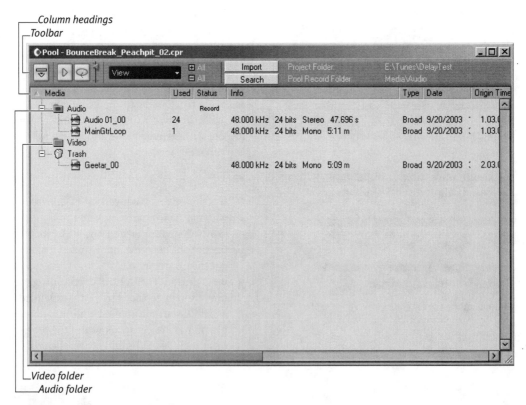

Figure 2.29 The Cubase SX 2 Pool.

VST instrument channels

Figure 2.30 A group of Mixer channels, including audio channels and VST instrument channels.

Channel strip   *Insert effects*   *EQ*   *Send effects*

Figure 2.31 The VST channel settings, used to edit all parameters for a single channel.

The Cubase SX 2 Mixer

Few parts of the program are more powerful than the Mixer (**Figure 2.30**). In fact, three full chapters in this book are dedicated to it. Cubase has a Mixer that can be customized beyond any hardware interface, and allows you to take extraordinary control over your mix. You can selectively show and hide elements of the Mixer, toggle automation on or off, and route audio through a wide range of software effects plug-ins or even to external effects hardware.

The Mixer in Cubase includes distinct channels for all MIDI and audio tracks in a project. All channels also have distinct windows that are used to edit all pertinent parameters for a single track (**Figure 2.31**). Unlike in a hardware mixer, in the Cubase Mixer, every single parameter, from mix levels to routing to effects, is instantly recalled the next time a project is opened.

THE CUBASE SX 2 MIXER

VST Instruments

Software-based synthesis and sampling is probably one of the most important capabilities in the history of audio computing. Cubase VST lead the way with VST instruments, which are plug-ins of various instrumental and percussive sounds that can be played by MIDI. This simple idea has led to an amazing variety of VST instruments, from dead-on emulations of famous synthesizers, to software samplers that rival the highest-end hardware samplers in complexity and creativity, to previously untried methods of sound creation and transformation.

Cubase uses a virtual rack to house VST instruments (**Figure 2.32**). The VST Instruments rack can have up to 32 software synthesizers or samplers running simultaneously. The amount of synthesis power is limited only by the power of the host computer. Cubase also includes support for automation of every parameter within a VST instrument and, of course, options to save presets of the sounds you create for use in future projects. Chapter 7 of this book is dedicated to VST instruments.

Figure 2.32 The VST Instruments rack, with five VST instruments loaded.

STARTING A PROJECT

3

Once you've installed and configured Cubase SX 2, the next step is to begin working on a project.

A project is the basic file type in Cubase, in the same way that a document is the basic file type in Microsoft Word. A Cubase project includes the audio, MIDI, automation, and settings for a piece of music. Most people create a new project for every song, though not everyone will work this way. Cubase allows a great deal of customization; someone working on audio postproduction or audio for video, for example, may set up a very different type of project than a person working on a country song.

In this chapter, you will learn how to start projects, including how to use the templates bundled with Cubase and how to create your own templates. You will also learn how Cubase manages the various files that are created as a project grows. Many music projects need tempo information to work properly, so you will learn how to set up a metronome click track. Finally, you will learn how to use the powerful audio-to-tempo matching features in Cubase, which allow you to sync the Cubase tempo to an audio snippet or audio drum loop.

Creating a Project

When you start a new project, Cubase automatically asks you where you want to store the files for that project. You can browse an existing folder or create a new one; often the easiest approach is to create a new folder for each song. As a project grows, Cubase creates new files and folders in this working directory, allowing you to easily manage files and, if necessary, move a project to a new machine. Be sure to create the working directory on a drive with enough free space to hold your audio files, and give the project and folder identical and logical names, so you can easily find and move the project if you ever need to do so.

In addition to a directory, you'll also be asked to select a template when you start a new project. Cubase offers a standard list to choose from, including 16-track and 24-track templates and MIDI and audio choices. If you don't want to start with a preexisting template, choose Empty. However, whether you're creating music for a soundtrack, a corporate video, a hip-hop tune, a live recording, or any number of other purposes, you'll likely find a template already set up and easily accessible for that particular job. See the sidebar "Templates Included with Cubase SX 2" later in this chapter for a description of the templates that ship with the Windows and Mac OS versions of Cubase. You can create your own custom templates as well.

Figure 3.1 Making a selection from the list of templates.

To start a project:

1. Choose File > New Project.

2. In the New Project dialog box, select a template from the Templates list (**Figure 3.1**).

3. For any new project, you will be asked to choose a directory to store it in. Select a directory or create a new one; then click OK.

   A new project is created.

4. Save and name your project using File > Save.

Templates Included with Cubase SX 2

Don't make the use of templates more complicated than it needs to be. Templates in Cubase work just like those in recent versions of many applications such as Microsoft Word; when a new file is created, the application opens a dialog box where you can choose from a group of templates that meet common needs. Word, for instance, offers templates for creating a resume, memo, or Web page, and it also includes a blank, empty document for creating whatever you want from scratch. Cubase operates in exactly the same way; out of the box, the program offers a group of templates that you can use to create new projects for common tasks.

Here is a quick rundown of the templates included with Cubase SX 2 and the most common uses for each. The templates you have available may differ depending on the version of the program and the platform you use, but this list should give you a good overview.

- **Empty** opens a completely empty project. You can use it to create a new project or a new template from scratch.

- **16 Track MIDI Sequencer** opens with 16 empty MIDI tracks. Use this template for MIDI-only projects or to add a few audio tracks as needed.

- **16 Track Surround Mix** is for projects that will be mixed in multichannel surround sound rather than stereo. Each of the 16 audio tracks is set up for panning in multiple-channel surround sound, not stereo.

- **24 Track Audio Recorder** is the best template option if you are going to record only acoustic instruments such as drums, guitars, and vocals. Each of the 24 tracks is ready to record audio and configured for stereo mixing.

- **Music for Picture NTSC** opens a project optimized for creation of audio for video using the NTSC video specification common in North America. Cubase can play back simple DirectShow video in sync with audio.

- **Music for Picture PAL** is identical to Music for Picture NTSC, but it is set to use the frame rate for European PAL video rather than the NTSC frame rate.

- **Stereo Mastering Setup** opens a project ready for postproduction of stereo mixes, such as those used to create a CD. This type of project is best for tweaking final mixes to make them sound their best before CD burning.

Figure 3.2 You can activate the audio click on the Transport bar.

Figure 3.3 In this example, the MIDI metronome note will be sent to an output on a MIDI interface.

Figure 3.4 Choose Metronome Setup from the Transport menu to configure the metronome.

About the Cubase Metronome

Some projects, such as audio for video or live recordings, do not have a consistent tempo from start to finish. Most musical projects, though, work best when they reference a solid tempo. Assuming that you'll be recording in a more or less tempo-centric sequencing environment, a solid timing reference is critical for good performances. Cubase has a built-in metronome that you can configure to send an audio click over the master output. You can also configure Cubase to send a MIDI note to trigger a sound.

To use an audio click:

◆ On the Transport bar, click the Click button (**Figure 3.2**).

If the audio click is active, the Transport bar will display *On* next to the Click button.

To use a MIDI note as a metronome:

1. From the Transport menu, choose Metronome Setup (**Figure 3.3**).

2. In the Metronome Setup panel, uncheck Audio Click and configure the proper channel and note number for the MIDI device and sound you want to use for the metronome (**Figure 3.4**).

3. Click OK.

✔ Tips

■ The metronome settings are global and are not saved with each project. You may have to change them if you move to a different computer.

■ The slider for the volume of the audio click is at the bottom of the Metronome Setup panel. By default, the click is *really* loud, perhaps too loud for your ears and speakers.

Setting the Project Tempo

Any new Cubase project has a particular tempo, which is audible using the metronome, but it might not be the right tempo for the song you want to create. If you're familiar with MIDI sequencers, you will be accustomed to setting tempos before starting to record. If you have recorded exclusively audio, however, this process may be new to you. One of the fundamental differences between MIDI and audio is that MIDI is at its core a tempo-based format. MIDI can't be recorded except in reference to tempo and meter information. If you plan to record only live instruments and will never do any MIDI sequencing or looping, you can pretty much ignore the tempo settings in Cubase and just start tracking. Otherwise, you need to set a tempo before you start recording.

To set a tempo:

1. Click the Transport bar and verify that the Tempo button is clicked and is set to Track, which references its tempo to the tempo track (**Figure 3.5**).

2. From the Project menu, choose Tempo Track (**Figure 3.6**).

    The Tempo Track editor opens.

Figure 3.5 When Tempo is selected, project tempo is controlled by the tempo track, and changes are edited for this track in the Tempo Track editor.

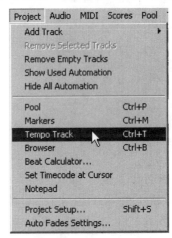

Figure 3.6 Opening the Tempo Track editor

Figure 3.7 Enter the desired tempo in the Tempo box.

3. *Do one of the following:*

▲ Click the Tempo box at the top of the editor and type the desired tempo (**Figure 3.7**).

▲ Use the up and down arrows next to the Tempo box to set the rate of the desired tempo. If you have a mouse equipped with a scroll wheel, you can use the wheel to increment and decrement many parameters, including the tempo setting in this dialog box.

4. Close the editor when the tempo is set as you want.

✔ Tips

■ Use the Tempo Track editor to make changes in the sequencer tempo. This editor is active and controls the tempo of a project only if the Tempo button on the Transport bar is set to Track. If you are absolutely sure that you will never want to change tempos in a song, you can click the Tempo button and set it to Fixed; you can now enter a tempo directly in the Transport bar field.

■ I strongly recommend that you use the Tempo Track editor to control the tempo of a project. It's much more flexible than the Fixed setting on the Transport bar, and if you use any ReWire instruments, you will definitely want the Tempo Track controlling the tempo of the project. ReWire applications are most effective when slaved to Cubase using the tempo track. You can learn more about ReWire instruments and Cubase in Chapter 15: "ReWire and Cubase."

SETTING THE PROJECT TEMPO

Importing a Loop

Over the past few years, loop-based music production has become increasingly common in all types of music. There are entire audio applications dedicated to working with audio loops, some built for use on stage and some for the recording studio. Cubase SX 2 is not exclusively a looping program, but it includes many tools for creating, importing, editing, and tempo-matching loops. The following section shows you how to use audio loops when recording, as well as how to match a loop to the tempo of a project or match your project tempo to a particular loop.

Using drum loops

Metronomes and audio clicks are certainly useful, but why record to a click when you can use a drum loop instead? A carefully selected drum loop, from a loop CD or other source, can help you get the feel of a track together right from the start. Setting up a loop across a project and setting the tempo of a project to match that loop involves some audio-editing tasks that are covered here somewhat out of order. Keep in mind that more advanced audio editing, tempo tricks, and file management are covered later in this book.

To import an audio drum loop:

1. Choose File > Import > Audio File.

2. In the Import Audio dialog box that opens, navigate to the loop you want to import (**Figure 3.8**); then click Open.

   The Import Options dialog box opens (**Figure 3.9**). Here, you can specify whether the audio file should be copied to the same directory as the current project and whether the file should be converted if it doesn't match the sample rate or bit depth of the current project. I recommend copying the file to the working directory.

Figure 3.8 Choosing the loop to import into the project; in this example, a drum loop is selected to be imported.

Figure 3.9 Normally, you will want to copy the imported loop to the working directory of the current project.

Figure 3.10 The loop, after it is imported, becomes an event on an audio track in the Project window.

3. Make your selections in the Import Options dialog box and click OK.

The file is imported to an audio track and is added to the Project window (**Figure 3.10**).

✔ Tip

■ The dialog box for importing audio, shown in Figure 3.8, has a small Transport bar on the lower right, which is handy for auditioning audio files before bringing them into a project.

Using Loops and Samples

You need to consider two issues when using drum loops and samples in a program like Cubase. One is technical: What file types and formats does the program support? The second is legal: What are you allowed to do with sounds created by someone else?

Cubase SX 2 supports all of the commonly used uncompressed audio file formats and supports the same file types on both platforms.

◆ WAV files are the most common audio files on Windows machines.

◆ AIFF files are the standard audio files on Macs.

◆ Sound Designer II (.sd2) files most often come from projects recorded using Digidesign software. Digidesign created .sd2 as its own proprietary file type; these files are widely found and supported in the audio world.

More often than not, samples you want to import will be in one of these formats. However, Cubase can also import compressed MP3 files and can even rip audio directly from an audio CD. In these two situations, the file will be converted to the default file format that the project is using.

The legal questions associated with the use of samples are much more complex. The law regarding sample use is still very much unresolved and can vary from case to case and from country to country. It is certain, though, that if you use an unlicensed sample, no matter how short, you expose yourself to problems if the music is ever released. Because of this, many people purchase sample libraries specifically created for use by musicians and video content creators. These libraries are much more expensive than regular CDs, but they include samples, loops, and sounds that you can use in your music productions, and you don't have to pay royalties to the sample CD creator upon release. Whatever you decide to do, always keep track of the samples you use, in case licensing questions arise down the road.

Matching the Tempo to an Audio Loop

On rare occasions, an imported loop will perfectly match the project tempo, but most of the time there will be at least some discrepancy between the tempo of an imported loop and the project tempo. In years past, fixing this problem in Cubase VST, and in many other programs, was a circuitous walk through some of the most confusing software panels you could ever have the misfortune to use. Thankfully, Cubase SX 2 makes the whole process *much* easier than before. You have two choices: you can match the project tempo to the loop or match the loop tempo to the project. We will look at both approaches.

To match the tempo of a project to an audio loop:

1. Listen to the loop and count its length in beats.

2. Select the loop in the Project window.

3. From the Project menu, choose Beat Calculator (**Figure 3.11**), which opens the Beat Calculator window.

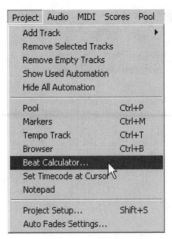

Figure 3.11 Open the Beat Calculator with the loop selected.

Figure 3.12 The Beat Calculator determines the tempo of the loop after you tell it the duration of the loop.

Figure 3.13 The loop in the Project window with the tempo matching exactly

4. In the Beat Calculator window, enter the number of beats in the selected loop.

In the example here, the loop is four measures long, or 16 beats (**Figure 3.12**).

The Beat Calculator updates in real time to show you the tempo that will result if the selected loop has the duration you entered.

After you've calculated the tempo, you need to enter it on the tempo track.

5. Usually when starting a project, you should set the tempo at the beginning of the project, so click the At Tempo Track Start button to enter the calculated tempo at the beginning of the project.

6. Close the Beat Calculator and return to the Project window.

You can see that the loop now fits into exactly two bars (**Figure 3.13**), but it's always a good idea to check with your ears.

7. Turn on a metronome or audio click to check the match.

It will be obvious immediately whether the tempo is matched correctly.

MATCHING THE TEMPO TO AN AUDIO LOOP

Matching a Loop to the Project Tempo

The most common approach to matching audio and sequencer tempo is the one just discussed: a loop will be the basis for a track, and the sequencer will need to use that tempo. In certain situations, though, you'll want the opposite approach. For example, a song may feel right at one tempo, but a great-sounding loop may not fit it properly. If this is the case, you will need to force the audio loop to match the project tempo.

To match an audio loop to the project tempo:

1. Listen to the loop and determine its length.

   As you can see in this example, the two-bar loop does not fit the project tempo because the two-bar loop starts at the beginning of bar 1 but ends before the end of bar 2 (**Figure 3.14**).

2. On the Project window toolbar, hold down the mouse on the arrow button. In the pop-up menu, select Sizing Applies Time Stretch (**Figure 3.15**).

3. In the Project window, click the audio part you want to resize and position the cursor at the end of it.

   The cursor will change icons to include the word *Stretch* so that you know what you are about to do (**Figure 3.16**).

4. Click the mouse on the handle on the part and move the handle to where you want the part to end.

   The Snap value applies here, and in this case, you want the part to be a two-bar loop from the beginning of bar 1 to the beginning of bar 3.

Figure 3.14 This loop is two bars long, but it does not match the project tempo.

Figure 3.15 Changing the action of the arrow cursor. In this mode, resizing an audio part will time-stretch the part instead of moving the boundary.

Figure 3.16 The cursor changes to a Stretch icon as the part handle is moved.

Figure 3.17 Cubase uses an offline process to change the duration of the audio file.

Figure 3.18 The processed audio file fits the project tempo perfectly. Compare this figure to Figure 3.14.

5. Release the mouse when the part is properly resized.

Cubase displays a status bar as it time-stretches or compresses the file (**Figure 3.17**).

In the Project window, the loop now matches the tempo of the project. In this example, the loop is now two bars long (**Figure 3.18**). Compare this to Figure 3.14, the loop now ends at precisely the end of bar 2.

✔ Tip

■ Cubase uses probably the best-sounding time-stretch algorithms in the world—the MPEX algorithms from Prosoniq—but there is a sonic penalty for changing the duration of an audio file. The artifacts vary depending on the source material and amount of time change, but they include audible effects such as phase shift in the high end, distortion, slight changes in timing and groove, and general "dirtiness" in the sound. Listen carefully to all such processed audio.

MATCHING A LOOP TO THE PROJECT TEMPO

Copying a Loop Throughout a Project

If you use an audio loop as a timing reference when recording, the loop needs to be copied throughout the project. Unlike a metronome, which will click away regardless of the point where the project is playing, a loop has to be copied for as long as you will need it. Once you've mastered looping, you'll be able to record without ever hearing a metronome again.

Figure 3.19 The audio loop has been moved to the start of the project.

To copy a loop throughout a song:

1. After the audio loop and project tempo are in sync, click the audio loop in the Project window and drag it to the start of the track (**Figure 3.19**).

2. With the loop selected, click the Edit menu and choose Repeat (**Figure 3.20**). The Repeat Events dialog box opens.

Figure 3.20 From the Edit menu, choose Repeat.

Figure 3.21 This setting will create 32 copies of the selected part.

Figure 3.22 The part copied and repeated in the Project window

3. Select the number of times that you want the loop to be repeated (**Figure 3.21**); then click OK

A short '60s pop tune will have roughly 80 measures, but most songs written today have significantly more than that.

In the Project window, the part will be copied the number of times you have specified (**Figure 3.22**).

✔ Tip

■ In the example in Figure 3.22, I copied a two-bar loop 32 times, or 64 measures. In addition, I left in the original two-bar loop as a lead-in to get the timing straight, so the loop now repeats for a total of 65 measures. Most rock, pop, hip-hop, electronic, and jazz music is based on phrases or parts that are some multiple of 4 measures long. Jazz standards are four 8-bar phrases, or 32 bars long; blues are three 4-bar sections, or 12 bars; pop songs are almost always based on 8 or 16-bar phrases. As listeners, we've come to expect music to be arranged in those dimensions. While rules are made to be broken, when building a song from loops or phrases, using 4-, 8-, or 16-bar phrases will make the song sound "right" to most people.

Importing a Cubase Project

You may have upgraded from an earlier version of Cubase VST or Cubasis and may have gigabytes of music created with the older program. Luckily for you, Steinberg built into Cubase SX 2 the ability to import songs and existing projects from previous versions of Cubase VST, Cubasis, and Cubase SL. Unfortunately, not all of an older Cubase song will be imported. Check page 770 of the *Cubase Operation Manual* to see specifics about what parts of Cubase songs are imported and what parts are not.

To import a song created with an older version of Cubase:

1. Choose File > Import > Cubase Song (**Figure 3.23**).

2. In the Import Cubase Song dialog box that opens, navigate to the file to be imported. Cubase songs previously used the .all file extension. When you have located the file, click Open (**Figure 3.24**).

   Cubase needs to create a new folder for the imported song. You use the same dialog box that opens for a new song to find the folder for the imported song.

3. Locate the folder for the new song and click OK.

   Cubase converts the old song to an SX 2 project and moves the audio and MIDI files to the directory for the new song. It does not automatically save the song.

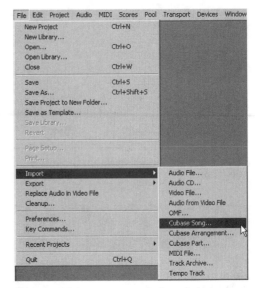

Figure 3.23 Cubase songs can be imported into Cubase SX 2.

Figure 3.24 The old Cubase song to be imported.

Figure 3.25 Saving the imported song to the new location.

4. To complete the import, choose File > Save (**Figure 3.25**).

✔ Tip

■ If you come from the comparatively enlightened world of text or Web publishing, where standards exist to ensure file interoperability between applications, you may be surprised to learn that such standards don't exist in the world of audio software. Projects created in one application are pretty much never usable in another application. Thus, your projects created in Pro Tools, Digital Performer, Logic, or another application can't be directly imported into Cubase. If you need to transfer projects from one application to another, you will have to export each MIDI file, audio file, and plug-in preset from the application in which the project was created. Then you'll have to import all of those pieces into Cubase and re-create the project as best you can.

Creating a New Template

You can also create new templates that fit
your specific needs. A template can include
nearly anything that a project can include,
meaning that you can set up one or more
projects just the way you like and have them
available immediately as a template. As you
get more experience in Cubase, you'll probably want to create your own templates to
save time.

To create a new template:

1. Set up a project exactly as you want it,
   including active inputs, routing, tracks,
   plug-ins, and virtual instruments.

2. Choose File > Save as Template
   (**Figure 3.26**).

3. In the Save as Template dialog box that
   opens, give the template a name and
   click OK (**Figure 3.27**).

4. To use the template, choose File > New
   Project and select it from the Templates
   list (**Figure 3.28**).

✔ Tip

- Templates save everything in a project,
  including audio files, MIDI files, and
  automation data. Sometimes this is precisely what you want; other times, you
  will want the project to have everything
  except such data. For example, you may
  want a set of common drum loops at certain tempos for sketching out songs, or
  you may want routings saved for headphone mixes for musicians. Just be careful to include or exclude the right things.

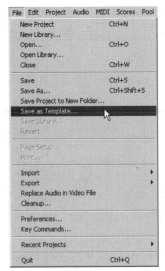

Figure 3.26
Creating a new
template.

Figure 3.27 Give templates meaningful names.

Figure 3.28 The new template is available in the
Templates list.

CREATING A NEW TEMPLATE

The Use and Abuse of Templates

During my time as a Cubase user, I have always been a loud advocate of templates. I used to create new templates all the time, trying to find the perfect one, but I wound up heavily modifying even my best templates according to the project at hand. Because of this, I've changed the way I work, and now I create a single template with minimal settings, adding tracks to it as I need them for each project.

Templates can include the following:

◆ Project window settings

◆ Effects plug-ins and virtual instruments

◆ Audio and MIDI files

◆ VST Connections settings

◆ Markers and navigation tools

◆ Anything else you use in a project

However, the basic template that I've settled on over time is simple: I set VST Connections to access my hardware in both stereo and surround modes, ReWire tracks for Reason and Live, and a couple of group tracks. Beyond that, I add audio, MIDI, and effects tracks as I need them. For me, this means I wind up with less Project window clutter, and being a fundamentally cluttered lad, that's a good thing.

What works for me might not work for you, though, so if certain types of projects wind up with the same setups, you might want to create your own templates. What you decide to include in your templates depends, of course, on what you plan to do with Cubase, but here are a few examples:

◆ If you use virtual instruments extensively with Cubase, you may want to have a number of them loaded and ready to go in your default template. The plug-ins are not actually running, so they take almost no CPU power, but with one click they are powered on and ready to use.

◆ If you use some track names over and over, a template can easily include them. For instance, you can name each part of a full drum kit on your first 12 audio tracks if you use a specific microphone setup on drums every time. When you name the track, the recorded audio files use this track name, which makes keeping track of files easier down the road.

Using the Empty Template

When none of the templates fit the needs of a project, you can use the Empty template to start completely from scratch. However, most of the time, you will find starting with a template easier, and if you spend some time making your own templates, you'll rarely find a situation where you have to use the Empty template. If you find yourself using the Empty template often, consider whether you can create a new template for at least some of the situations where you are now starting from a blank slate.

To create a new project with the Empty template:

1. From the File menu, choose New Project, which opens the New Project dialog box (**Figure 3.29**).

2. Select the Empty project, which creates a blank project with no audio or MIDI tracks; then click OK.

3. In the Select Directory dialog box that opens, navigate to the folder where you want to save a new song or create a new folder (**Figure 3.30**); then click OK.

4. A new, unnamed project opens. Save it right away by choosing File > Save As and naming it (**Figure 3.31**).

✔ Tip

■ Cubase automatically creates folders for audio files, fade files, and other files. Every file created during the life of a project will be stored somewhere in the working directory.

Figure 3.29 The New Project window opens, including the list of available templates; select the Empty template to start a project from scratch.

Figure 3.30 Locate a folder for the project or create a new one.

Figure 3.31 Saving the new song in the folder you created.

RECORDING AUDIO

Let's move on to the more creative and rewarding tasks of creating some new tracks. If you've spent time recording on any hard-disk recording system, many Cubase functions will seem familiar and intuitive. If instead you have worked with tape decks or are new to recording, some functions may take a bit of time to get used to— but soon you will become comfortable with operations that may seem a bit strange and fiddly at first.

You'll start this chapter by learning how to configure the inputs and outputs of your sound and then how to record a single mono track from sound card input. Then you'll learn how to record multiple tracks and how to record in stereo. You'll also learn how to set up Cubase to automatically start and stop recording at selected points in time and how to record more than one take while looping, so you can then select the best takes without interrupting the flow of the recording process. In addition, you'll learn how to record using the Stacked mode, new to SX 2; this mode is specifically designed for creating one great take out of many individual ones.

One of the primary goals of the Cubase interface is to provide as much power and control as possible in the main Project window, where you'll do most of your work. You'll also learn about particular situations where another window may be easier to use.

Creating an Audio Track

Before you can record any audio, you need an audio track to which you can record. Cubase SX has many kinds of tracks that you can use, including audio tracks, MIDI tracks, and automation tracks. They can be added singly or in groups.

To create a single new audio track:

1. In the Project window, right-click (Windows) or Control-click (Mac OS) the track list.

   A menu opens to let you create a new track (**Figure 4.1**).

2. From the menu, choose Add Audio Track.

3. The Add Audio Track dialog box opens, (**Figure 4.2**) allowing you to choose the kind of audio track you want to create. Choose either Stereo or Mono and click OK. For now, ignore all of the other options.

   A new audio track is added in the Project window (**Figure 4.3**).

Figure 4.1 You can use this menu to create any kind of track in Cubase.

Figure 4.2 Use this menu to define the kind of track to be created: mono, stereo, or some type of surround track.

Figure 4.3 A track has been added to the Project window.

Figure 4.4 Select this option from the contextual menu to add more than one track.

Figure 4.5 Clicking OK will add eight mono audio tracks to the project.

Creating Multiple Audio Tracks

Sometimes, you'll need multiple tracks. For example, you may want to transfer an eight-track live recording for mixing, or you may be setting up to record a full rock band with 16 or more tracks for each take. In these situations, it's much easier and faster to add more than one track at a time.

To create more than one audio track:

1. Right-click (Windows) or Control-click (Mac OS) the track list in the Project window.

2. From the menu that opens, choose Add Multiple Tracks (**Figure 4.4**).

3. When the Add Multiple Tracks dialog box opens, select Audio on the Track, which opens a submenu. Then choose Mono or Stereo on the configuration menu and specify the number of tracks you want to create in the Count field.

   The settings in **Figure 4.5** will create eight mono audio tracks.

4. Click OK.

   The tracks are added to the project.

Setting Audio Recording Preferences

Before you click the Record button and start recording, you need to be sure that Cubase will record the files at the bit depth and sample rate you want.

To set properties for audio recording:

1. From the Project menu, select Project Setup (**Figure 4.6**).

   The Project Setup panel opens (**Figure 4.7**). The bottom pane includes three options that enable you to set the sample rate, bit depth (recording format), and type of file to be recorded. The fourth option, for setting the stereo pan law, changes the way tracks are attenuated when they are panned further and further from center; unless you have a good reason to change it (and know what you are doing), it should be left at the default.

2. Select your preferred settings. If you don't know where to start, try 44.100 Hz, 24 bit, and Broadcast Wave.

3. Click OK.

Figure 4.6 Opening the Project Setup panel, where you can configure many project parameters.

Figure 4.7 Typical settings for a project: in this case, 24-bit, 44.1-kHz Broadcast Wave files will be recorded.

✔ Tips

- A Broadcast Wave file is a WAV file that can have extra text added to it, such as the name of the author and the date the file was created. Broadcast Wave files are also time-stamped, meaning that when the file is recorded, the start and end positions of the file relative to the start of the project are embedded in the file. For example, if a file starts 1 minute and 30 seconds from the start of a project, that information is stored with the WAV file, and the file can be re-spotted at that exact location in another project. This makes transfer of files between different projects simple, because you can place a Broadcast Wave file in a new project at precisely the point where it started in the original project.

- Cubase SX 2 adds support for files in the Wave64 format, an extension of the WAV file specification created by Sonic Foundry. Wave64 files are just like normal WAV files but can be much longer, so you can use them if you plan to record one continuous file for a very long time. Because the file header of a Wave64 file uses 64-bit values instead of the 32-bit values in a standard WAV file, a Wave64 file can be much longer than the 2GB limit set for a standard WAV file. You can use Wave64 files, for example, to record entire live performances that might last hours instead of minutes.

SETTING AUDIO RECORDING PREFERENCES

File Resolution

The arguments about which sample rate to use may go on forever. On paper, 16-bit, 44.1-kHz audio would seem to cover the entire range of human hearing, leaving no reason ever to use a higher sample rate of 88.2 or 96 kHz or a word length of 24 or 32 bits. That said, instruments undoubtedly make noises above the range of human hearing. Some people claim that the absence of this information degrades the quality of 44.1-kHz audio.

The most commonly used sample rates are 44.1, 48, 88.2, and 96 kHz. The sample rate for CDs is 44.1 kHz, many DAT decks sample at 44.1 or 48 kHz, and DVDs can sample at either 96 or 88.2 kHz, depending on the format and decisions made in production. Though there are arguments about what is the "best" sample rate to use, there is little argument about one thing: converting sample rates after the fact is generally a very bad idea. The math involved in turning a 48-kHz file into a 44.1-kHz file is very complex and conversion often leaves ugly, harsh artifacts in the resulting file.

My recommendation is to use the sample rate that the intended release format uses, unless you have a very good reason to do otherwise. This means that if a project is destined for CD release, track it at 44.1 kHz. If you are still worried about not catching enough of your instruments at that sample rate, at least choose 88.2 instead of 96 or 48 kHz. Not surprisingly, the math to turn 88.2 into 44.1 is comparatively simple. Keep in mind, though, that 88.2 kHz doubles the number of samples the system uses, which makes that sample rate precisely twice as demanding on the computer as 44.1. This means half the number of tracks, plug-ins, software synths, and so on at the higher sample rate.

Bit depth for a file is much easier to choose. Nearly every sound card these days can record at 24 bits, and turning a 24-bit file into a 16-bit file for CD release is a benign process. It is strongly recommended that you record 24-bit audio, regardless of the sample rate you choose.

Figure 4.8
Opening the VST Connections panel.

Figure 4.9 There are two tabs for VST connections: one for configuring inputs and one for configuring outputs.

Figure 4.10 The many options for creating new busses. Most musicians use only mono and stereo.

Figure 4.11 The newly created mono bus (next to the pointer).

Creating a VST Connection

One of the major changes in Cubase SX 2 is the way it works with the audio inputs and outputs on your sound card. Previous versions of Cubase, and most other audio applications, simply allow the program to activate and use the physical inputs and outputs. In the new version of SX, VST connections create virtual connections in addition to the physical ones and are another layer between the software and your audio hardware. This approach may seem a little unintuitive at first, but it allows you to employ many powerful routing and mixing options, particularly with surround mixing.

By default, Cubase SX 2 creates one pair of inputs and outputs, using the first two physical inputs and outputs on your sound card. You'll learn a lot more about VST Connections in the audio sections of this book, but as an introduction, you will create a new input bus to record a mono track.

To create an input bus using VST Connections:

1. From the Devices menu, select VST Connections (**Figure 4.8**).

2. On the VST Connections panel, select the Inputs tab if it is not selected (**Figure 4.9**). Most likely it will be the default when the panel opens.

3. Click the Add Bus button (refer to Figure 4.9).

4. In the Add Bus dialog box, choose the kind of input bus that you want to create. For now, select Mono.

   Figure 4.10 shows all of the options available in the menu.

5. Click OK.

   A new input bus is created on the VST Connections panel (**Figure 4.11**).

Configuring VST Connections

Selecting Cubase's VST Connections to work with sound card inputs and outputs offers many advantages. For example, more than one input bus in VST Connections can refer to the same hardware input on your sound card. This allows you, for example, to have an input bus called simply "Stereo In" that refers to analog inputs 3 and 4 on your sound card, but also to create a new mono input bus called "Keyboard" that uses input 3 on your soundcard, where your keyboard is plugged in. Using VST Connections, each input and output bus can be named and can refer to any hardware inputs and outputs, and more than one bus can use the same audio hardware.

In the following example, you will configure the mono input bus created in the previous task.

To configure a bus in VST Connections:

1. Open the VST Connections panel and create a new bus, as described in the previous task.

2. Click twice (click slowly) on the bus name in the Bus Name column of the VST Connections panel. The name will become highlighted (**Figure 4.12**); type a new name for the bus.

3. Click the setting in the ASIO Device Port column.

    A pop-up menu opens showing all the available inputs on your currently selected ASIO card (**Figure 4.13**).

4. Click to select the input you want on the sound card.

    After you select the input, the VST Connections panel will look something like **Figure 4.14**, which shows a mono input bus named "Keyboard" using Analog input 3 on the sound card.

Figure 4.12 Clicking twice on a bus name lets you rename it.

Figure 4.13 Selecting one of the hardware inputs on the ASIO card for the mono bus.

Figure 4.14 An example of a configured input bus.

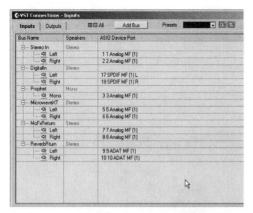

Figure 4.15 The VST Connections panel with a fully configured Input panel, including multiple buses all named.

Add preset

Figure 4.16 Clicking this button will create a new preset.

Figure 4.17 Naming the preset.

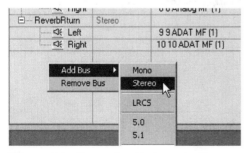

Figure 4.18 Another way to add a bus, using the contextual menu.

Saving VST Connections Settings

When you save a project or create a template, all changes to VST Connections are saved with that template or project. If you quit Cubase without saving a project, or if you create a new Empty project, changes to VST Connections settings are lost. Because of this, if you use a set of inputs and outputs regularly, you may want to save them as a preset in the VST Connections panel. After you create a preset, you can use it to recall all of the settings in the VST Connections panel in any project you create in Cubase.

To save a VST Connections preset:

1. Configure all input and output buses as you want, including names and routing.

   Figure 4.15 shows one example of a panel ready to be saved.

2. Click the Add (+) button, at the top right of the VST Connections panel (**Figure 4.16**), to add a preset.

3. In the Type in Preset Name dialog box that opens (**Figure 4.17**), type the name for the preset you want to create.

4. Click OK to save the preset name.

   The preset will now be available in the drop-down Presets menu at the top right of the VST Connections panel (refer to Figure 4.15).

✔ Tip

■ Another way to add a bus in the VST Connections panel is to right-click (Windows) or Control-click (Mac OS) and select Add Bus in the contextual menu (**Figure 4.18**). This contextual menu can add stereo, mono, or the surround busses that will be discussed later in this book.

Recording a Single Track

The simplest way to start recording is to use the Transport bar exactly the way you would if you were using a tape deck. There are lots of options that we'll cover later; for now, we will simply put a bass loop over a drum loop.

To record a single track using the Transport bar:

1. From the track list, select the track you want to record. Double-click the track name and rename it. In this example, the track is renamed Bass.

2. Check to be sure that the Record Enable button is red (**Figure 4.19**).

3. In the Track inspector, select the correct input on your sound card.

   In this example, the bass is patched into the left input of the first VST connection (**Figure 4.20**).

4. On the Transport bar, be sure that the AQ (autoquantize), Punch-In, Cycle, and Punch-Out buttons are not selected.

5. Click the Record button on the Transport bar.

   This starts both recording and playback. The selected track turns red to show that it's recording, and you'll see the new audio file being created (**Figure 4.21**).

6. Click the Stop button on the Transport bar when you are done recording.

Figure 4.19 The track name is set to Bass, and the Record Enable button is on.

Figure 4.20 The left side of a stereo input is selected in the Track inspector for this mono track.

Figure 4.21 Recording in progress. The track being recorded is highlighted (it's actually red); note the audio file image being created in the track.

No Signal?

You may still have trouble getting Cubase to recognize your input device. If the meters don't show any input signal when the Record and Monitor buttons are selected, or if your audio tracks remain empty when you try to record in them, make sure that your audio input device is selected on the VST Multitrack tab of the Device Setup dialog box under the Device menu. (You may need to quit Cubase and relaunch it after you make your selection.) Make sure that your drivers are installed in the correct locations on your computer, that your VST Connections settings are specified in Cubase, and that the input patch on your sound card matches the input selection number on your Track inspector. For additional setup instructions, refer to Chapter 1, "Installing and Configuring Cubase SX 2."

Remember also that working with multi-track audio on a computer inevitably involves a certain number of configuration hassles. You are asking your computer, a highly specialized sound card with equally specialized drivers, and Cubase all to deal with each other happily. There will be frustrating moments, but the problems almost always can be fixed. Nevertheless, even the people who get paid good money as consultants to fix these problems have moments of confused and embarrassed head scratching.

✔ Tips

- The spacebar on your keyboard starts and stops playback, and the asterisk (*) key on the numeric keypad starts and stops recording, so another quick way to start recording is to press the spacebar and then * on the numeric keypad when you want to start recording. There are numerous shortcuts for recording using both the Transport bar and the computer keyboard. If you find some recording operation frustrating, there's a good chance that Cubase has a way to make it easier; check the included documentation.

- It's common when recording yourself to play back and record to previously created material, building up a song one track at a time. If this is what you're doing, try setting the beginning of your song at bar 3 or 5. Then you can start Cubase recording and have a few measures of your loop or drum part playing before you start recording new material.

Recording Multiple Tracks

In many situations—from capturing the simple stereo output from a synthesizer to capturing the setup for a full rock band with dozens of microphones—you will need to record more than one track at a time. One cannot live on mono alone.

To record multiple audio tracks:

1. For each track to be recorded, select a distinct input in the Track inspector.

   Cubase won't enable tracks for recording if they have the same input selected.

2. Select the tracks to be recorded by doing one of the following:

   ▲ To select multiple tracks one by one, hold down the Ctrl (Windows) or Command-Option (Mac OS) key and click each individual track to be recorded.

   ▲ To select a group of tracks, click the first track in the group; then hold down the Shift key and click the last track in the group (**Figure 4.22**).

3. Check that the Record Enable button is red for all of the tracks.

4. Click Record on the Transport bar.

   The selected tracks will turn red to indicate that they are recording (**Figure 4.23**), and the project will play back.

5. When you are done recording, click Stop on the Transport bar or press the space-bar on your keyboard.

Figure 4.22 The track list has been resized to show four tracks selected for recording.

Figure 4.23 All of the selected tracks in the track list are red to indicate that they are recording; note that the top track was not selected and so is not recording.

Figure 4.24 Each track with an activated Record Enable button will be recorded, even if the track was not selected.

✔ Tips

- Tracks actually don't need to be selected for you to record them. As long as the Record Enable button is selected, a track will start recording when Record is engaged, regardless of whether the track is selected (**Figure 4.24**). Assuming that the input is available, selecting a track will enable it for recording, so sometimes the easiest and quickest approach is to select a track, while other times the best approach is to just click the Record Enable button.

- You can hear the audio while recording by selecting the Monitor button, which is next to the Record Enable button.

Recording Stereo Tracks

The mechanisms for recording stereo tracks are the same as those for recording mono tracks, but to record in stereo you need to have a stereo track, and you need to select a stereo input for recording. Remember that when you create tracks, they are defined as mono or stereo tracks. Stereo tracks can use only stereo inputs, while mono tracks can use mono inputs or one side of a stereo input.

Figure 4.25 Mono and stereo tracks are named clearly in the track list.

To record stereo tracks:

1. Select the stereo track.

    The Track list displays the type of track. **Figure 4.25** shows two tracks selected. Above the pointer on the upper track, the word *Mono* shows that it is a mono track, while the track below is a stereo track.

2. Set the input selector for the stereo pair that you want to record (**Figure 4.26**).

3. Click Record on the Transport bar.

    The track will turn red to indicate that it's recording.

4. When you're finished recording, click Stop on the Transport bar.

Figure 4.26 Only a stereo pair can be selected for input on a stereo track.

Figure 4.27 The two markers and highlighted section of the ruler indicate the loop selection. In this case, the loop selected is all of bar 2.

Figure 4.28 The left marker (which is the punch-in point) has been dragged to the first beat of bar 5.

Figure 4.29 Punch-in recording activated on the Transport bar.

Recording Automatically: Punch Recording

So far, we've been talking about recording manually using the Transport bar or the keys on the computer keyboard. This is an intuitive way to record because you click buttons much like you click tape deck controls, something nearly everyone has used. Cubase provides far more than tape deck functionality, though, letting you start and stop the recording process automatically. This is commonly known as punch recording, and it's particularly useful when you have to be engineer, tape operator, and performer all at the same time.

All of the tasks in the next few sections use the ruler and the loop markers (**Figure 4.27**). The left and right locators are useful for such operations as setting loops points and selecting part of a project, but for now just keep in mind that the left marker indicates the punch-in point (where recording automatically starts), and the right marker indicates the punch-out point (where recording automatically ends).

To start recording audio automatically:

1. Configure one or more stereo or mono tracks to record.

2. On the ruler, click the left loop locator (the right-pointing triangle) and move it to the location where recording should start (**Figure 4.28**).

   The cursor will turn into a small hand as the left point is moved.

3. On the Transport bar, click the button to activate punch-in recording (**Figure 4.29**). For now, do not click the Cycle or Punch-Out button.

continues on next page

4. Click the ruler somewhere before the punch-in point.

5. On the Transport bar, click Play.

Playback begins. When Cubase reaches the punch-in point, recording will begin.

6. When you are done recording, click Stop on the Transport bar.

The newly recorded track is highlighted (**Figure 4.30**).

Figure 4.30 The newly created track starting at bar 5 is recording.

✔ Tip

■ You can use a keyboard shortcut to set the left and right locators. To set the left locator, Ctrl-click (Windows) or Option-click (Mac OS) the ruler. To set the right locator, Alt-click (Windows) or Command-click (Mac OS) the ruler.

Punching out

Punching out while recording audio is accomplished in much the same way as punching in, but uses the right locator to define the punch-out point. By far the most common way to punch record is to set both punch-in and punch-out points. This lets you define very specifically where audio recording will take place. With punch-in and punch-out points set in this way, you can start playback before the punch-in point, and Cubase will run the recording operations for you.

Setting up good punch-in and punch-out points can provide very convenient, automatic, hands-free tracking.

Figure 4.31 The ruler with the punch-in point set to bar 5, beat 1, and the punch-out point set to bar 7, beat 1.

Figure 4.32 The punch-in and punch-out settings both are activated.

Figure 4.33 A two-bar punch, with the just-recorded part still selected

To start and stop recording automatically:

1. Configure a track or tracks, stereo or mono, to record.

2. Place the left locator where recording should start and the right locator where recording should stop (**Figure 4.31**).

3. Activate both punch-in and punch-out recording on the Transport bar (**Figure 4.32**).

4. Click the ruler at some place before the punch-in point.

5. Click Play on the Transport bar.

    Recording begins at the punch-in point and ends at the punch-out point.

6. To stop playback, click Stop on the Transport bar after the recording has punched out.

✔ Tips

- In these examples, Snap has been turned on and set to either Bar or Beat. With this setup, the locators snap to the nearest snap point when they are moved. Snapping provides a quick and easy way to create a clean two-bar overdub (**Figure 4.33**). However, snapping can be turned off and the punch-in and punch-out points set manually. This allows you to specify surgically precise punches, if that's what you want.

- Double-clicking the L and R settings on the Transport bar allows you to enter the left and right locator positions manually, by typing the bar, beat, or time location using the number keys on the keyboard. This approach can be very handy if you know exactly where you want to punch.

Recording Automatically: Cycle Recording

Cycle recording offers another way to automate audio recording and playback in Cubase. Unlike punch recording, cycle recording records in a loop, where each *pass*, or *take*, creates its own part in the editor. Although these takes seem to be unique, stand-alone pieces of audio, Cubase creates a single long audio file during cycle recording. That full audio file can be viewed and edited as a group of takes, which makes editing bits and pieces of different passes into a final version much easier.

For now, we'll use the default setting, Create Regions. Choose this setting unless you have a reason to choose differently.

To cycle record audio:

1. Activate the Cycle button on the Transport bar (**Figure 4.34**) as well as the Punch-In and Punch-Out buttons.

2. If you want to hear a click while cycle recording, click the Click button on the Transport bar.

3. Record–enable the tracks you want to record.

4. Click the ruler to start playback somewhere before the start of the loop.

5. Click Play on the Transport bar.

   The audio will play back until it reaches the punch-in point at the start of the loop, at which point recording will start.

   The track will record over the loop indefinitely, creating a new region with each loop.

6. When you're finished recording, click the Stop button on the Transport bar. Only the most recent cycle will appear in the Project window (**Figure 4.35**), but all of the cycles can be played back and edited.

Figure 4.34 The Cycle button is active on the Transport bar.

Figure 4.35 All of the individual takes are "behind" this finished part created with cycle recording.

Cycle Recording References

Exactly what Cubase does while cycle recording depends on the preferences that you choose. Cubase will always record the whole audio file in the same way, but the recording can create audio events, audio regions, or both.

◆ If you choose to create events, then each pass in the cycle creates a new event, and all events are stacked on top of each other like note cards. This means that each take can be moved and edited individually as an event.

◆ When each take creates a new region, the looped section in the Project window can quickly point to any of the regions created by cycle recording. You may prefer working with regions instead of events, particularly if you use the Pool for exporting parts of files for use in other programs, which can be easier when regions are recorded in cycle mode.

◆ You can also choose to create both events and regions in the preferences.

For reasons we'll get to later, using regions when you cycle record can make creating composite tracks a bit easier, but you can still create comps using events, so don't worry if you have a lot of events created by cycle recording. This setting can be changed by selecting File > Preferences and clicking the Record tab (**Figure 4.36**).

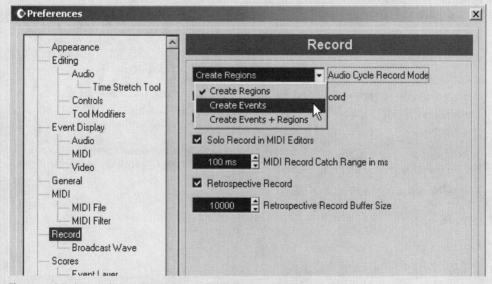

Figure 4.36 Cycle recording settings in the Audio Preferences panel.

Playing Back Cycle-Recorded Parts

Much of the power of cycle recording audio is in the ability to create master takes of solos or instrumental parts out of bits and pieces of various different takes. The idea is that a perfect solo is a rare thing, so it's handy to be able to replace the occasional clunker note or slack timing with a good part from another take. We'll discuss how to create such a composite take (often called a *comp*) later in the book. For now, we'll explore how to listen to the various takes that were just recorded in cycle mode. After you stop recording, Cubase always plays back the most recently recorded loop, but you can easily hear any of your takes.

To listen to the loops in a cycle-recorded part:

1. Right-click the cycle-recorded part in the Project window.

2. On the menu that opens, select the Set to Region option (**Figure 4.37**).

   The last take is selected because it was just recorded.

3. Select a different take in the Set to Region menu and click it (**Figure 4.38**). This other region will appear in the Project window and start playing back (**Figure 4.39**).

✔ Tip

- If you're recording yourself, a good way to start getting tracks is to set the locators so that you can cycle record the whole song. Play or sing the tracks a few times, and often that will give you good material to work with.

Figure 4.37 This menu determines which cycle-recorded take is played back.

Figure 4.38 Take 2 is selected.

Figure 4.39 Both the waveform in the Project window and the audio playback will switch to the selected take.

Figure 4.40 Use this menu to select Stacked mode when recording.

Figure 4.41 The three takes recorded in Stacked mode are all visible on the track.

Recording in Stacked Mode

New to Cubase SX 2 is stacked recording, which is a little like cycle recording on steroids. The most common use for cycle recording is to record a number of takes over a short loop and then pick the best take or pieces of multiple takes for the final version. You do this by opening the cycle-recorded audio part in the Audio Part editor. Stacked recording does something quite similar, but stacks each take vertically in the track, directly in the Project window. Both methods are described here and in Chapter 8, "Basic Audio Editing."

To record a track in Stacked mode:

1. Set the left and right locators just as you would for cycle recording and click both the Punch-In and Punch-Out buttons on the Transport bar. Record-enable the track or tracks you want to record.

2. Click the Cycle button if it is not already selected.

3. At the lower left of the Transport bar, click the pop-up menu for the Cycle record mode and select Stacked (**Figure 4.40**).

4. Start playback before the punch-in point, and record a few takes over the selected loop.

5. When you're done recording, click Stop on the Transport bar or press the space-bar on your computer keyboard.

   Each take will be displayed on the track you just recorded (**Figure 4.41**).

Playing Back Stacked Tracks

After a track is cycle recorded, you can use the contextual menu to select the take that you want to bring to the front for playback. You can also edit the takes in the Audio Part editor as described in the section on comping in Chapter 8. With stacked parts, you can do many of the things in the Project window that previously involved the Audio Part editor.

Both methods, stacked and cycle recording, are covered extensively later in this book, but here are a few points about playing stacked tracks, just so you have an idea of what stacked recording can do.

◆ The take closest to the bottom of the screen is the one that plays back. In **Figure 4.42** this is Take 3 of Bass_04. On the screen, this take is highlighted with a different color to indicate that it is the take that's playing back.

◆ If you click a take and press the Backspace key on your computer keyboard, that take will be deleted, and the next take above will play (**Figure 4.43**).

◆ If you drag a take or takes, a combination of takes will play back. **Figure 4.44** shows one possible combination of all three takes playing back. Note again that the parts of each take that are highlighted will be the ones that you hear when the project plays.

Figure 4.42 The bottom track, under the mouse pointer, will play back.

Figure 4.43 After you delete the bottom track, the next track up will become highlighted and play back.

Figure 4.44 A more complex playback scheme, where some parts of each take play in the project.

RECORDING MIDI

The audio recording and editing capabilities of Cubase get so much attention that you may forget that the program also includes world-class tools for recording, editing, and manipulating MIDI data. MIDI tracks live in the Project window next to audio tracks, group tracks, and folder tracks, but they have their own recording and editing tools—along with their own special quirks.

The most common kind of MIDI data is note data. A MIDI controller, such as a keyboard or a wind controller, creates MIDI note-on and note-off events as the instrument is played. A sequencer is used to record and play back these MIDI notes. MIDI offers a great deal of flexibility, allowing you to easily change both the tempo and pitch of MIDI data, and its appeal derives largely from these abilities. You can use MIDI for much more than just recording the note data of a performance on an instrument—you can also use it to control synthesizers, effects, drum machines, and even other software.

In this chapter, you'll learn to record MIDI in Cubase, using the MIDI inputs and outputs on your computer. You will also learn how to record in Loop mode, how to punch in parts automatically, and how to record more than one track at a time. Finally, you will learn how to record MIDI continuous controller (CC) data and sysex data.

Naming MIDI Inputs and Outputs

Before you begin to record MIDI in Cubase, you should give your MIDI inputs and outputs meaningful names. A complex project can route multiple tracks to multiple pieces of MIDI hardware, as well as route automation settings and MIDI data to software instruments and effects. Having recognizable names is a big advantage as the complexity of a project or your recording setup increases. For example, in my studio, I have a Yamaha Motif synthesizer, and it's a lot easier to figure out where MIDI data is going when I have the option to rout it to "Motif" instead of "Midex8 3." Cubase gives you the option to organize your MIDI devices by names, simplifying the task of keeping track of MIDI comings and goings.

Figure 5.1 Opening the Device Setup panel from the Devices menu.

To name MIDI inputs and outputs:

1. From the Devices menu, select Device Setup (**Figure 5.1**).

2. In the Device Setup dialog box, *do one of the following:*
   - ▲ In Windows, from the Devices list, select DirectMusic (**Figure 5.2**).
   - ▲ In Mac OS, from the Device Setup dialog box, select MIDI System.

3. The right panel of the Device Setup window lists all installed MIDI inputs and outputs. Click any of the generic names and then type a new name for that MIDI device (**Figure 5.3**).

4. Click OK in the Device Setup window to save the changes and close the window.

Figure 5.2 Select DirectMusic in Windows to see all available MIDI inputs and to rename them.

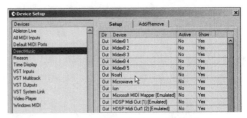

Figure 5.3 Select a generic name, such as Midex8 7, and then simply type a new, more descriptive name, such as the one shown here.

Figure 5.4 Using the track list to add a MIDI track.

Creating MIDI Tracks

Cubase uses specific track types to record specific types of data. Audio tracks will record audio, automation tracks will record automation, and so on. The default projects that come with Cubase, as well as the projects you create, will often have the correct type of track already available. If not, you can create MIDI tracks in the same way as any other type of track.

To create a MIDI track:

1. Right-click (Windows) or Control-click (Mac OS) the track list.

2. From the context menu that opens, select Add MIDI Track (**Figure 5.4**).

What Is MIDI?

MIDI stands for Musical Instrument Digital Interface. Regardless of what you may have heard, it does not stand for Masterfully Incoherent Digital Interface or Mostly Inscrutable Destroyed Inspiration. Honestly. MIDI was created in the early 1980s by a consortium of manufacturers to allow a synthesizer made by one company to communicate with a synthesizer made by a different company. At the time, this was a revolutionary idea. Much-missed American synth legend Sequential Circuits was one of the prime movers behind this open standard that has enabled so much innovation and creativity in the use of synthesizers and sequencers. MIDI is one of the greatest arguments in the world for technology standards. Almost two decades after its creation, MIDI is still a music production cornerstone, and you could take a synthesizer from the earliest days of MIDI and connect it to a sequencer using a cable you bought today in a music store. Try that with any other piece of technology in your house more complicated than a coffee maker—and good luck!

In some situations, you will want to add several MIDI tracks at once. This is very easy with Cubase, as you'll see in the next task.

To create multiple MIDI tracks:

1. In the Project window's track list, right-click (Windows) or Control-click (Mac OS).

2. From the context menu that opens, select Add Multiple Tracks (**Figure 5.5**).

3. When the Add Multiple Tracks window opens, select MIDI as the type of track to add. Then, in the Count field, enter the number of MIDI tracks you want to create.

   The example settings in **Figure 5.6** will create eight MIDI tracks.

4. Click OK.

   The MIDI tracks will be added to the project.

✔ Tip

- A great feature of Cubase is its extensive use of time-saving context menus. However, if you prefer the regular menus, you can choose Project > Add Track instead of opening the context menu from the track list.

Figure 5.5 Using the track list context menu to create more than one track.

Figure 5.6 The type of track to be created is MIDI; the number of tracks is 8.

Figure 5.7 The Show Inspector button in the Project window.

Figure 5.8
Selecting a MIDI input.

Configuring a MIDI Track to Record

After adding the appropriate tracks to your project and giving meaningful names to your MIDI inputs and outputs, you need to take one final step before clicking the Record button: you need to select the correct MIDI inputs and outputs. The easiest way to do this is by using the Track inspector.

To select MIDI inputs and outputs:

1. In the track list, select the MIDI track you want to record. If the inspector is not already open, click the Show Inspector button at the top left of the Project window (**Figure 5.7**).

2. The top tab of the inspector (the one with the name of the track) is used to display the most common parameters for a track. Click the MIDI input setting to display a drop-down list (**Figure 5.8**).

3. From the MIDI input list, choose your MIDI controller or select All MIDI Inputs.

continues on next page

4. Click the MIDI output setting to open another drop-down list, and in this list, select the MIDI synth, sound module, or VST instrument to which you want the MIDI data sent (**Figure 5.9**).

5. If you want the MIDI data sent to a particular MIDI channel, click the setting marked chn: and select the channel (**Figure 5.10**).

✔ Tip

■ The All MIDI Inputs setting for the MIDI input of a track is a great shortcut. This setting gathers all incoming MIDI data from any active input and uses it as the source for recording. If you are working on your own, this is the easiest setting to use, because you can just grab any MIDI device and record its output on the selected track. More complex MIDI setups, with many players or complex routings, require you to specify inputs.

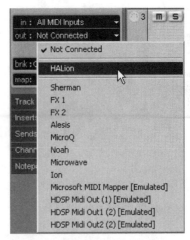

Figure 5.9 Selecting a MIDI output.

Figure 5.10 This menu specifies a particular channel for the MIDI output.

Figure 5.11 Record-enabling a MIDI track; note that you can also change the MIDI output settings here, in the track list.

Figure 5.12 Renaming a track; recorded MIDI parts will automatically have this name.

Figure 5.13 The Transport bar while recording.

Recording a Single MIDI Track

The track is now ready for recording. A few more clicks and you will be underway.

To record a MIDI track:

1. In the track list or inspector, click the Record Enable button for each track you want to record (**Figure 5.11**).

   Usually, it's best to give a track a name before recording, so you can more easily monitor MIDI tracks and events as your project progresses.

2. In the track list, double-click the name of the track and then type a new name (**Figure 5.12**).

3. Move the cursor to a location before where you want to start recording.

4. To start recording MIDI data, click the Record button on the Transport bar (**Figure 5.13**).

   The track in the track list will turn red to indicate that it's recording, and MIDI notes will appear as they're recorded in the Event display.

5. When you finish recording, click the Stop button on the Transport bar.

✔ Tip

■ Just as when recording audio tracks, you can use the computer keyboard to start and stop playback and recording. By default, the spacebar starts and stops playback, and the * key on the numeric keypad toggles recording on and off. You may find typing at the keyboard easier than clicking the Transport bar with the mouse.

No Sound When Playing MIDI?

Most of the examples in this book assume that you are using a MIDI controller and one or more sound modules. Many people will use a single synthesizer with built-in sounds as the sound module, plus the MIDI controller. Some will have a keyboard synthesizer that has its own sounds, which they also use to trigger sounds from other synthesizers or samplers. Others, though, may have nothing but a keyboard, with no built-in sounds, connected via MIDI or USB to the Cubase computer. These users will be able to view and record MIDI data but won't hear any sound, which is a less-than-thrilling experience.

If you are one of these people, probably the best thing to do is to learn a little bit about VST instruments, which are software-based synthesizers and samplers that run inside of Cubase. Chapter 7, "Using VST Instruments," is dedicated to VST instruments and includes descriptions of the VST instruments included with Cubase. Refer to that chapter to learn how to open the rack of virtual VST instruments and how to load and activate a VST instrument. Once a VST instrument is active, you will be able to select it as an output for a MIDI track, and this will let you trigger software-based sounds with nothing other than a MIDI controller.

Keep in mind also that some VST instruments are multitimbral, and some others are not. Multitimbral synths can generate a different sound on each MIDI channel: a keyboard on channel 1, a synth on channel 2, and so on. Many VST instruments, though, are not multitimbral, which means that the synth can make only one sound. If you want both a bass sound and a synth sound from such a VST instrument, you need to have two instances of it running at the same time. Again, refer to Chapter 7 for a lot more information about VST instruments in Cubase.

Figure 5.14 Moving the left locator; when the mouse pointer becomes a hand, you can click to grab the locator to move it.

Figure 5.15 You can also move the left locator manually by typing a new location here.

Figure 5.16 Only the Punch-In button is active. Cubase will not loop, and you will have to stop recording manually.

Punching In Using the Locators

The left and right locators can make MIDI recording much easier and more convenient, particularly if you are recording alone. The locators for MIDI tracks work the same as the locators for audio tracks, so if you can use one set of locators, you can easily use the other. You can use the locators to automatically start, stop, and loop MIDI recording and playback. Using the locators for recording involves both the ruler in the Project window and the Transport bar.

The simplest use of locators is to start recording at a certain time. If you set the locator correctly, you can start playback anywhere before the punch-in point, and Cubase will automatically start recording at the locator.

To automatically start recording MIDI:

1. Set the left locator to the point where you want to begin recording *by doing one of the following:*
   - ▲ Drag the locator on the ruler (**Figure 5.14**).
   - ▲ Double-click the setting on the Transport bar and enter the location manually (**Figure 5.15**).

2. On the Transport bar, click the Punch-In button to activate automated recording. Also be sure that the Punch-Out and Loop buttons are not selected (**Figure 5.16**).

3. Click the Record Enable button for each MIDI track that you want to record..

4. Start playback at a point before the punch-in point defined by the locator.
   When the playback head reaches the locator, all record-enabled tracks will begin recording.

5. When you are finished recording, click Stop on the Transport bar.

✔ Tip

- Also remember that you can set the left locator by Control-clicking (Windows) or Option-clicking (Mac OS) the ruler. Set the right locator by Alt-clicking (Windows) or Command-clicking (Mac OS) the ruler.

Punching Out Using the Locators

Naturally, just as you can for audio recording, you can set MIDI recording to automatically punch out at a certain time. You can use the right locator to set a point in the project when all tracks will stop recording.

To automatically stop recording MIDI:

1. Set the right locator *by doing one of the following*:
   ▲ Drag the right locator on the ruler (**Figure 5.17**).
   ▲ Double-click the right locator setting on the Transport bar and enter a position manually.

2. On the Transport bar, click the Punch-Out button if it is not already active (**Figure 5.18**).

3. Start recording at a point in the project before the punch-out point.
   When recording reaches the right locator, it will stop.

✔ Tips

- Remember that the status and setting of the Snap value always determine how the locators move on the ruler.

- Punching out is most commonly paired with punching in. Set the left and right locators and click both the Punch-In and Punch-Out buttons on the Transport bar (**Figure 5.19**) to define a section of the project where recording automatically starts and stops.

Figure 5.17 Moving the right locator.

Figure 5.18 The Punch-Out button is selected; recording will automatically stop at the right locator.

Figure 5.19 The most common punch setting; Cubase will automatically punch in at the left locator and punch out at the right locator.

Figure 5.20 You toggle the Record mode setting here, at the top left of the Transport bar.

MIDI Recording Mode Options

One way in which working with MIDI is unlike working with audio is that you can add data—both notes and continuous controller data—to a MIDI track after it has been recorded. For example, when you're working with an audio track, you can't add an extra harmony note to an existing file; the harmony note must be recorded on a different audio track and then mixed with the original. Cubase has three different modes for recording MIDI: Normal, Merge, and Replace. You toggle the mode by clicking at the far left of the Transport bar (**Figure 5.20**).

Normal mode records MIDI like audio. If you are recording and reach a place in the project where MIDI has already been recorded for that track, Cubase creates a new MIDI part and leaves the original untouched. The parts can later be edited and spliced, but they remain distinct MIDI events.

Merge mode merges new MIDI data with whatever has been previously recorded for that track. This is the mode to use when you want to build up a part from multiple takes, playing the kick drum on one pass, the snare drum on another pass, and so on. It is also the mode to use when you want to add continuous controller data to a track you have already recorded: for example, if you have a synthesizer part and want to add changes to the volume, pan, filter cutoff, or some other parameter.

continues on next page

Replace mode writes over a MIDI part if one is encountered while recording. In contrast to Normal mode, which adds a new part and stacks it on top of the existing part, Replace mode removes the MIDI parts previously recorded and records over them.

It's not too difficult to figure out which recording mode is best for a certain situation, but it's also easy to forget to change the setting before recording starts. Always do a quick mental check before recording MIDI to be sure you are using the right mode for the current task.

Another Way to Record MIDI

This chapter explains how to record MIDI using an external MIDI device, and in the next chapter, you'll learn how to draw MIDI notes from scratch using the mouse in the Key editor. There is one other option for recording MIDI, though, which is sort of in between the two. If you open the Key editor, you can click the keyboard on the left side of the editor to trigger MIDI notes. You can start recording in Cubase, and it will record those notes, just as if you had played them on an external controller, although you may find it more difficult to maintain the tempo while clicking the screen.

Figure 5.21 The left and right locators set for a two-bar cycle.

Figure 5.22 Cycle recording is active, and the left locator is set to punch in recording.

Figure 5.23 The Rhodes track is recording in Cycle mode.

■ You don't have to set the starting point for MIDI playback manually. If you just click the Record button on the Transport bar, a count-off will begin, and recording will start at the left locator. This can be a very convenient shortcut.

Recording MIDI in Cycle Mode

Just like audio, MIDI can be recorded while a specific section of a project is looping. The Cubase term for this loop-style recording is cycle recording. Setting up the program to cycle record MIDI is much like setting up to cycle record audio, though there are some extra considerations for MIDI cycle recording, discussed later in this chapter.

To cycle record MIDI:

1. Set the left and right locators to select the section that you want to cycle (**Figure 5.21**).

2. On the Transport bar, click to turn on Cycle mode and also click to make the Punch-In button active (**Figure 5.22**).

3. Move the cursor to a point before where you want the loop to start; then start playback.

   When Cubase reaches the point where it will loop, recording will automatically be punched in, and playback/recording will continue indefinitely (**Figure 5.23**).

4. When you're done recording, click Stop on the Transport bar to stop playback.

✔ Tips

■ When cycle recording, you don't want both the Punch-In and Punch-Out buttons selected. That setting will punch out recording after the first pass, though the section will continue to cycle playback.

■ You don't need to use the punch-in button to cycle record. If you're playing along to a section that is in Cycle mode and get a part you like, start recording manually, and you'll be cycle recording.

Cycle Recording: Mix Versus Overwrite

When you cycle record audio, you create a new audio part for each cycle of the loop. But when you're recording MIDI, the nature of MIDI allows some choice over how cycle recording works. You can toggle cycle recording between Mix mode and Overwrite mode using the Transport bar.

Mix mode (Figure 5.24) acts much like Merge mode for non-cycle recording. Incoming MIDI is added to the already recorded MIDI for that track. This allows a part to be built up over multiple passes, playing the hi-hat on one cycle, the kick drum on the next cycle, and so on. When recording is stopped, all MIDI played during all cycles is included in the single MIDI part.

Overwrite mode (Figure 5.25) overwrites any MIDI recorded in previous cycles whenever new MIDI is played. In effect, playing anything during a cycle erases what was played before and creates a new MIDI part. Use this mode when you want to keep playing a part until you get the performance you want, and then stop playback to keep the most recent, good take.

✔ Tip

- If you're cycle recording in Mix mode to build up a drum part or a pad, you should loop a fairly long part. Looping 16- or 32-bar sections will give you numerous shots at a part that often will be a 1-bar loop when recording multiple MIDI tracks.

Figure 5.24 The Transport bar set for Mix mode when cycle recording.

Figure 5.25 The Transport bar set for Overwrite mode when cycle recording.

Figure 5.26 The top two tracks already have audio recorded, while the next track down is an empty MIDI track, ready for stack recording.

Figure 5.27 Clicking this setting in the menu will activate Stacked mode.

Figure 5.28 After recording, each of the five takes is shown as a distinct lap on the MIDI track.

Recording MIDI in Stacked Mode

One of the exciting new features in Cubase SX 2 that was unavailable in the first version of SX is the ability to record MIDI in Stacked mode. This mode was discussed briefly in Chapter 4, "Recording Audio." When you record in Stacked mode, each pass creates a new take visible on the track being recorded. After you record the takes, you can edit them into one single take made up of the best parts of each individual take. Recording MIDI in Stacked mode is similar in many ways to recording audio in Stacked mode.

To record MIDI in Stacked mode:

1. Set the left and right locators where you want the MIDI parts to begin and end (**Figure 5.26**).

2. On the Transport bar, click the Cycle button.

3. Select Stacked from the Cycle recording menu on the Transport bar (**Figure 5.27**).

4. Click the Record button on the Transport bar to start Cycle recording; play through the loop a few times.

5. When you're done recording, click Stop on the Transport bar or press the spacebar on the keyboard.

   Each take will be visible on the track that was just recorded (**Figure 5.28**).

Playing Back Stacked MIDI Tracks

Recording MIDI in Stacked mode isn't exactly like recording audio in Stacked mode, but it's reasonably close. A new take is created with each pass, and each take is visible right in the project window, where takes are called laps. The main difference between audio and MIDI recording in Stacked mode has to do with the inherent difference between audio and MIDI. Each audio track in Cubase can play back one audio stream at a time, whereas each MIDI track can contain almost unlimited numbers of notes and other data. In theory, every MIDI part recorded in Stacked mode can play simultaneously, but only one part or one section of the audio recorded in Stacked mode can play back at a time.

Cubase gets around this problem by muting each take, or lap, except the last one. **Figure 5.29** shows the same track (with the same set of takes) that is in Figure 4.28 except that it has been edited a bit. All but one lap is darkened, which means that Cubase has muted the others. If you wanted, you could unmute every take, but then instead of a single track of mediocre keyboard playing, Cubase would play back a cacophony of five simultaneous takes of mediocre keyboard playing, all at the same time.

Editing MIDI is covered extensively in Chapter 10, "Editing MIDI," and if you want to know how to work with stack-recorded MIDI, you should look there. Just keep in mind that you can perform all of the editing operations on each lap of a stack-recorded MIDI part that you can perform on any other MIDI part, including copying, resizing, processing, and moving.

Figure 5.29 A stack-recorded MIDI track, which in this case will play lap 4 while all others are muted.

Figure 5.30 Three tracks record-enabled; all will record at the same time.

Figure 5.31 Each track that will record is set to its own MIDI output; this is the view in the track list.

Figure 5.32 All four tracks are recording at the same time.

Recording Multiple MIDI Tracks

Up until now, you have been learning about recording single tracks. That is the most common way MIDI is recorded, but Cubase also can record more than one track at a time. There are many situations in which this is a good idea, such as when you want to record more than one musician, to record the same part to more than one destination, or to record MIDI instruments that transmit on more than one channel.

To record multiple MIDI tracks:

1. Record-enable all tracks that you want to record (**Figure 5.30**).

2. In the inspector for each track, select the MIDI input you want to use. This may be the same for all tracks, or it may be different, depending on your situation.

3. In the Track inspector or on the track list, select a MIDI output for each track to be recorded (**Figure 5.31**).

   When you start recording, all record-enabled tracks will record MIDI from their selected MIDI inputs (**Figure 5.32**).

4. When you are finished recording, click Stop on the Transport bar or use the keyboard to stop recording.

✔ Tip

■ All of the features available for recording single MIDI tracks are available for recording multiple tracks. When recording more than one track, you can still cycle, punch in, punch out, and do everything that's possible with single-track recording.

About Multitimbral MIDI Devices

Many synthesizers and samplers are *multi-timbral*, which means that they can play back different sounds triggered by different MIDI channels—that is, MIDI channel 1 will trigger the piano part, MIDI channel 2 will trigger the bass line, MIDI channel 10 will trigger the drum part, and so on.

Some MIDI controllers can also play back on different MIDI channels simultaneously. This capability can be used to create keyboard splits; for example, you can set up a split where one part of a keyboard triggers a bass sound on MIDI channel 1, and the rest of the keyboard triggers a piano sound on MIDI channel 2. Other parameters can be used to trigger different channels depending on the controller, but the issues remain the same regardless of the particular controller and setup.

Figure 5.33 When recording multiple tracks and using multi-timbral devices, it's usually best not to select All MIDI Inputs.

Multitimbral Recording Considerations

◆ When recording a multitimbral MIDI controller, you don't want All MIDI Inputs selected as the source. Define a unique channel and device for each track that is to be recorded (**Figure 5.33**).

◆ All multitimbral MIDI devices must have the ability to save setups where the whole state of the synthesizer can be recalled. These are often called multis or combis or something similar. If you will be using multitimbral synths, get familiar with the way that each device manages multitimbral setups. It's easy to get lost in the multitimbral MIDI maze, and knowing how the gear works will keep that from happening.

Figure 5.34 A track with previously recorded notes is record-enabled.

Figure 5.35 Selecting Merge mode to add the CC data to the track.

Recording MIDI Controller Data

MIDI is more than just notes. The MIDI specification also includes continuous controller (CC) data, or even sysex data. CC data provides one of the fantastic features of MIDI: it allows you to use the tactile knobs and sliders on a MIDI controller to modify parameters like volume, pan, and filter cutoff on MIDI devices, or within your sequencer, in real time. You can usually use CC to control almost any MIDI parameter, but a common use where tactile control via CCs is preferable is to modify the cutoff on a synth filter. It's much more intuitive to turn a physical knob to find just the right spot for filter cutoff than to do the same thing with the mouse. Cubase can record this data much like it records note data, and if you change a controller during recording (by moving the pitch wheel on your synth, for example), Cubase will record the CC data with the MIDI notes.

CC data is recorded with a performance, but often you can also use it to add dynamic elements to a performance after the fact. For example, you can use the modulation wheel on a MIDI controller to control the behavior of a filter in a synth.

To record MIDI CC data:

1. Record-enable the track to which you want to add the CC data (**Figure 5.34**).

2. Check that recording mode is set to Merge on the Transport bar (**Figure 5.35**) so the CC data is added to the current MIDI track.

3. Start recording manually, or set a punch-in point to start recording automatically.

4. Move the modulation wheel on the controller.

continues on next page

The Event display shows the data as it is being recorded (**Figure 5.36**).

5. When you're finished recording, use the Transport bar or computer keyboard to stop playback.

You'll see the recorded CC data along with the note data (**Figure 5.37**).

✔ Tip

■ Nearly all MIDI hardware made in the recent past has powerful tools for editing CC sources and destinations. Learning about your MIDI hardware and software will allow you to use the modulation wheel on your MIDI controller to control nearly any parameter on nearly any MIDI device in your studio.

Figure 5.36 The CC data is visible in real time as it is recorded.

Figure 5.37 The track after recording CC data; the thin horizontal lines are the MIDI notes for the track, and the vertical lines are the recorded CC data.

Recording MIDI Sysex Data

All MIDI devices understand note and CC data in pretty much the same way. However, the smart people who put together MIDI also realized that manufacturers would sometimes need to implement specialized abilities not covered by the basic MIDI specification. This data is called system-exclusive MIDI data, or sysex data for short.

Sysex data is MIDI data that can be understood only by the particular make and model of MIDI device that created it. For example, all synthesizers should respond to the CC data for volume in the same way, but sysex data from a Roland synth will do nothing when sent to a Waldorf synth.

Sysex has many uses if you are willing to spend the time to learn about it, but be ready to put your MIDI geek hat on, because sysex is about as technical and computerlike as MIDI gets. There is one use for sysex, however, that nearly everyone should know about: a bulk dump.

Almost all synths, samplers, and other MIDI hardware have the ability to send their complete current state as sysex data. Cubase can record this sysex bulk dump, and then it can be transferred back to the device to return it to the precise state it was in when the sysex dump was recorded. To restore the device settings, the sysex data only needs to be played back from a MIDI track in Cubase routed to the MIDI hardware.

To record MIDI sysex data:

1. By default, Cubase filters out sysex data when recording. To enable recording of sysex data, *do one of the following:*

   ▲ In Windows, choose File > Preferences and then select MIDI Filter (**Figure 5.38**).

   ▲ In Mac OS, choose Cubase SX > Preferences and then select MIDI Filter.

2. Uncheck Sysex to allow MIDI sysex data to be recorded (**Figure 5.39**). Otherwise, any MIDI parameters selected on this panel will be filtered out and not recorded. Click OK to save the changes in the preferences.

3. Record-enable a MIDI track and start Cubase MIDI recording.

4. Initiate a sysex dump.

   Each MIDI device has a slightly different method for initiating a sysex bulk dump. Usually, you either push a few buttons simultaneously on the front panel of the device or choose an option in the Global section for the MIDI device. Consult the documentation that came with the MIDI hardware.

   The MIDI In indicator on the Transport bar will light to indicate that MIDI is being received, and Cubase will record the sysex data.

5. When the sysex bulk dump is finished, the MIDI In light will stop flashing. Use the Transport bar or computer keyboard to stop recording.

✔ Tips

- The easiest way to be sure that sysex data was recorded is to play back the part that contains the sysex data and see if the MIDI Out light on the Transport bar lights to show MIDI activity. You can also check in the MIDI List editor, which is discussed in Chapter 10.

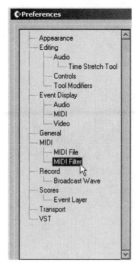

Figure 5.38 Selecting the Filter section of the MIDI tab on the Preferences panel lets you choose whether Cubase includes or ignores some kinds of MIDI data.

Figure 5.39 Sysex has been unchecked, so that sysex data will not be filtered out. Now Cubase can record sysex data.

- Sysex has some voodoo to it, and a lot of data is transferred at the same time. Always check sysex bulk dumps to be sure they work properly. Also, you should record and play back sysex data at the beginning of a song, since many MIDI devices will not play notes while sysex data is being received.

- Dealing with sysex data can seem difficult and irritating, but it's still a lot easier than using pencil and paper to write down every parameter of a MIDI device!

ENTERING MIDI MANUALLY

You don't have to use an external device to record MIDI data in Cubase. While this is often the best way to get music into Cubase, there are some situations when you simply won't have a controller handy for recording. In addition, some people find creating certain parts, such as bass lines and programmed drum beats, easier to do manually by entering them from the computer keyboard or with the mouse.

Cubase offers many ways to enter MIDI data by hand, but the most commonly used tools are the Key editor and the Drum editor. This chapter will get you going with these editors, showing you how to create MIDI notes and how to edit basic parameters to change the way the notes sound.

You will start by creating an empty MIDI part in the Project window. Then you will learn how to open it in the Key editor and to enter notes with the mouse. You will also learn about the tools Cubase provides to control the duration of notes and how to edit the volume and pan and other properties in the Key editor. In addition, you will learn about the specialized Drum editor, a powerful editor with tools specifically designed for creating programmed beats from scratch.

Creating a MIDI Part

When you record MIDI data on a MIDI track in Cubase, the application automatically creates a MIDI part for the incoming data. However, when you enter MIDI notes using one of Cubase's built-in editors, you first need to create a part, or container, for it. There are two primary ways to create new, empty parts: with the locators and with the Draw tool.

To create a MIDI part using the locators:

1. In the Project window, set the left and right locators where you want the MIDI part to start and end (**Figure 6.1**).

   You can set the locators by moving them on the ruler or by entering their locations on the Transport bar.

2. Select the Object Selection tool (the arrow) and double-click the MIDI track, between the locators, where you want to create the new part.

   A new, empty MIDI part is created and is selected (**Figure 6.2**).

Figure 6.1 The locators set to create a MIDI part.

Figure 6.2 After you double-click with the arrow, a one-bar part is created.

Contextual Menu Bug

As of this writing, Mac users (in OS 10.3) cannot access the contextual menus for MIDI parts using the Control-click method. If you don't have a two-button mouse, choose the equivalent selections from Cubase's main menus above the Project window.

Figure 6.3 You can select any of the tools, including the Draw tool, from this contextual menu.

Figure 6.4 After you drag with the Draw tool, this MIDI part is created.

Sometimes, you will want to create a part that does not begin and end precisely at the locators. In this case, you can use the Draw tool, as you'll see in the next task.

To create a MIDI part with the Draw tool:

1. In the Project window, right-click (Windows) or Control-click (Mac OS) and select the Draw tool from the contextual menu (**Figure 6.3**), or choose the Draw tool from the toolbar.

2. With the Draw tool selected, hold down the mouse on the location where you want the part to begin and drag to the location where you want the part to end. Release the mouse.

   A new part is created and selected in the Project window (**Figure 6.4**), with its length determined by the distance you dragged the mouse.

✔ Tip

- When you use the Draw tool, Snap applies. Turn Snap off to draw a part freehand; keep Snap on to easily create a part of a particular length.

CREATING A MIDI PART

113

Opening an Editor

The Project window has only minimal tools for editing MIDI data and no tools whatsoever for creating MIDI data. To put something in an empty MIDI part, you need to open the part in an editor. One method is simply to double-click the MIDI part with the Object Selection tool—the arrow. This opens the MIDI Key editor, which is commonly used for editing MIDI. However, Cubase also includes Drum, List, and Score editors, which may be more appropriate for your needs. You'll learn what these editors do later in the chapter. Here's how to open any of these editors.

To open a MIDI part in an editor:

1. In the Project window, click the part you want to open, to select it (**Figure 6.5**).

2. Right-click (Mac users with one-button mice must use the MIDI menu at the top of the Project window) the part to open the contextual menu.

3. Choose MIDI and then select the editor you want to open (**Figure 6.6**).

   The MIDI part opens in the editor you select.

✔ Tip

■ By default, Cubase uses the MIDI Key editor when a part is double-clicked. If you prefer to open a part in a different editor when you double-click, you can change the default behavior. Choose File > Preferences (Windows) or Cubase SX > Preferences (Mac OS). In the dialog box that opens, under Event Display, select MIDI. In the right panel of this dialog box, open the drop-down Default Edit Action menu and choose a different default MIDI editor (**Figure 6.7**).

Figure 6.5 It's hard to see in this illustration, but a red outline surrounding this MIDI part shows that it is selected.

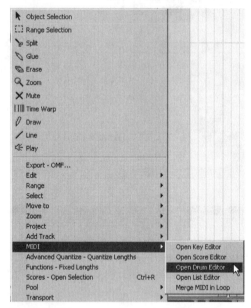

Figure 6.6 This contextual menu includes many options, including options to open a part in any MIDI editor.

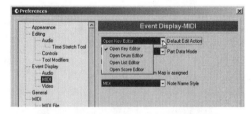

Figure 6.7 The default editor, the one used when you double-click a part in the Project window, can be changed here.

About the Key Editor

The Key editor lets you enter data through a visual representation of a piano keyboard. (You can also record MIDI data in the Key editor just as you can in the Project window.)

Creating MIDI data in the Key editor involves extensive use of the toolbar and Info line. **Figure 6.8** shows the toolbar with a MIDI note selected, with information about this note displayed on the Info line.

Solo button: When this button is selected, only the MIDI data in the current editor is audible. All other MIDI data and audio is muted.

Show Info button: Toggles the Info line on and off.

Acoustic Feedback (formerly "Audition") button: Toggles auditioning on and off. When you create a new note with auditioning turned on, the note plays back. When auditioning is off, notes do not play back when they are entered.

Edit tools: The various tools used to create and modify MIDI data. See the next section, "About the Edit Tools," for more information on these tools.

Autoscroll button: When this button is selected, the window follows along as the project plays back.

Insert Velocity menu: Sets the velocity used when a new MIDI note is entered.

Snap button: Toggles Snap on or off for the Key editor.

Quantize menu: Sets both the Snap and Quantize values for MIDI data.

Length Quantize menu: Sets the duration used when a new MIDI note is entered.

Mouse time value: Shows the current location of the mouse pointer in both song position and pitch.

Colors menu: Specifies whether and how MIDI notes are color-coded.

Figure 6.8 The toolbar and Info line in the MIDI Key editor.

About the Edit Tools

The edit tools are particularly important when creating MIDI parts. **Figure 6.9** shows the edit tools on the toolbar.

Object Selection tool: Selects one or more notes in the Note or Controller display. This book also refers to this tool as the arrow.

Draw tool: Creates notes and controller data and is often referred to as the pencil tool.

Line tool: Used to draw multiple notes in Paint mode and to draw shapes for controller and automation data. Previously a subset of the Draw tool, in SX 2 the Line tool is distinct.

Eraser tool: Erases notes when they are clicked with this tool.

Zoom tool: Shows more or less information in the editor by enlarging or shrinking the view.

Mute tool: Stops a note from playing back until it's unmuted. Clicking a note with this tool does not erase it permanently (unlike when you use the Eraser tool).

Scissors tool: Splits a MIDI note into two notes.

Glue tool: Combines two MIDI notes into a single note.

Time Warp tool: Used for graphically editing the tempo track.

Figure 6.9 The MIDI edit tools on the Key editor toolbar, with the Draw tool options displayed.

Figure 6.10 Use the toolbar to select the Draw tool.

Figure 6.11 Clicking enters a MIDI note. Notice also that the note about to be entered is visible on the keyboard; in this case, the A key is highlighted.

Figure 6.12 After you click, the A is created in the Note display.

Entering a MIDI Note

The most basic task when creating MIDI data is entering a note. The Draw tool in the Key editor makes this very easy.

To enter a note in the Key editor:

1. Click the Draw tool on the toolbar to select it (**Figure 6.10**).

2. Using the piano-like keyboard on the left side of the Key editor as a guide, place the tool at the pitch and meter position where you want to enter a note (**Figure 6.11**).

3. Click once.

   The note is entered in the Key editor (**Figure 6.12**).

✔ Tip

■ If you hold down the mouse after clicking, you can drag to the right to make the duration of the note longer.

Hearing MIDI Notes

When entering notes in the Key editor, you can choose whether to hear them or not. When the Acoustic Feedback (Audition) button is enabled, Cubase sends each MIDI note as it is created to the device selected for the MIDI part currently in the Key editor. When this button is not enabled, notes do not sound when entered.

Each method is best in different situations. If you are looping a drum part in an editor and building the groove by adding notes as the loop plays, you usually won't want the notes to sound; you will want to hear the added note the next time the loop passes that point in the groove. If you are entering MIDI data for another sound, such as a bass line or a synth bell, and are not also looping the part, you may prefer to hear the pitches as they are entered.

It's easy to figure out when to turn Acoustic Feedback on or off. Essentially, leave it on unless it bothers you. The situations where it's inconvenient to have the notes sounding are usually pretty obvious.

Expanding the Note Display

Most windows in Cubase let you zoom the view on both the vertical and horizontal axes. Because of the way the Key editor works, the vertical axis is particularly important when entering MIDI notes. With too much showing, it's easy to enter the wrong note; with too little showing, it's hard to find the note you want to create. You can set the Key editor so that the keyboard on the left displays from one to seven octaves. Viewing more octaves makes it easier to see what is going on with the music, but it's much easier to click the correct note when the Note display is zoomed in.

To change the Note display:

1. Click the Zoom slider at the right side of the Key editor (**Figure 6.13**).

2. Drag the slider up to see more notes in the Note display, to get an overview of the whole MIDI part (**Figure 6.14**).

3. Drag the slider down to see fewer notes in the Note display, to see them in the most detail (**Figure 6.15**).

Figure 6.13 The Zoom slider in the Key editor, here at roughly its default position.

Figure 6.14 With the Zoom slider all the way up, many notes can be viewed, but they are quite small on the vertical axis.

Figure 6.15 The Zoom slider is now all the way down, showing far fewer notes, but the notes are much larger.

Using the Mouse Time Value Display

Figure 6.16 This is the location and pitch we want: F♯ at the first tick of beat 2 of measure 2.

Mouse Pointer display

Figure 6.17 Clicking the Note display adds the C at beat 4 of measure 5, as shown in the Mouse Time Value display.

As mentioned previously, one way to see what note you're entering is to look at the highlight on the Key editor's keyboard. However, the Mouse Time Value display (formerly known as the Mouse Pointer display) at the top of the Key editor window gives you even more feedback. This display shows the current position of the mouse pointer, with the position constantly updated as you move the mouse around the Note display. It also shows the note that will be entered and the song position where the note will be entered. The song position is shown in *bars.beats.ticks*, so 4.3.1 means bar 4, beat 3, tick 1. This notation makes it easy to place a note precisely, even without looking at the Note display. For example, assume that you want to enter an F♯ at the second beat of bar 2. Here's how.

To enter a note using the Mouse Time Value display:

1. Select the Draw tool and move it over the Note display.

2. Watch the Mouse Time Value display as you move the cursor to the location where you want to enter the note (**Figure 6.16**).

3. Click at that location, and the note will be entered at precisely the point you wish (**Figure 6.17**).

Snap and the Key Editor

Like nearly everything else in Cubase, the state and setting of Snap has a great deal to do with what exactly happens when your mouse-clicking starts. Having Snap on is convenient when you want to enter notes exactly in time. Snap must be turned off if you want to put notes at places other than at exact meter divisions.

For example, if you want to enter a part exactly on the eighth notes, the easiest way to do this is with Snap.

To enter notes using Snap:

1. Set the meter division you want to use.

   In this example, in the Key editor the Quantize value is being changed to 1/8 Note (**Figure 6.18**).

2. If Snap is not turned on, click the Snap button to turn it on (**Figure 6.19**).

3. Select the Draw tool.

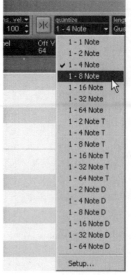

Figure 6.18 Setting the Quantize value (used by Snap in the Key editor) to an eighth note.

Figure 6.19 Snap is turned on.

Figure 6.20 The Draw tool is not precisely at the first beat.

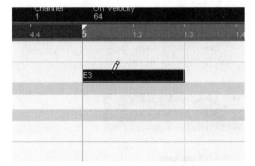

Figure 6.21 Clicking at the location shown in Figure 6.20 snaps the note to the exact start of the measure.

Figure 6.22 With the Draw tool positioned as in Figure 6.20 and Snap turned off, the note will start where the Draw tool is clicked.

4. Starting on the left side of the Note display in the Key editor window, click the note you want to enter.

   Clicking where the Draw tool is positioned in **Figure 6.20** will snap the note to the nearest eighth note—in this case, the very beginning of the measure (**Figure 6.21**).

5. Continue to enter notes with Snap on across the whole measure.

   Each note will be placed precisely on an eighth note.

✔ Tip

- If you turn off Snap when entering the note with the Draw tool positioned exactly as in Figure 6.20, the result is **Figure 6.22**.

Setting Note Length

In the previous example, you entered eighth notes across a bar using Snap to place the notes precisely. When you enter notes in the Key editor, the default note duration will be equal to the Snap value. If Snap is set to eighth notes, then clicking the Note display with the Draw tool will enter an eighth note. In some situations, this is desirable, but not always. For example, you may want to program a techno-style pulsing bass line that is still straight eighth notes, but with each note lasting only the duration of a sixteenth note. You can alter the duration of the note through quantizing.

To change the duration of notes created with the Draw tool:

1. Turn Snap on if it not already on, and set the Quantize value to 1/8 Note.

2. Select the Draw tool.

3. In the Length Quantize drop-down menu, select 1/16th Note (**Figure 6.23**).

4. With the Draw tool, click the note and meter location where you want the line to start.

    A note of sixteenth-note duration will be entered at the nearest eighth note (**Figure 6.24**).

5. Continue clicking across the whole measure, skipping one sixteenth and then adding a note at the next sixteenth The result will look like **Figure 6.25**.

Figure 6.23 This setting will insert sixteenth notes, regardless of the Snap setting, when you use the Draw tool.

Figure 6.24 This setting enters a sixteenth note at the start of the MIDI part. The figure shows the first part of measure 5.

Figure 6.25 A few more clicks, and the Snap and Length Quantize settings create this simple line.

Figure 6.26 Click the Insert Velocity field and then change it by typing a value on the computer keyboard.

Figure 6.27 This setting will create notes with the maximum velocity for MIDI notes: 127.

Figure 6.28 After you enter and then select a note, check the Info line to see whether the Insert Velocity setting was applied correctly.

Figure 6.29 You can click the arrows to increase or decrease the velocity of inserted notes.

Setting Note Velocity

MIDI involves more parameters than just pitch and duration. One of the more important parameters is velocity. Velocity relates back to the keyboard and synth origins of MIDI; it is a measure of how hard a key is struck. For non-keyboard sounds, the velocity essentially controls how loudly a note is sounded, though of course not every sound or synth responds in the same way to velocity information.

Like most things MIDI, velocity is recorded using a not terribly intuitive scale that ranges from 1 to 127. By default, the Cubase Key editor uses a velocity of 100 for notes entered by hand with the Draw tool. You'll learn how to change velocity for an individual note later in this chapter, but in some cases you will know ahead of time that you want notes to have a particular velocity. For a techno bass line, for instance, you may want to use maximum velocity, or 127, for each note.

To enter notes with a specific velocity:

1. Select the Draw tool.

2. Click the Insert Velocity field to highlight the setting (**Figure 6.26**).

3. Type a new value; in this example, enter 127 to create notes with the maximum velocity allowed by MIDI (**Figure 6.27**).

4. Use the Draw tool to enter a note in the Note display.

   When that note is selected, the Info line will show its velocity (**Figure 6.28**).

✔ Tip

■ You can also use the small up-and-down arrows beside the Insert Velocity field (**Figure 6.29**) to increase or decrease the velocity by one unit per click. If you have a wheel mouse, you can also click the note and use the wheel to change the velocity.

Painting Multiple Notes

Cubase makes great efforts to provide short-cuts to let you create music quickly and easily. One of these shortcuts gives you the ability to enter multiple notes in the Key editor with the Line tool by putting it in Paint mode. When the Line tool is in Paint mode, dragging will enter notes anywhere and everywhere that the tool is dragged. In fact, you can combine the Snap setting, the Length Quantize setting, and the Insert Velocity setting with the Paint mode shortcut to create in one pass the eighth-note techno bass line we've been working with.

To paint notes:

1. Click the Line tool on the toolbar to select it. Click it again after it is selected to open a drop-down menu; select Paint (**Figure 6.30**).

2. Turn on Snap by clicking the Snap button.

3. Set the Quantize, Length Quantize, and Insert Velocity values to control the way that notes are entered. For this example, set 1/8 Note for Quantize, 1/16 Note for Length Quantize, and 121 for Insert Velocity (**Figure 6.31**).

4. Click with the Line tool (which turns into a paint brush) the place where you want to start entering notes and drag to the right to enter notes for as long as you wish. Release the mouse when you're finished (**Figure 6.32**).

Figure 6.30 Setting the Draw tool to Paint mode.

Figure 6.31 The Snap, Quantize, and Velocity settings—the same ones used in the previous example.

Figure 6.32 Dragging to paint notes on the Note display.

Figure 6.33 Using the contextual menu to select the Erase tool.

Figure 6.34 When you click the note, the note is deleted.

Muting and Deleting Notes

As easy as it is to make mistakes playing a musical instrument, it's probably even easier to make mistakes when entering notes with a mouse. The painting action described in the preceding section is also particularly prone to occasionally creating unwanted notes. Fortunately, you can use the Eraser and Mute tools in Cubase to fix your mistakes by deleting notes or by muting a note or two in a part without actually losing the MIDI data. As their names suggest, the Eraser tool deletes data completely, and the Mute tool prevents the selected note from sounding during playback.

To delete MIDI notes with the Eraser tool:

1. In the Note display, right-click on the note and select Erase from the contextual menu (**Figure 6.33**), or select the Erase tool from the toolbar.

   The pointer turns into an eraser.

2. Click any note to delete it (**Figure 6.34**).

To mute notes with the Mute tool:

1. In the Note display, right-click the note and select Mute from the contextual menu, or select the Mute tool from the toolbar (**Figure 6.35**).

2. Using the Mute tool, which looks like an X, click any note that you don't want to hear.

   Muted notes turn white (**Figure 6.36**) and will not sound at playback.

✔ Tip

■ You can use the Mute tool to create interesting effects in existing MIDI tracks, whether the tracks are entered manually or recorded from a MIDI controller. Often in music, less really is more, and setting a project to loop while muting notes a few at a time can lead to much more interesting MIDI lines.

Figure 6.35 Selecting the Mute tool from the toolbar.

Figure 6.36 The two white notes are muted and will not sound.

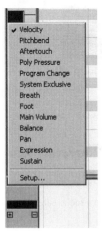

Figure 6.37 Clicking to the left of the Controller lane opens the pop-up menu for selecting the CC you want to display.

Figure 6.38 Choosing Pan as the CC to be viewed and edited.

Figure 6.39 CC data for Pan is now visible in the Controller lane.

Viewing Continuous Controller Data

Continuous controller (CC) data can be used for an enormous range of tasks with MIDI devices. It can be used to send modulation to synthesizers, change settings on effects devices, and add expression to performances after the fact. There is no room to cover all of that in this chapter—you will learn much more about CC data in Chapter 10, "Editing MIDI"—but basic CC skills are useful when creating a MIDI part in Cubase, and that's what we'll focus on here.

There are 127 possible CC messages. Many are known only by number (CC 59), but some are standardized and are generally referred to by name: for example, Velocity, Pan, Modulation, Main Volume, and Pitchbend. Pretty much every MIDI synth made should respond to these standardized controllers, and the Key editor lets you make changes to any CC data you wish. By default, the Key editor shows only one CC at a time, so you need to choose which one to view.

To select a continuous controller to view in the Key editor:

1. Click the pop-up menu at the left of the Controller lane (**Figure 6.37**).

2. In the menu that opens, select the CC you want to view and edit (**Figure 6.38**).

   The controller is visible in the Controller lane (**Figure 6.39**) and is ready for editing.

Entering CC Data with the Draw Tool

Figure 6.40 Selecting the Draw tool to create CC data.

Although you can use the various Line tool modes when creating or modifying MIDI CC data, you'll use the simple Draw tool most often when creating new data. For example, still using that eighth-note pulsing bass line, you can use the Draw tool to pan each note slightly to the left and right by entering CC data.

Figure 6.41 Dragging with the Draw tool creates new controller data.

To enter CC data with the Draw tool:

1. Select the Draw tool by clicking it on the toolbar (**Figure 6.40**) or by right-clicking and selecting it from the contextual menu.

2. Set the Controller lane so it displays the CC you want to edit. In this example, select Pan.

Figure 6.42 With Snap set to eighth notes, you can easily draw a slight pan for each eighth note with the Draw tool.

3. Turn on Snap to create data according to meter. In this case, set Quantize to 1/8 Note.

4. With the Draw tool, drag the Controller lane.

   The bar being drawn with the pointer in **Figure 6.41** shows the CC value entered.

5. Repeat step 4 for each eighth note you want to modify.

   Figure 6.42 shows CC data that pans each note alternately slightly to the left and slightly to the right.

✔ Tip

■ MIDI CCs are your friends. You can use them to modulate and modify your synths, samplers, and effects for greatest impact. Learn about CCs in all of your gear, and you will be rewarded.

About the Drum Editor

The Key editor is often the best tool for putting together a MIDI part from scratch. Most of the time, it's the easiest editor to use for building up instrument lines and bass lines and performing similar tasks. One thing it is not terribly good for, though, is creating drum parts. Luckily, Cubase has a dedicated Drum editor with some unique features and tools specifically for drum parts. The Drum editor was one of the first features that set Cubase apart from other sequencers, way back in the Atari computer days, and it is still a superior tool for building up a good drum loop.

Under normal circumstances, sending MIDI data to a particular device on a particular channel will trigger one sound at different pitches. If you send MIDI data to a synth with a bass patch on that channel, every note will trigger the bass sound, and the notes will control the pitch played back. However, with drum tracks, each note plays back a different sound: one note will be a kick drum, another note a hi-hat, and so on. The Drum editor is specifically designed for creating and editing

such sounds. **Figure 6.43** shows the parts of the Drum editor. With a few exceptions, it is very much like the Key editor.

Toolbar: As in the Key editor, the toolbar has controls for viewing, creating, and editing MIDI data, as well as Snap and Quantize settings.

Note display: Unlike in the Key editor, notes in the Drum editor are represented by diamonds. This makes them easier to see on a grid, a more intuitive arrangement for viewing drum parts.

Drum Sound list: Because each note triggers a different sound, the Drum editor lets you name your drum sounds and edit the properties of those sounds. The Drum Sound list is closely related to the drum map.

Controller lane: The Controller lane in the Drum editor is basically identical to the Controller lane in the Key editor.

Drum Map settings: You can use the pop-up menus to select drum maps and display drum map names.

ABOUT THE DRUM EDITOR

Drum Map settings   Toolbar   Global Quantize button

Drum Sound list   Controller lane   Note display

Figure 6.43
The Drum editor.

Opening the Drum Editor

You access the Drum editor in the same way as all of the other MIDI editors in Cubase. You can open any MIDI part in the Drum editor, regardless of how it was created. Even MIDI parts created in another editor, such as the Key editor, can be opened and edited in the Drum editor if you wish.

To open a MIDI part in the Drum editor:

1. In the Project window, click the MIDI part you want to edit (**Figure 6.44**).

2. Right-click to open the contextual menu for that MIDI part, or open the MIDI menu from the Project window.

3. Select MIDI > Open Drum Editor (**Figure 6.45**).

   The Drum editor opens, displaying any MIDI data already in that part.

Figure 6.44 A MIDI part selected in the Project window.

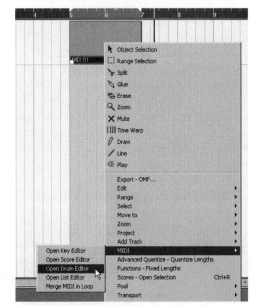

Figure 6.45 Selecting Open Drum Editor from the contextual menu.

Figure 6.46 Clicking this button selects the Drumstick tool; you can also select it by right-clicking the Note display if you have a two-button mouse.

Figure 6.47 Snap is turned on, as is Global Quantize, and 1/4 Note is selected from the Quantize menu.

Figure 6.48 Clicking at the first beat enters a note; it appears as a diamond, as do all notes in the Drum editor.

Figure 6.49 The MIDI part after all four quarter notes have been entered.

Using the Drumstick Tool

The Drumstick tool is the primary means of entering note data in the Drum editor. If you sequence a lot of drums, you'll get to know the Drumstick tool better than some members of your immediate family. Clicking the Note display with the Drumstick enters a note at that location, and clicking an existing note with the Drumstick erases it. Put simply, the Drumstick toggles notes on the display grid on and off. To see a very simple example, you can program a kick drum on all four quarter notes of a one-bar loop.

To enter notes with the Drumstick tool:

1. Click the Drumstick tool on the toolbar (**Figure 6.46**) or select it from the contextual menu.

2. On the toolbar, click the Snap button to turn on Snap; click the Global Quantize button and set the Quantize value to 1/4 Note.

   These settings are explained in the next few pages. For now, just set them as shown in **Figure 6.47**.

3. Hold the pointer over the Note display until it turns into the Drumstick tool (in other parts of the window, the pointer will be an arrow, used for selecting buttons, values, and menus). Move the Drumstick tool to roughly the beginning of the MIDI part and click to enter a note (**Figure 6.48**).

4. Click beats 2, 3, and 4 to create the other notes.

   The result will look like **Figure 6.49**.

Global Quantize vs. Individual Settings

The Drum editor has more Snap and Quantize options than any other editor in Cubase. For example, the Drumstick tool can use either of two Snap and Quantize settings, depending on what you want to do. The Drum Sound list includes a Quantize setting for each sound, and clicking a setting opens a drop-down menu of meter settings (**Figure 6.50**). You can either assign each drum sound its own unique Quantize setting or override these settings using Global Quantize.

The Global Quantize button determines how notes are entered with the Drumstick tool regardless of their individual Quantize settings. In the previous task, you turned on Global Quantize and set it to 1/4 Note, so that the Drumstick tool enters notes only on a quarter note in the Note display. If Global Quantize is turned off, the Quantize setting for the particular sound will be used instead of the global setting. In the following task, you'll add an eighth-note pattern to the quarter-note pattern you created earlier.

To enter notes with the Drumstick tool without Global Quantize:

1. Select the Drumstick tool.

2. Turn off Global Quantize but leave Snap on (**Figure 6.51**).

3. In the Drum Sound list, click the Quantize setting of the sound you want to use. In this case, select 1/8 Note from the menu that opens (**Figure 6.52**).

Figure 6.50 The Quantize setting for an individual sound is used by the Drumstick tool if Global Quantize is turned off.

Figure 6.51 With Snap on but Global Quantize off, the Quantize setting for the individual sound will be used.

Figure 6.52 This setting selects eighth notes for this sound.

Figure 6.53 Only eighth notes can be added with these settings. In this situation, the Drumstick tool acts a bit like the Paint tool, creating multiple notes as the tool is dragged.

4. Using the Drumstick tool, click at the beginning of the part and drag the tool to the right.

   Notes are entered according to the Quantize setting for that sound (**Figure 6.53**).

5. Continue dragging to the right until you have created all of the notes you want.

Drum Maps

Cubase uses drum maps to match names and MIDI notes of drums. Not every synthesizer and sample uses the same note to trigger the same sound, so Cubase allows individuals and synth manufacturers to create their own drum maps to address this issue. With a properly configured drum map, you can use the name of a sound, such as Bass Drum, to enter sounds instead of specifying the note, which could be nearly anything.

Cubase comes with some included drum maps, including the General MIDI (or GM) drum map. General MIDI is a set of parameters for sounds that synth manufacturers have agreed on so that there is a base set of sounds that a GM synth follows. This makes it possible to create a sequence with one GM synth and then play it back with a different GM synth and have it sound roughly the same. Part of the GM setup is a standard drum map, where certain pitches trigger certain sounds. Nearly all newer synths have at least one GM drum kit, as do many software drum machines and software samplers. Also, the manufacturer of your synth may have drum maps available; check the disks that came with it or the manufacturer's Web site.

You can also make your own drum maps if you wish. For more information on loading, saving, creating, and using drum maps, look at the "MIDI Editors" chapter in the electronic documentation that comes with Cubase SX 2.

Changing Velocity in the Drum Editor

Creating and editing continuous controller data in the Drum editor is very similar to performing the same tasks in the Key editor. The Controller lane is in the same place and is configured to show CC data in the same way. The main difference is that since each note triggers a different sound, the Controller lane shows data for only that selected sound.

One of the most common parameters for drum and percussion sounds, velocity, needs to be changed fairly often in the Drum editor. Rarely do drum sounds always play back at the same volume. In the preceding examples, all notes were entered with a velocity of 127 (the setting for the Insert Velocity parameter). Using the Controller lane, you can easily change the quarter-note part to a slightly lower velocity, with the eighth-note pattern lower yet.

To change velocity in the Drum editor:

1. Click the Drumstick tool to select it.

2. To the left of the Controller lane, click the drop-down menu and select Velocity if it is not already selected (**Figure 6.54**).

3. In the Drum Sound list, click the sound that you want to edit.

   In **Figure 6.55**, the Bass drum sound is selected, and the Controller lane shows four vertical stalks, which represent the velocity of the four notes entered.

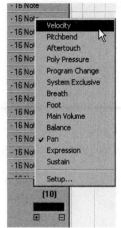

Figure 6.54 Use this menu to select the CC that appears in the Controller lane.

Figure 6.55 With the Bass Drum sound selected, only the velocity of the four quarter notes appears in the Controller lane.

Figure 6.56 Editing the velocity with the Drumstick tool. The display with the number 86 shows the current value for the Drumstick tool.

Figure 6.57 Clicking the next sound, the hi-hat, brings the velocity settings for notes on that sound into the Controller lane.

4. In the Controller lane, click one of the stalks with the Drumstick tool and drag the stalk up or down to the setting you want.

A numerical display to the left of the Controller lane shows the current value of the Drumstick tool. In this example, it shows velocity (**Figure 6.56**).

5. Click the next sound in the Drum Sound list whose velocity you want to edit.

The Controller lane now shows the velocity for those notes (**Figure 6.57**).

6. Edit the velocity sticks with the Drumstick tool. Continue selecting sounds in the Drum Sound list and editing with the Drumstick tool until you are finished.

✔ Tip

■ Cubase has lots of tools in addition to the Drumstick tool for editing CC data. For more information on CC editing, refer to Chapter 10 of this book and to the electronic documentation that comes with Cubase.

Deleting and Muting Notes

Most of the time, Drumstick is the easiest tool to use to delete notes in the Drum editor. The whole point of the Drumstick tool is that it lets you toggle notes on and off in a grid, and clicking a note is the easiest way to delete it. One of the best uses of the Drum editor, though, is to set a project to loop over the length of the part currently in the editor and then to build up a part by clicking the Drum editor grid. It can be very helpful in such a situation to selectively mute notes, just to see how the pattern sounds without them, without deleting the notes completely.

To mute notes in the Drum editor:

1. In the Note display, open the contextual menu and select the Mute tool (**Figure 6.58**), or select the tool from the toolbar.

2. Click the note you want to mute. Muted notes turn white (**Figure 6.59**) to indicate that they will not sound.

3. To unmute a note, simply click it again with the Mute tool.

✔ Tip

- In some music styles, programmed drums are crucial to the sound. In particular, if you make electronic music of any kind, you will spend what seems like lifetimes working in the Drum editor. Learn as much about it as you can from the Cubase documentation, your own experimentation, and other Cubase users.

Figure 6.58 Selecting the Mute tool in the contextual menu.

Figure 6.59 The white notes have been muted with the Mute tool. They will unmute and turn back to a color if they are clicked again with the Mute tool.

Using VST Instruments

A VST instrument—usually called a VSTi—is a piece of software that uses the processing power of your computer to generate sounds, turning your audio computer into an actual instrument. Before VST instruments, the computer could record, edit, play, and mix audio with effects, but all sound generation had to happen outside of the computer. VST instruments changed that and gave the computer an even greater role in music production.

If you are familiar with VST instruments at all, you probably think of VST instruments as famous pieces of hardware re-created as software plug-ins triggered by MIDI. That is certainly one role they fulfill, but many VST instruments are only slightly related to hardware. There are loop tools, specialized drum samplers, strange other-worldly sound generators, and even applications that let you hand-build your own VST instruments. Don't make the mistake of thinking that VSTi is only for synth geeks without the budget for "real" synthesizers.

In this chapter, you will learn how to open VST instruments, change their settings, and save your own sounds. You will get an overview of each VST instrument that ships with Cubase so you can begin your own exploration of what each instrument can do. You will also learn how to use MIDI to get more out of some VST instruments.

What Is a VST Instrument?

A VST instrument is really nothing more than a piece of software that outputs audio when it receives MIDI. This audio can be from any number of sources: some VST instruments are emulations of famous analog synthesizers, some are general-purpose sample players, and others are completely bizarre and unique sound-generation tools that are combinations of synthesizers, samplers, and effect devices.

VST instruments come from many sources. Cubase ships with a group of VST instruments—for instance, the a1 (**Figure 7.1**) is an analog-style synthesizer. In addition, many commercial software companies make all sorts of other VST instruments, such as the superb sample-based synthesizer Atmosphere from Spectrasonics (**Figure 7.2**).

Not all VST instruments are bundled with Cubase or come from traditional software manufacturers. There is a vibrant community of VSTi users and creators, and this community is providing some of the most exciting sounds and instruments in audio software. A great place to learn more about available VSTi options is www.kvr-vst.com, where you will find information and forums about everything imaginable regarding free, cheap, and expensive virtual instruments.

Figure 7.1 The a1 VSTi is a powerful, complex analog-style synth that runs completely from the CPU of your computer. It's one of the VST instruments bundled with Cubase.

Figure 7.2 A very different kind of VSTi is a third-party synth, from Spectrasonics, called Atmosphere. It's a powerful sample-based synthesizer.

Why Use VST Instruments?

VST instruments have both an upside and a downside. You may not want to use them for all of your synthesis and sampling, but you may nevertheless find them very useful.

VST instruments have these advantages:

◆ **Project integration:** Using software for synthesis and sampling means that every setting and change to a device is saved, transparently and automatically, with the project. You never need to use sysex dumps or to write down settings, saving you significant amounts of time.

◆ **Cost and variety:** The most expensive software instruments cost less than all but the cheapest hardware instruments. You can get very good shareware VST instruments for less than $100, which means they cost about as much as the cables needed to hook up a new sound module or keyboard. VST instruments are also cheaper to make than hardware, meaning that a developer can bring to market as a software instrument a unique idea that would be prohibitively expensive to create as a hardware device.

◆ **Features that leverage the computer:** Every VSTi gets more power when you upgrade your computer. A faster CPU means more synths, more samplers, and more voices from each.

VST instruments have these disadvantages:

◆ **Latency:** Digital synthesizers and samplers have almost no latency (delay) between the time you initiate a sound or modification and when it's audible. The latency of a VSTi is determined by the time it takes to generate and route the sound through your computer and sound card to your speakers or headphones, which can be a problem when the combination is not state of the art. See Chapter 1, "Installing and Configuring Cubase SX 2," for more information on latency and sound cards.

◆ **Sound quality:** Many VST instruments sound fantastic, some even better than their hardware equivalents, but not all do. Particularly in the realm of emulated analog synthesis, some people find software synths lacking.

Figure 7.3 Use the Devices menu to open the panel for setting plug-in preferences.

Installing and Managing VST Instruments

Cubase comes with a set of its own VST instruments. These bundled VST instruments are automatically available the first time you run Cubase, and you don't need to worry about where they are installed. Over time, you'll probably add third-party VST instruments made by commercial software companies or shareware developers.

When you install a new VSTi, you'll need to follow the instructions that come with the software. Each installation procedure can have its own requirements. For example, in Windows, Cubase lets you designate a particular folder as the shared plug-ins folder. VST instruments are plug-ins, and this folder can provide a convenient way to keep track of your VST applications; VST effect plug-ins and VST instruments in this shared plug-ins folder will be available to any application that supports those protocols.

To assign a shared plug-ins folder (Windows only):

1. Open the Devices menu and select Plug-in Information (**Figure 7.3**).

   The Plug-in Information window opens. The default tab shows all currently installed VST instruments. At the top of the window, there is also a setting for Shared VST Plug-ins Folder.

continues on next page

2. Click the Change button (next to the Shared VST Plug-ins Folders setting; **Figure 7.4**) to open the Select Directory dialog box.

3. On the Select Directory panel, navigate to the folder that you want to designate as the shared VST plug-ins folder (**Figure 7.5**). Click it and then click OK to close the panel.

This folder is now set as your shared plug-ins folder.

✔ Tip

■ As this is written, the Mac version of Cubase does not have a shared VST plug-ins folder. This may or may not change in the future.

Figure 7.4 Click the Change button to select a preferred folder for VST plug-ins and VST instruments.

Figure 7.5 Double-click a folder in this window to set it as the shared plug-ins folder.

Figure 7.6 Select this option to open the VST Instruments rack.

Opening a VSTi

Many of the features of Cubase covered in the rest of this book involve virtual racks. These are software versions of the standard-sized rack-mount systems used for mounting hardware in recording studios. The VST instruments mount on a virtual rack.

To open a VSTi:

1. Open the Devices menu and select VST Instruments (**Figure 7.6**).

   The VST Instruments panel, or virtual rack, opens (**Figure 7.7**). The rack has 64 slots, though not many computers can run 64 simultaneous VST instruments.

2. Click any of the slots labeled No VST Instrument.

   A pop-up menu opens, showing all of the currently installed VST instruments.

3. Select the instrument you want to use.

   In **Figure 7.8**, the a1 synth is being selected from the Synths submenu.

✔ Tip

■ Figure 7.8 shows all of the VST instruments installed on my own version of Cubase. Unless you happen to have a setup exactly like mine, your menus will look somewhat different. Later in this chapter, you will read about each of the VST instruments included with Cubase.

Figure 7.7 In this figure, all 64 slots in the VST rack are unused.

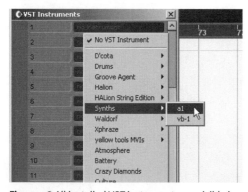

Figure 7.8 All installed VST instruments are visible in this menu. Your own menu will likely look different.

OPENING A VSTI

Opening the VSTi Editor

Every VSTi has a window for editing the sound parameters for the instrument. Some instruments are photorealistic renderings of real-world hardware, some are strange, never-before-seen tools for manipulating sounds, and some are just a bunch of sliders and knobs. Regardless of what kind of VSTi you use, you access the panel that controls its parameters in the same way.

To open the editor for a VSTi:

1. Open the VST Instruments panel if is not already open.

2. Find the slot in the virtual rack that contains the VSTi that you want to edit. Click the Edit button—the cursive *e* at the far left of the slot with the instrument name (**Figure 7.9**).

   The editor for that VSTi opens (**Figure 7.10**).

3. When you are done editing the instrument, close the editor.

✔ Tip

■ The F11 button is the keyboard shortcut for opening the VST instrument rack.

Figure 7.9 Click the Edit button—the cursive *e*—to open the editor window for the VSTi in that slot.

Figure 7.10 The VSTi editor for the selected instrument.

Figure 7.11 The two buttons with arrows step through presets for that VSTi. Click the name to open a menu that shows all available presets.

Figure 7.12 The same menu and arrows for presets is available in the edit panel of the VSTi, just as it is in the VST Instruments panel shown in Figure 7.11.

Selecting VSTi Presets

Most VST instruments include some number of presets, just like hardware synths come with some sounds already programmed. Listening to the presets for a VSTi is a great way to become familiar with what the VSTi can do. A VSTi that emulates an analog synth might have a selection of sounds already programmed for bass, lead, and pad sounds, and auditioning them can be a good way to get a feel for the style and range of a VSTi. You can listen to the presets by stepping through them one after the other, or you can start by viewing a list of all of the presets for the VSTi.

To step through presets:

1. Open the VST Instruments panel or the editor for the VSTi.

   The currently selected patch will be visible.

2. Click the up and down arrows on the right of the patch name to change the preset. You can also click the preset name to open a menu that you can browse.

   Both the panel and the editor have two arrow buttons and the menu. **Figure 7.11** shows these buttons on the VST Instruments panel; **Figure 7.12** shows them in the editor.

✔ Tip

■ Keep in mind that more than one MIDI track in the Project window can trigger the same sound. If you set a VSTi to a certain preset, you can point more than one track to it in the Project window.

Playing a VSTi

Using a VSTi is not much different than using a hardware synth. The routing and settings are almost identical. VST instruments can be played live if you want; the only potential problem is the latency of your sound card. As this is written, the highest-quality sound cards can achieve latencies below 3 milliseconds, which is as low as most hardware synths and samplers. Not all systems are capable of this quality, though, and you will need to test your system to see if you can comfortably play VST instruments.

Figure 7.13 The most common setting for MIDI input is All MIDI Inputs. It will take MIDI from any available device.

To play a VSTi:

1. In the track list, click the track that you want to use for the VSTi.

2. Open the Track inspector. The settings for the selected track will be visible.

3. On the top tab of the Track inspector, check whether the correct setting is chosen for the MIDI In field.

   Figure 7.13 shows All MIDI Inputs selected for the selected MIDI track.

4. Click the MIDI Out setting to open a menu listing available MIDI outputs.

   All active VST instruments are listed, along with any MIDI hardware devices that have been configured (**Figure 7.14**).

5. Select the VSTi you want to play.

6. Play your MIDI controller; it will trigger the VSTi.

Figure 7.14 If you choose the Out setting, any active VST instruments will be listed and can be selected as the output of that MIDI track.

✔ Tips

■ If you don't want to open the Track inspector, the same options are available in the track list (**Figure 7.15**).

■ In Cubase, MIDI is MIDI, regardless of what it triggers. All of the procedures for recording, creating, and editing MIDI data apply in exactly the same way when you're working with a VSTi.

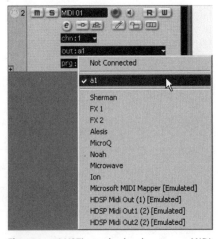

Figure 7.15 A VSTi can also be chosen as a MIDI destination in the track list.

PLAYING A VSTI

Figure 7.16 The sliders on this VSTi work just like mechanical sliders and can be edited simply by dragging them.

Figure 7.17 This breakpoint editor works differently than any mechanical device.

Figure 7.18 If you move one of the breakpoints, the corresponding knob (Attack) moves as well.

VSTi Visual Editing Tools

Part of what makes VSTi so great is that the designer can create a software tool that operates according to whatever rules the designer wants. Some VST instruments look and act just like hardware, while others look and act like nothing you have ever seen before. This makes it impossible to say for sure how every VSTi will work, but here are a few examples of the more common interface tools used to change parameters for a VSTi. Always consult the documentation that comes with a software instrument to find out more about how to edit its sound.

◆ **Knobs:** You've encountered them in the real world, and they do just the same jobs in the virtual world. Many (though not all) knobs on software instruments work differently than their hardware counterparts. Often you change the value of a knob by clicking it and dragging your mouse up or down, which controls the direction the circular knob moves on the screen.

◆ **Sliders:** Whereas knobs are sometimes tricky to turn on a computer screen, sliders (**Figure 7.16**) are easy to drag up and down to set values.

◆ **Buttons:** Like sliders, buttons translate well to the computer screen. Often buttons are backlit and change color when they are selected.

◆ **Breakpoint editors:** These are visual, intuitive tools for editing parameters that are normally assigned to knobs. In **Figure 7.17**, the Attack setting is all the way to the left, at zero. Attack is the parameter used to determine how quickly the envelope reaches its maximum setting. With a computer-based synth, it's easier to click the first breakpoint and drag to the right (**Figure 7.18**). This changes the Attack time, and the setting on the Attack knob reflects this.

Saving and Reusing VSTi Settings

Remember that VST instrument selections and settings are saved with projects, which is one of the great advantages of using them. You don't need to worry about setting the knobs and buttons each time you use the VSTi—they will be set in precisely the same way when you open the project the next time.

In addition, sometimes you may want to save the settings of a VSTi as a preset. For example, you may want to use the same sound in more than one project, or you may want to send the instrument settings to a friend who is using the same VSTi. Cubase refers to these user settings as *instruments*, and Cubase can save these presets as discrete files that you can load into another project or e-mail to another Cubase SX user.

To save a VSTi instrument:

1. Set up the VSTi exactly as you want to save it.

2. In the editor window of every VSTi and on the VST Instruments panel are a set of menus and buttons that control features such as presets; click the little graphic that looks like a floppy disk to open the File menu.

   A menu opens with options for saving and opening various file types (**Figure 7.19**).

Figure 7.19 Click the floppy disk icon when you want to save your current settings as a distinct file, outside of the current project, and then load them into another project if you want.

Figure 7.20 This menu option will save the current settings of the VST instrument to a preset on your hard drive.

Figure 7.21 Use a standard operating system dialog box to name and save an instrument.

3. Choose Save Instrument (**Figure 7.20**).

4. When the Save dialog box opens, name and save the instrument as a file. Type a name for the instrument, navigate to the folder where you want to keep it, and then click Save (**Figure 7.21**).

You can save an instrument wherever you want.

✔ Tips

■ You follow the same procedure to load instruments, but in reverse. Click the floppy disk button, select Load Instrument from the menu, and navigate to the file you want to open.

■ A bank is a file that includes multiple instruments. You save and load a bank in exactly the same way as you do single instruments.

The vb-1 VSTi

The vb-1 is a software bass instrument that can produce a wide range of bass sounds. Though its interface strongly mimics a modern electric bass, it can also produce synth bass and even some non-bass sounds when configured to do so.

The vb-1 interface (**Figure 7.22**) has two parameters that at first glance may not seem editable. In fact, you can change the location of both the pick and the pickup simply by dragging them. For instance, **Figure 7.23** shows the vb-1 after the pick and pickup have been moved. You move the pickup by grabbing it under the strings of the bass, as the pointer indicates in Figure 7.23.

The Shape parameter controls the basic type of bass sound used by the plug-in. This is the primary parameter for changing the bass sound from an electric bass to a synth bass. The Damper setting controls the sustain of each string—the more damper that is applied, the shorter each note will sound.

The presets (**Figure 7.24**) are a great place to discover what the vb-1 can do.

Figure 7.22 The vb-1 VSTi is used mostly for bass sounds.

Figure 7.23 You can move the pickup and pick, and the timbre of the bass sound will change as each is moved.

Figure 7.24 The presets menu for the vb-1 has sounds that show its sonic variety.

Figure 7.25 The a1 VSTi is the most complex of the analog-style synths that come with Cubase.

Figure 7.26 Choosing the oscillator shape for Oscillator 1.

Subtractive Synthesis

The a1 uses what's called subtractive synthesis, one of the most popular styles of synthesis in history. Famous synthesizers like the Minimoog and the Prophet 5, and many others, create sound in this way. The basics of a subtractive synth are an oscillator that generates sound, which feeds into a filter that shapes the timbre of the sound, and an amplifier that controls the volume of the sound after the filtering. Usually, some kind of modulation is involved as well. Modulators are things like envelopes and low-frequency oscillators (LFOs) that automatically change parameters on a synth.

The a1 VSTi

By far the most complex and powerful VSTi included with Cubase is the a1 (**Figure 7.25**). The a1 can play up to 16 simultaneous voices and receives MIDI on all channels. This means that you don't have to worry about routing a particular channel to the a1—just use the Track inspector to select it as the output for a track.

Learning to create expressive sounds with a subtractive synth like the a1 is as much a combination of art and science as learning to play any other instrument. It's far too complex to be covered in depth in this book, but a quick look at the a1 includes insights such as the fact that you can choose a shape for each oscillator. You use the buttons (**Figure 7.26**) at the right of the controls for Oscillator 1 and Oscillator 2 to select an oscillator waveform, and Oscillator 2 can have a different shape than Oscillator 1. This feature offers a great deal more sonic flexibility when combined with the features of the Mixer section, which can mix any amount of each oscillator together before the signal goes into the filter.

The filter in the a1 is a multimode filter that includes more variety than any of the other included VST instruments. The a1 includes the same four different filters: low pass, high pass, band pass, and notch.

The a1 is a complex analog-style synth, with lots of features and great sounds. It offers a huge number of presets for bass, lead, polyphonic, pad, and special-effects sounds. The keyboard at the bottom of the interface is very handy for auditioning the presets: you simply click the keys.

The lm-7 VSTi

The final VSTi included with Cubase is the lm-7 drum machine (**Figure 7.27**). Each lm-7 preset bank has 12 sounds, each of which can be slightly modified with the sliders and knobs. Clicking any of the virtual drum pads triggers a particular drum sound, and the pads provide a good way to audition the preset drum kits.

Each pad also has a corresponding pair of sliders: one marked Vol, and one marked Tone. The Vol slider determines the relative volume for that pad, and the Tone slider controls the pitch of the drum sound. Cymbal sounds like hi-hats and bass drum sounds are often pitch shifted for effect in dance and electronic music.

When a sound is triggered, the light above the pad turns green to indicate that it is playing; when the sound is done playing, the light turns yellow. You can use the Panorama knob on the right side of the lm-7 interface to modify the drum with the yellow light (**Figure 7.28**). The Panorama knob controls the left-right pan of that pad in the stereo drum mix. You can set each pad to its own pan position.

The lm-7 has three preset kits by default. Compressor uses samples from an acoustic drum kit and is best for rock and pop music, and 909 samples a famous dance music drum machine. The samples in the Percussion bank are from hand-percussion instruments such as congas and claves. If you use the Load Bank option and navigate to your VST plug-ins folder, you will find a folder called Drums with a bank containing three more drum kits. You can load these into the lm-7 to use Modulation, Fusion, and Drum'n'Bass kits.

Figure 7.27 The lm-7 is a dedicated drum VSTi.

Figure 7.28 You can edit the pan setting of the pad with the yellow light above it. In this black-and-white image, the yellow light is the one that appears lighter than the rest.

Controlling VST Instruments with MIDI

By definition, VST instruments respond to MIDI notes. Some, but not all, VST instruments go one step beyond this and also respond to MIDI CC messages. A VSTi that responds to these messages is not only more fun to work with, but is much easier to control with familiar tactile controls like knobs, sliders, and wheels.

Most hardware MIDI controllers—such as keyboards—allow their knobs and sliders to send CC messages. By matching the CC message being sent by the controller to the parameter that you want to change on the VSTi, you can control any parameter on a VSTi with a physical, tactile controller.

The a1 VSTi has deeper MIDI controls than any of the other VST instruments bundled with Cubase. The following task shows you how to use an external controller to modify a parameter on the a1. The a1 displays controller information in its editor window.

To control a VSTi using MIDI:

1. Select an a1 instrument for a slot in a VSTi rack and open the editor window.

    If you hold the mouse over any knob or button, you will see the CC message for that parameter in the data display. For example, **Figure 7.29** shows the mouse over the Envelope knob in the Filter section, and the data display indicates that CC 18 controls that parameter.

2. Move the mouse over the knob that you want to control and note the controller number.

    For example, filter resonance, a commonly edited parameter, is CC 71 (**Figure 7.30**).

3. Configure your MIDI controller to send the CC number, or open the Key editor and manually enter the CC data.

    For instance, configure your MIDI controller to send CC 71, or open the Key editor and manually enter CC data for message 71.

4. Play the MIDI controller, or use the data in the Key editor.

    The VSTi parameter will change to match your setting.

✔ Tip

■ Most VST instruments aren't as easy to set up for CC editing as the a1. Usually, you will have to consult the documentation that came with the VSTi to find out what parameter is mapped to what CC.

Figure 7.29 When the mouse is over the Envelope parameter, the data display shows that CC 18 will modify that parameter.

Figure 7.30 Resonance is controlled with CC 71 in the a1 VSTi, and you can use a MIDI controller to send that CC data and manually control resonance.

Freezing a VST Instrument

Freeze is a new feature in SX 2 that you can use to "print" the output of a VSTi to an audio file. After freezing a track, Cubase simply plays back that audio file instead of calculating the output of the VSTi in real time. It's almost always easier on the processor to play back an audio file than it is to generate sound with a VSTi synth of sampler. Previously you could manually export an audio file of the VSTi output and manually import it back to an audio track in SX. Freeze automates that entire process, making it no more difficult than clicking a single button.

There are two negatives when a VSTi track is frozen. First, because Cubase is playing back an audio file instead of calculating the VSTi in real time, you can't change the parameters on the VSTi to modify the output; however, you can still unfreeze, edit the VSTi, and then refreeze if you want. Second, when you freeze a VSTi, an audio file is created. MIDI files are tiny, usually only a few kilobytes. A frozen VSTi creates the highest-resolution audio file that Cubase can use, and these files can be huge. Large hard disks are dirt-cheap these days, but if you are running low on disk space, freezing lots of VST instruments may not be the best idea.

continues on next page

Freezing a VSTi

I am an unabashed fan of VST instruments. I use them all the time in my music and think you should do so as well. I maintain a handful of specialized or vintage keyboard gear, but otherwise, I use software for all of my synthesis and sampling—I don't even own a hardware sampler anymore.

As great as VST instruments are, they take up a lot of CPU resources. Even with the fastest computer made, a project that includes lots of VST instruments can overload the processor. Cubase SX 2 has a function called Freeze, which you can use with processor-intensive VST instruments to streamline processor usage. When you freeze a VSTi, three things happen:

◆ SX 2 saves the output of the VSTi, including all MIDI tracks routed to it, as an audio file in the current project folder.

◆ All of the MIDI tracks that are routed to the VST are muted, and the VSTi itself is turned off.

◆ When the project plays back, the sounds of the VSTi that you froze are played back from the "invisible" audio file. The VSTI output remains routed to its mixer channel, meaning that all effects and routings that you have set for the VSTi output will be heard. The effects on the mixer channel still operate in real time, and you can change them, but instead of calculating the output of a processor-intensive VSTi, Cubase has to play back only a simple audio file.

FREEZING A VST INSTRUMENT

To freeze a VSTi:

1. Set up the VSTi and its MIDI track (or tracks) exactly as you want them to sound.

   Figure 7.31 shows a simple loop-based project with three tracks all triggering VST instruments.

2. Open the VST instruments panel by selecting it from the Devices menu or by pressing F11 on your computer keyboard.

3. In the VST Instruments panel, click the Instrument Freeze button (**Figure 7.32**) for the VSTi you want to freeze.

   A status bar will show the progress of the freeze process (**Figure 7.33**).

✔ Tips

- You can unfreeze a track by clicking the same Instrument Freeze button again. This will delete the frozen audio file and let you change the MIDI tracks that trigger the VSTi. You can repeat the freeze/unfreeze process if you wish to make further edits.

- When you freeze a track, the audio output is saved to a file in a folder called Freeze in the project folder. This is nothing more than a 32-bit float audio file, so for a nifty trick, you can import that file back into Cubase. You can then edit it like any other audio track.

Figure 7.31 This project includes only three MIDI tracks, each of which is triggering a VSTi.

Figure 7.32 Clicking this button starts the freeze process for the individual VSTi.

Figure 7.33 A status bar shows the progress, and the VSTi is frozen.

FREEZING A VST INSTRUMENT

BASIC AUDIO EDITING

Figure 8.1 The Project window showing two loops on audio tracks.

For most of the history of recorded audio, editing involved a razor blade, a cutting block, and some tape. Editing individual tracks was difficult or impossible, and one bad edit with that razor blade could mean redoing the entire song from scratch.

Editing digital audio is a completely different story. Cubase stores audio files on a hard drive, and the visible audio waveforms in the Project window that we call events and parts are actually just pointers to those audio files. This means that any part of any file can play back at any point in a project—there is complete freedom to rearrange and modify the parts of a project. Cubase SX 2 is a world-class audio editing platform.

The techniques that you'll learn in this chapter and in Chapter 9 are accomplished by using advanced editing tools right in the Project window (**Figure 8.1**).

Unlike some other audio applications, Cubase lets you do a huge percentage of the audio editing in the Project window. Its other editors, such as the Audio Part editor and the Sample editor, are available for more advanced tasks. You can often accomplish the same thing in many ways.

Contextual menus are a powerful part of Cubase. You open a contextual menu by right-clicking on the screen (**Figure 8.2**). If you have a two-button mouse, you'll use contextual menus extensively while you work.

In this chapter, you will learn how to edit audio events and parts, starting with how to move, copy, and mute them. You will also learn more about Snap and how to use it to move audio precisely in a project. You'll learn the different methods for changing the duration of events and parts. Finally, you'll learn how to fade events in and out, how to crossfade between two audio events, and how to use the Scissors tool.

Figure 8.2 The contextual menu with the Process option selected. You'll be using contextual menus often.

What's the Difference Between an Event and a Part?

The differences between audio events and parts can be confusing even for expert Cubase users. If you record an instrument in Cubase, you've created an audio event in the Project window—the thing with a waveform that you can click, move, edit, and modify. For some projects, you may use nothing but events for your audio. Some events may be as long as the full song, and other events may be loops or single, short snippets of sound.

Parts are used mainly for two purposes. First, you may want to create a part when you have a group of events that you want to use together as a single entity. For instance, if the vocal line in a song is great but the last note is wrong, you can find another place where the singer hit that note right, snip it out, and then align the two events so the good note replaces that bad note in the first event. This leaves you using two events to play back a single line. To make your work easier, you can combine these events into a single part, so you can move and process the events as a single entity.

The second main use of parts is in creating comps. Comps are explained later in this chapter, but in general, comping involves using bits of numerous events to achieve a better take.

One reason that parts and events may seem confusing is that different audio programs work with audio in quite different ways. For example, in previous versions of Cubase, all audio events had to be in an audio part. This is no longer true in SX; events can be played, edited, and processed directly in the Project window. If you are learning Cubase after using another audio application or an earlier version of Cubase, you may want to take some time to be sure you understand the differences between parts and events.

The final tricky part of distinguishing between parts and events is that in the Project window, audio parts and audio events look very similar. One easy way to tell the difference is to click something to select it. If you see the blue handles (which are used to change volume and fade), you've clicked an event. If you don't see them, then you have a part on your hands.

Don't fret if the distinction between parts and events seems a bit arcane at first. Parts and events both follow logical rules, and after you've tried a few of the examples in this chapter, you'll understand intuitively which is which and when to use one or the other.

Converting Events to Parts

When you start editing audio in Cubase, it might be hard at first to see the difference between events and parts. Both can be used in the Project window, and both can be edited directly in the Project window. However, some of what is described in this chapter relates only to audio events, some is useful only with audio parts, and some works with both events and parts.

Audio event: An audio event is a reference to an audio file that has been recorded or imported into Cubase. It is not the audio file itself, but an indication to Cubase to play an audio file (or a part of an audio file) at a particular time in a project.

Audio part: An audio part is a container that can hold one or more audio events. Audio parts are used to more easily manage one or more events in the Project window. If it is convenient to deal with a group of events as a single entity, it's usually best to create a single part that holds all of the events.

To convert audio events to an audio part:

1. Using the Arrow tool, drag over the events you want to convert to a part (**Figure 8.3**).

   This selects the events in the Project window.

2. With the events selected (they will be outlined in red), open the contextual menu by right-clicking one of the selected audio parts.

3. From the contextual menu (or the main menu for people with one-button mice), select Audio > Events to Part (**Figure 8.4**).

   In the Project window, a new part will be created that is large enough to hold all of the selected events (**Figure 8.5**).

Figure 8.3 Selecting four events on the same audio track.

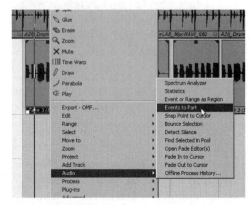

Figure 8.4 This menu command creates a new audio part.

Figure 8.5 The newly created part, with each of the events visible within the part.

✔ Tip

■ You also can select multiple events in the Project window by holding down the Shift key and clicking each one.

Figure 8.6 Selecting the audio part in the Project window: You can't see this easily here, but the part is outlined in red to show that it is selected.

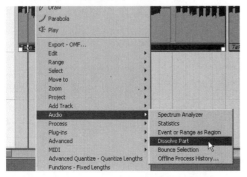

Figure 8.7 This command dissolves a part into events—the reverse of combining events into a part.

Figure 8.8 Each event in the part is now a discrete element again.

Breaking Parts into Events

Sometimes it's easier to work on smaller events instead of a whole part. If you want to work directly in the Project window on events that are within a part, you can break the part into its constituent events.

To convert an audio part to the audio events it contains:

1. Select the part by clicking it with the Arrow tool (**Figure 8.6**).

2. Open the contextual menu by right-clicking the part.

3. In the menu that opens, select Audio > Dissolve Part (**Figure 8.7**). If you don't have a two-button mouse, use the main menu.

   The events that were in the part will now be displayed in the Project window (**Figure 8.8**).

Muting Events and Parts

One of the simplest editing operations in the Project window is muting, which simply tells Cubase not to play back the muted event or part during the playback of a project.

To mute parts or events:

1. Select the Mute tool by clicking the Mute button on the toolbar (**Figure 8.9**) or selecting Mute from the contextual menu in the Project window.

2. Using the pointer (it will turn into an X), click any parts or events that you want to mute.

   They will be dimmed to show their muted status (**Figure 8.10**).

   To unmute a muted part or event, simply click it again.

   The part or event will now play back normally (**Figure 8.11**).

Figure 8.9 The Mute tool on the toolbar.

Figure 8.10 The second, third, and fourth events are muted; only the first event will play in the project.

Figure 8.11 The third event is unmuted.

Figure 8.12 The Use Quantize setting enables more Snap options.

Figure 8.13 With these settings, Snap will constrain movements to quarter notes.

Figure 8.14 The beginning of this event moves along a quarter note grid.

Moving Parts and Events Using Snap

You can move any part or event in Cubase to another place in a project simply by dragging it to a new location. If Snap is turned off, parts and events can be moved anywhere, without relation to a beat or grid. When Snap is turned on, parts and events are moved according to the grid created by the Snap settings. In the following task, you will move an event a quarter note at a time to change its place in a beat, but keep in mind that parts are moved exactly the same way.

To move an event using snap:

1. Turn on Snap by clicking the Snap button on the toolbar.

2. From the Snap Settings menu, select Use Quantize (**Figure 8.12**).

3. From the Quantize menu, select 1/4 Note. The snap settings will look like those in **Figure 8.13**.

4. Drag the audio event, which is now constrained to movements of 1/4 note (**Figure 8.14**).

✔ Tips

- Many people turn Snap on and off constantly. If you are one of those people, you should know that the J key on your computer keyboard is the default shortcut key for Snap; using it will save you a lot of mouse trips to the toolbar and back.

- Notice the numerical display in Figure 8.14. It shows the current location of the event (4.3.1) and its song position relative to its position before it was moved (+0.2). You can use this information to keep track of the movement of parts and events.

Moving Events and Parts Using the Cursor

Snap provides a convenient method for moving parts and events along a grid. Sometimes, though, it's easier to use the cursor to move a part or event. Using the cursor, you can more easily line up an event or part at the beginning or end of another event or part. The cursor can also help you place events or parts when you are synching dialogue and effects to video material. In this example, you will use the cursor to place an audio event at bar 13, beat 1.

To move an audio event using the cursor:

1. Position the cursor where you want to move the audio event by clicking the ruler, or by using the Fast Forward and Rewind buttons, or by manually entering the location on the Transport bar.

2. Click the event that you want to move.

3. If you have a two-button mouse, right-click the event to open its contextual menu.

   Choose Move to > Cursor (**Figure 8.15**). One-button mouse users should choose Edit > Move to from the main menu.

   The audio part will move to wherever the cursor is located (**Figure 8.16**).

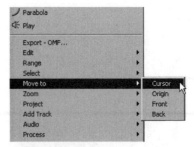

Figure 8.15 The menu option to send the currently selected event or part to the cursor location.

Figure 8.16 The audio event after it is moved to the cursor location.

Figure 8.17 This event is selected. It has a red outline around it (not visible in the illustration).

Figure 8.18 When the event is moved to a different track (it's in transit here), it keeps its position in the project.

Figure 8.19 When released, the event is on a different track, but at the same point in time.

Constraining Vertical Movement

Moving an event or a part to a different track is a common operation in Cubase, but in many situations you need the part to play back at the same time in the project as before it was moved. You can constrain the movement of an event or part to a vertical axis when you relocate it. In the following task, you will move an audio event to a new track but won't change its meter position.

To move an event or part while retaining its playback position:

1. Press and hold the Ctrl key (Windows) or the Command key (Mac OS).

2. Click the event or part you want to move (**Figure 8.17**).

3. While still holding the Ctrl or Command key, drag the event or part down or up in the Project window (**Figure 8.18**).

4. When you reach the track to which you want to move the event or part, release the mouse.

   The event or part will move to the new track at the same playback position in the project as before it was moved (**Figure 8.19**).

✔ Tip

■ The use of the Ctrl or Command key is one of a small number of operations in Cubase where Snap does *not* matter. In Figures 8.17 through 8.19, you can see that Snap is on, with a beat-based grid, but the part does not snap to the nearest beat when moved.

Setting the Snap Point

By default, the snap point for a part or event is the starting point of the part or event. More often than not, this is the most sensible way for Snap to work. In fact, the only way to change the snap point for an audio part is to resize the part itself. The snap point for an audio event, however, does not have to be its starting point.

The snap point for an event determines where Cubase moves the event when Snap is on. Although by default, the snap point is at the beginning of the event, it can be set to any point. Often a different setting is useful for snapping events that do not begin at a musically significant point. An event may have an obvious place where it is rhythmically anchored, and this may be the best place to use as the snap point. In the next task, an event with the downbeat close to its end will be snapped to the beginning of the measure. You will set the snap point with the cursor.

To move an event using the snap point:

1. Turn off Snap while setting the snap point.

2. Determine where in the event the snap point should go.

   It's usually easiest to snap events to quarter notes or, if possible, to the first beat of a measure. In **Figure 8.20**, the last note is the downbeat.

3. Click the Zoom tool on the toolbar to see clearly where the note starts and use the tool to drag over the part of the event where you want to set the snap point (**Figure 8.21**).

4. Move the cursor to the start of the note, where the snap point will be located.

5. If the event is not selected, choose the Arrow tool and click the event to select it.

Figure 8.20 In this event, the last note is the first beat of a new measure.

Figure 8.21 Using the Zoom tool to view a small part of the event.

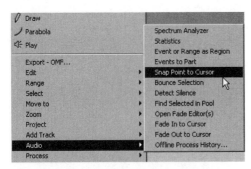

Figure 8.22 This command sets the snap point.

Figure 8.23 Using the newly set snap point, the event can be snapped so that the last note falls at the start of a measure.

6. Right-click to open the contextual menu for the event, or select Audio > Snap Point to Cursor from the main menu (**Figure 8.22**).

7. Zoom back out to see the whole event.

   The newly created snap point will appear as a thin blue line in the event.

8. Before moving the event, turn Snap back on so Cubase will use the snap point.

9. Click the event and drag it to its new location.

   The event now plays from the snap point instead of the beginning. In **Figure 8.23**, the event has been moved so that the downbeat is at measure 21.

SETTING THE SNAP POINT

Copying Audio Parts or Events

Events and parts are copied in the Project window using the common system-level key commands for click-and-drag copying. Hold down the Alt key (Windows) or the Option key (Mac OS), click the object to be copied, and move the copy to its new location. Cubase does include, however, a few of its own shortcuts and additions that make copying events and parts easier in some situations.

Shortcuts and tricks for copying events and parts

◆ If you want to copy an event or part to a new track but keep its position in the project, press Shift+Alt+Ctrl (Windows) or Shift+Option+Command (Mac OS) to create a time-constrained copy (**Figure 8.24**).

◆ Select an event or part and choose Edit > Duplicate to copy the selected part or event and place the new copy exactly after the original. This is another of the rare operations that ignores Snap. The two events in **Figure 8.25** were created using the Duplicate command with Snap on and set to Beat. The new event did not snap to the nearest beat.

Figure 8.24 An event copied to a new track but constrained vertically.

Figure 8.25 Snap was on and set to 1/4 Note, but Duplicate puts the copy directly after the original.

Figure 8.26 This event has been selected; the two triangles and small box at the top of the event will be moved to create a fade-in.

Figure 8.27 The pointer is at the place where the fade-in point can be moved.

Figure 8.28 Dragging the fade-in point to where the fade-in should end.

Creating a Fade-In

All music and sound production uses effects called fades. A fade-in takes a sound from a lower level and raises it in volume so that it can be heard. A fade-out takes a sound that is playing and decreases its volume until it is not heard. Most people notice fades only when a full mix is faded out at the end of a song on, say, a CD, but parts are faded in and out of mixes constantly.

Cubase has many ways to create fades. One very graphical way to create fades is to use the mouse in the Project window to fade individual events in and out. Only events can be faded in this way. If you need to fade a part, you probably should do that when you are mixing the project.

To fade in an audio event:

1. With the Arrow tool, in the Project window, select the event that you want to fade in.

   The event will have two blue triangles at both top corners and a blue square at the top middle (**Figure 8.26**).

2. Still using the Arrow tool, position the pointer over the top-left blue triangle.

   The pointer will change to a pair of arrows pointing in opposite directions (**Figure 8.27**).

3. Drag to the right to move the blue triangle ahead into the event (**Figure 8.28**).

4. When you reach the point where you want the fade-in to end, release the mouse.

   The triangle shows where the fade-in ends, and the audio waveform will update to show the change in the volume of the part.

Creating a Fade-Out

To create a fade-out, you reverse the procedure that you used to create a fade-in.

To fade out an audio event:

1. Click with the Arrow tool to select the event that you want to fade out.

2. Position the pointer over the blue triangle in the upper-right corner of the event.

   The pointer changes to a pair of opposing arrows (**Figure 8.29**).

3. Drag the triangle to the left (**Figure 8.30**).

4. Release the mouse at the point where you want the fade-out to begin.

   The blue triangle shows where the fade-out starts, and the waveform will update to show the change in volume (**Figure 8.31**).

✔ Tip

- The way that the waveform updates when you set a fade is more than just cool looking. The waveform provides excellent visual feedback for setting fade points.

Figure 8.29 The fade-out point is ready to be moved.

Figure 8.30 Dragging to the left to move the fade-out point.

Figure 8.31 The fade-out is set; note that both the fade-in and fade-out are reflected in the change in the waveform.

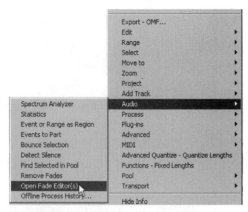

Figure 8.32 This menu item opens the window where fades can be edited.

Figure 8.33 The default fade-in is a simple linear fade.

Figure 8.34 One of the fade curves that is available as a preset in Cubase.

Editing Fades

Cubase uses a simple linear fade by default. This default is the rough equivalent of turning a volume knob for the event at precisely the same speed throughout the fade. Although this default fade quite often does the job, Cubase does not restrict fades to this linear shape. Fades can be almost infinitely edited by using the Fade editors.

To edit the curve of a fade:

1. Using the Arrow tool, click an event in which a fade has been created.

2. Right-click (or single click) and select Audio > Open Fade Editor(s) (**Figure 8.32**).

   This opens the Fade In editor, the Fade Out editor, or both. Each editor opens only if the event has the type of fade it can edit.

   The fade editor shows the portion of the event that is faded in or out. **Figure 8.33** shows the Fade In editor with the default linear fade-in.

3. Click the buttons at the bottom of the editor pane to change the shape of the fade (**Figure 8.34**).

4. When the fade has the shape you want, click OK.

   The curve will be applied to the event in the Project window.

✔ Tips

- If the presets for a fade-in or fade-out are not what you want, you can drag the breakpoints in the fade editor to create your own shape. You can even create new breakpoints by clicking the line of the fade if you wish. Most situations, though, are well covered by the preset fades.

- You can also open the fade editors by double-clicking the overlapping section that is to be faded.

EDITING FADES

171

Changing the Volume Level for an Event

While you can use the two blue triangles in a selected event to create fade-ins and fade-outs, you can use the blue square to graphically edit the overall volume level for an event when it is played back. This option, in combination with the fade-in and fade-out options, gives you deep control of dynamics for any event in the Project window.

To set the overall volume level for an event:

1. Click an event with the Arrow tool to select it.

2. Position the pointer over the blue square in the middle of the event (**Figure 8.35**).

   The pointer becomes two opposing vertical arrows.

3. Drag up to increase the overall volume level of the event, or drag down to decrease the overall volume level (**Figure 8.36**).

4. When the volume level is set where you want it, release the mouse.

   The blue square will show the relative volume level of the event, and the waveform will update to show the result of the change (**Figure 8.37**).

✔ Tip

■ You can also raise the volume level of an event several decibels above its original level using this method.

Figure 8.35 The pointer is over the blue box and can now set the overall volume level of the event.

Figure 8.36 Dragging down decreases the volume level.

Figure 8.37 After the mouse is released, the waveform changes to reflect the new, lower volume level of the event.

Three Ways to Resize Audio Events

You might have heard the term *nonlinear editing* used when describing how a multi-track editor like Cubase works. Unlike a tape-based system, in which recorded audio plays back only at the time when it was recorded, a digital editor gives you complete freedom to choose which pieces of audio play when. You can take the second phrase of the great-sounding backing vocal you sang over the first chorus and easily copy it to every other chorus.

When you are making these type of edits, you'll nearly always need to take only certain sections of an event or events: a phrase here, two beats there, and so on. To do that, you'll often need to change the duration, or size, of an event. Cubase offers three ways to change the size of an event, all selected via a drop-down menu on the object selection tool. Each mode is fully described in the pages that follow, but here's a quick comparison to keep in mind as you use the different modes:

♦ **Normal Sizing** might also be called masking. Using this mode, you move the start or end point of the event to play only part of the audio. If you like only the second part of a phrase in a performance, for instance, you use this mode to move the starting point of the event so it plays only the second half of the phrase.

♦ **Sizing Moves Contents** allows you to keep the start or end of an event the same while you push around the audio content inside the event. This mode can be useful when you're trying to move a drum hit or sound to a particular beat, or when you want to correct a performance that's a little ahead of or behind the beat.

- ◆ **Sizing Applies Time Stretch** lets you drag the start or end point of an event to make the duration of the event longer or shorter. Used in conjunction with Snap, this mode is invaluable for forcing an audio event to match the project tempo.

The mode you will most commonly use is Normal Sizing. This mode lets you mask and unmask any part of the audio in an event. For instance, you can take a guitar part that spans an entire five-minute song and resize the event so that it plays only a single note. Like all editing in Cubase, this is purely non-destructive; you can always resize again and hear the entire event or a different part of it.

Figure 8.38 The pointer changes to two arrows to show that it is ready to resize an event.

To resize an event using Normal Sizing:

1. Using the Arrow tool, click the event that you want to resize to select it.

2. Position the pointer on the bottom corner of the beginning or end of the event (**Figure 8.38**).

    The pointer changes to a pair of opposing horizontal arrows.

3. Drag to the place where you want the event to begin or end (**Figure 8.39**).

4. Release the mouse when the file is resized as you want.

    Compare Figures 8.38 and 8.39; after the resizing, only the first two of the four notes in the phrase will be played.

Figure 8.39 Dragging in this direction moves the beginning of the event forward, acting as a mask.

✔ Tips

- If Snap is on, the event will be resized according to the Snap setting.

- To temporarily override Snap without turning it off, hold down Ctrl (Windows) or Command (Mac OS) while resizing the event.

What About Resizing Parts?

Parts are resized in exactly the same way as events, using exactly the same tools. There is really no difference in the way the audio is handled, except when you use Resize Applies Time Stretch. If a part with more than one event is resized in this mode, Cubase has to time stretch each event in the part. Other than this minor difference, the tools for resizing events work in the same way for resizing parts and produce the same results.

Figure 8.40 Choose a mode for the Arrow tool to change the way that resizing affects an event.

Figure 8.41 Note the different phrase in each bar. The pointer will now resize the event.

Using Sizing Moves Contents

You can also use the Arrow tool in the Sizing Moves Contents mode. When an event is resized using this mode, moving the start or end point pushes the audio itself back and forth inside the event. This allows the event to start or end at the same place in the project, but moves the audio inside the event forward or backward in time. In the following task, you will resize a two-measure section, using this mode to move the second bar ahead in time by one measure.

To move the contents of an event by resizing:

1. Click the Arrow tool on the toolbar to select this tool and then click it again to open the contextual menu. Select the Sizing Moves Contents option (**Figure 8.40**).

2. Turn Snap on or off, depending on your preference.

   In the example shown here, Snap is on.

3. Move the pointer to the lower-right corner of the event to be changed.

   The arrow changes to two opposing horizontal arrows (**Figure 8.41**).

4. Drag to the left to move the end of the event forward in time.

   The event being resized in these figures is the same event that was used in Figures 8.38 and 8.39.

continues on next page

5. When the event is resized as you want, release the mouse.

The audio in the event is moved forward in time, with the end of the event as an anchor (**Figure 8.42**). Compare Figures 8.42 and 8.39. Instead of masking part of the event as in Figure 8.39, the last note in Figure 8.42 has been moved ahead in time; however, the event will start at the same point.

✔ Tips

■ Resizing using Sizing Moves Contents is very useful, but the process isn't always easy to understand. Try resizing the same part in the exact same way using each resize mode. The techniques will become clear quickly.

■ You can use either the event's starting point or ending point when resizing an event using the Sizing Moves Contents mode .

■ Again, holding down Ctrl (Windows) or Command (Mac) defeats Snap temporarily.

Figure 8.42 The second phrase has now been moved to where the first phrase was originally. The event is also half as long as it was before.

Figure 8.43 This phrase is one bar long, but it does not fit into a bar of the current project.

Figure 8.44 The change in the pointer indicates that the event will be time stretched.

Figure 8.45 The event fits in one bar now; compare this figure to Figure 8.43.

Resizing an Event by Time Stretching

The third mode for resizing an event, Sizing Applies Time Stretch, doesn't change the amount of the audio that the event plays or the place where the event plays it. Instead, it alters the tempo or duration of the audio to fit the new size of the event. This approach was introduced in Chapter 3 in the context of fitting a drum loop to the tempo of a project. To see how this mode works, you will shorten a one-bar line that does not fit correctly in the project (**Figure 8.43**). You will commonly need to do this when you have samples taken from CDs or vinyl that do not match the tempo of the song in which they will be used.

To resize an event by time stretching:

1. Click the Arrow tool on the toolbar to select this tool and then click it again to open the contextual menu. Select Sizing Applies Time Stretch.

2. Turn Snap on or off, as you prefer.

3. Click the event to be resized, to select it.

4. Position the pointer at the bottom corner of the start or end of the event.

   If you are using Windows, the pointer becomes a pair of opposing arrows with the word *Stretch* beneath them, indicating that the event will be time stretched if it is resized (**Figure 8.44**). If you are using Mac OS, the pointer will not change.

5. Drag the start or end of the event until it is the length you want it.

6. Release the mouse.

   Cubase begins processing the event. A status bar will show the progress of the change operation. When the processing is finished, the duration of the event will be changed (**Figure 8.45**).

Creating a Crossfade

A crossfade is a special combination of a fade-in and a fade-out. Crossfades are used in many ways, but their primary use is to create a smooth transition between two different events on the same audio track. For instance, if two takes of a solo part were recorded, and the first half of one take sounds great while the second half of the other take sounds great, the two events can be edited together. In some situations, the transition between the two events will be audible and unpleasant. Crossfading the events together makes the transition nearly inaudible. In this task, you will crossfade two events for just such a transition.

Figure 8.46 These two events need to be joined seamlessly with a crossfade.

Figure 8.47 Position events so that they overlap in a place in the performance where a fade will not be too obvious.

Figure 8.48 After you choose the Crossfade command from the Audio menu, the lines in the crossfade indicate the two fade curves.

To crossfade two events:

1. Resize both events so the section to be crossfaded is at the very end of the first event and at the very beginning of the second event (**Figure 8.46**).

2. Resize the events over each other so that the sections to be crossfaded overlap.

   The area where the events overlap is indicated by a darkened section (**Figure 8.47**).

3. Select both events by clicking them with the Shift key held down, or use the Arrow tool to draw a box over both events.

4. Select Audio > Crossfade. You can also press the X key on the keyboard as a shortcut.

   The overlap of the events is outlined in blue, and the fade curves are displayed in blue (**Figure 8.48**).

✔ Tip

■ Creating good crossfades is a craft, if not an art; it takes practice to find the best fade points. The general rule of thumb, however, is to find a place for the crossfade where not much is going on. The less action at the fade point, the more likely it is to be inaudible.

Figure 8.49 The Crossfade panel.

Figure 8.50 The Equal Power box is selected, creating a preset fade curve for both fade-in and fade-out.

Figure 8.51 The fade curves have changed now that Equal Power is selected in the Crossfade panel.

Changing the Shape of a Crossfade

A crossfade, after all, is nothing but a fade-out of one event and the fade-in of another. Therefore, you can edit a crossfade much like any other fade. Crossfades have a few additional editing options as well.

To edit the shape of a crossfade:

1. After you create a crossfade, select either or both events that are part of the fade.

2. Select Audio > Crossfade, or double-click the events where they overlap.

3. When the Crossfade dialog box opens (**Figure 8.49**), select a curve to adjust the fade-in, fade-out, or both; or select either of the check boxes: Equal Gain and Equal Power.

   In **Figure 8.50**, Equal Power is selected.

4. Click Close.

   When you return to the Project window, the crossfade will reflect the changes made in the Crossfade panel (**Figure 8.51**).

✔ Tips

- An Equal Power crossfade maintains the energy, or power, of the sounds throughout the crossfade. An Equal Gain crossfade maintains the gain across the crossfade. A huge percentage of crossfades will sound perfect when using one of these two settings. When in doubt, give them a test-listen.

- In the Crossfade Audio window, you can preview the results of each individual fade and the crossfade by clicking the Play Fade Out, Play Crossfade, and Play Fade In buttons. Hearing all or part of the fade can really help you if a fade doesn't sound right and needs to be adjusted.

Splitting Events and Parts

Crossfading and resizing often are applied to snippets of larger takes, either to grab a loop to be repeated in the song or to create a single version of a line or solo with the best sections from multiple takes. For both looping and editing multiple takes together, the Splits tool can be invaluable. Using the Split tool, you can chop audio parts and events into smaller bits that are easier to work with. In the following task, you will see how to split a two-bar loop into smaller, one-bar sections.

To split events with the Split tool:

1. Click the Split tool on the toolbar.

2. Turn on Snap and select Bar.

   Snap matters when using the Split tool, so it needs to be turned on or off depending on the job. In this case, two-bar loops are the goal, so you need snap to align them (**Figure 8.52**).

3. Position the pointer over the event to be snipped.

   A thin line shows where a cut will be made if the mouse is clicked at the current location (**Figure 8.53**).

4. Move the pointer until the line is on the location where you want to snip the audio event; then click.

   The event is split into two pieces (**Figure 8.54**), with the name of each event now displayed.

✔ Tips

- Parts can be snipped just like events. The only real difference is that when a part is split with the Split tool, the corresponding events are also split to create a new part.

- Remember that after a part is snipped with the Split tool, all of the audio from the original event is still there, and you can view or hear it by resizing the event.

Figure 8.52 Setup to use the Split tool: The tool is selected on the toolbar, and Snap is turned on and set to Bar.

Figure 8.53 The thin, light line at measure 6 indicates the place where the Split tool will cut the event if the mouse is clicked.

Figure 8.54 The darker line in this illustration shows where the event was cut. The line is actually blue in Cubase.

SPLITTING EVENTS AND PARTS

Figure 8.55 The Audio Part editor with two events shown.

The Audio Part Editor

Audio parts are useful for a number of reasons; in particular, after a group of events has been edited together into a part, you can move, copy, process, and otherwise treat them as a single entity. You use the Audio Part editor (**Figure 8.55**), as you might guess, to edit audio parts.

The Audio Part editor creates composite takes, or *comps*. A comp is a single musical phrase, line, or groove that is composed of pieces from more than one performance. Sometimes a comp is created to cover a mistake, such as a single flat note by a singer in an otherwise solid performance. Comps can also be heavily edited masterpieces of audio artifice. The following pages walk you through the basics of creating a comp in the Audio Part editor.

Keep in mind that an audio part is just a container in which audio events are kept, so much of what you do in the Audio Part editor you could also do in the Project window.

The Audio Part Editor vs. Stacked Mode

By far the most common task done in the Audio Part editor is comping tracks. Comping is also the most common reason for using Stacked mode to record a track, and then editing the track in the Project window. So it's reasonable to ask: which is the best choice?

If you've used the previous version of SX for a while, you may be more comfortable working in the familiar Audio Part editor than in Stacked mode. Also, I find the Audio Part editor to be a little more spacious for comping; with more room to move things around in lanes. Stacked mode is great, though, because there's never a reason to leave the Project window. Try a similar comp using both approaches to see which you find easier and more effective. Chapter 9, "Advanced Audio Editing," discusses how to edit tracks recorded in Stacked mode.

Preparing Events for a Comp

A comp can be created from many sources. For example, a single long take can be cut into pieces for comping. Events or regions created with cycle recording are also very common sources. Comps can also be created out of completely unrelated and distinct pieces of audio, although this is not a common practice. In the task here, a longer event was snipped into two-bar loops and will be comped from these pieces. You will get the events ready for comping.

To arrange events for comping in the Audio Part editor:

1. Set the start and end points for the loop so they correspond to the length of the section to be comped. In this case, set a two-bar loop (**Figure 8.56**).

2. On the Transport bar, click the Cycle button to turn on looping.

3. Drag all of the events that will be used into the range of the loop (**Figure 8.57**). This puts together all of the constituent events that will be used to create the comp.

✔ Tip

■ When comping, and particularly when arranging elements for a comp, you may find it useful to set the lanes in the Audio Part editor so that they are quite narrow and allow the editor to show more events. To adjust the height of the lanes, you use the vertical slider at the lower right of the Audio Part editor (**Figure 8.58**).

Figure 8.56 A two-bar loop, from measures 9 to 11, is set in the Audio Part editor.

Figure 8.57 Each of these events has been created from a longer take by using the Split tool.

Figure 8.58 Use the vertical slider to adjust the lanes when you are managing a lot of events in the Audio Part editor.

Figure 8.59 The Eraser tool just deleted the bottom event; the event newly on the bottom will now play.

Figure 8.60 Muting an event has the same effect as deleting it, except that a muted event can be unmuted easily.

Figure 8.61 The resized event will not play until the cursor moves to the point where it is the bottom event in the editor.

Hearing the Events in a Comp

When you are creating a comp, you can hear each of the events in the Audio Part editor. The Audio Part editor plays back only one event at a time, and—if you have events stacked vertically—the event at the bottom of the Audio Part editor is the one that will play back. In Figure 8.57, for example, the bottommost part will play back throughout the loop. However, there are multiple ways to hear events that are not on the bottom:

◆ Use the Eraser tool to delete the event that's closest to the bottom (**Figure 8.59**).

◆ Apply the Mute tool to the bottom event to leave it in its current location and hear the event directly above it (**Figure 8.60**).

◆ Resize the bottom event so that a section of the event above it will be heard (**Figure 8.61**).

In Figures 8.59 through 8.61, at least a section of the middle event from the top will play instead of the bottom event. Of course, muting, deleting, or resizing any of the events can change which one gets priority in playback.

Finishing a Comp

In Cubase, probably the best way to create a comp is to start playing the loop and listen to each part play by alternately muting each of the other parts. The good parts will usually be pretty obvious, and the bad parts can be resized or muted out of the comp. **Figure 8.62** shows one possible comp that was created from the lines in Figures 8.59 through 8.61. The top event plays for the first measure, and then the bottom event plays part of a line, which is then finished by the middle event.

When the Audio Part editor is closed, the comped part looks like **Figure 8.63**. The thin lines displayed in the audio part show where the different events that make up the comp start and end.

✔ Tip

- Comping is another editing operation that is a blend of art, science, and craft. The Audio Part editor in Cubase is one of the better software comping tools currently available. Comping practice will pay off mightily over time.

Figure 8.62 This is one of a nearly infinite number of possible comps.

Figure 8.63 In the Project window, the comp looks like this. It plays back just as shown in Figure 8.62.

ADVANCED AUDIO EDITING

Audio applications are generally divided into two main categories: multitrack recording applications and sample editors. Sample-editing applications give users lots of control over a single stereo or mono audio file; multitrack applications substitute nicely for multitrack tape decks but have limited options for editing and processing the tracks.

Cubase, however, breaks free of these categories, allowing you to perform both sample editing and multitrack recording in the same window. What's more, Cubase provides tons of processing options, and you can perform a lot of processing with almost no strain on your CPU. Additionally, because all editing in Cubase is nondestructive, you can save a history of the effects you've applied so that, if necessary, you can undo them afterward.

In this chapter, you will delve deeper into the audio-editing abilities of Cubase, learning how to process and change the audio you have recorded. You will learn about some of the audio processing options that come bundled with Cubase and how to apply them to events and parts in a project. You will also learn about third-party VST plug-ins and their uses, and how to manage and modify all of the changes made to an event, even after the fact. Finally, you will learn about the high-resolution Sample Editor and some of its regions-based editing options.

Types of Audio Editing

You can perform two main types or styles of audio editing in Cubase. The first type, discussed in Chapter 8, "Basic Audio Editing," involves changes to parts and events, including changes in duration, location, and basic sonic parameters such as fade and level. The second type of audio editing makes changes to the audio itself so that it doesn't sound the same after it has been edited. This second kind of audio editing involves such modifications as changes to the gain structure of a sample, addition of reverb, time correction, and pitch shifting.

Once again, if you have a two-button mouse, you will be spending a lot of time with the contextual menus that open when you right-click an event or part. Most of the actions in this chapter use the Process menu (**Figure 9.1**) or the Plug-ins menu (**Figure 9.2**). For those readers who are on Macs and have one-button mice, I'll show alternate routes.

Even though the work you do in this chapter will involve mucking around with the way your audio sounds, as mentioned earlier, all editing in Cubase is nondestructive. When Cubase processes a piece of audio, it always keeps the original, and you can return to this original sound if you decide you want it back. Later in this chapter, you'll learn how to restore your original files using the Offline Process History feature of Cubase.

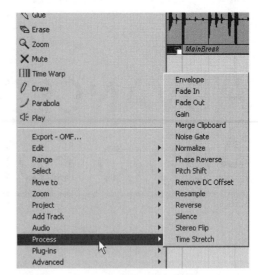

Figure 9.1 The Process menu includes many of the utility processing tools that are bundled with Cubase.

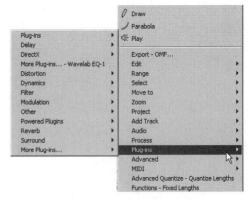

Figure 9.2 The Plug-ins menu lists all installed VST/DirectX plug-ins—both those bundled with Cubase and those from third parties.

Figure 9.3 Selecting the Zoom tool on the toolbar.

Figure 9.4 Drag over a section of an event to zoom in and display it in closeup view in the Project window.

Figure 9.5 The Events display after zooming.

Using the Zoom Tool

Until now, the actions described in this book have been on a comparatively large scale. More advanced audio editing, however, often necessitates a much closer look at the event or part being edited. For this purpose, the Zoom tool is invaluable. You can select the Zoom tool from either the toolbar (**Figure 9.3**) or the contextual menu opened by right-clicking. You can use the Zoom tool to zoom in on a particular section of the Project window.

To zoom a section of the Project window:

1. Select the Zoom tool by clicking the Zoom button on the toolbar or choosing Zoom from the contextual menu.

   The pointer turns into a magnifying glass.

2. Using the magnifying glass, drag over the section of the Project window that you want to see more closely (**Figure 9.4**).

   The section appears zoomed and centered in the Events display (**Figure 9.5**).

✔ Tip

■ Holding down the Shift key while clicking anywhere with the Zoom tool will zoom the project significantly.

Extracting Events from Parts

You can use the Range Selection tool for more controlled editing in the Project window or the Audio Part editor, for example, to select a specific section of an audio event or part. After you select the range, it functions as if it were its own event. This gives you incredible flexibility when working with events and parts. In the task here, you will see how to copy a single drum hit from an event using the Range Selection tool. The event will not be resized at all.

To extract a section of an event with the Range Selection tool:

1. Zoom in closely on the section you want to select.

   This example uses the drum hit on beat 2, under the pointer in **Figure 9.6**.

2. Turn off Snap.

   Snap matters with the Range Selection tool—you can turn it on or off as you wish, but in this example, it should be off.

3. Click the Range Selection button on the toolbar or select the tool with the contextual menu.

   The pointer turns into a cursor.

4. Using the cursor pointer, drag over the section of the event you want to select (**Figure 9.7**).

   The pointer becomes a small hand.

5. Hold down Alt (Windows) or Command-Option (Mac OS) and drag the selected range to an adjacent track.

6. Release the mouse.

   A new event is created from the selected material (**Figure 9.8**).

Figure 9.6 The solid, dark drum hit will be selected.

Figure 9.7 Only this one note in the larger event is selected. In Cubase, the selection will be blue.

Figure 9.8 The single sample has been copied to a new track, with no need to resize or modify the event.

Figure 9.9 The same drum hit that you saw in Figure 9.6: The start of the selection will be fine-tuned.

Figure 9.10 Zooming in close to the start of the selection.

Figure 9.11 The start point of the selection has been modified.

Adjusting a Range Selection

The range stays selected only when the Range Selection tool is active. Once you click the Zoom tool, the range selection is gone. If you make a range selection and decide that it is not what you want, you have to start over again. In addition, you may need a very exact range that is also fairly long, making it nearly impossible to select without the use of different zoom levels. The only way to make an exacting change in a selected range is to zoom using the ruler and cursor. The following task shows you a couple of navigational shortcuts you can use to select with precision the single drum beat selected in **Figure 9.9**.

To zoom in and adjust a range selection:

1. Unselect Snap if it is on.

   When you make exacting edits, Snap almost always needs to be off.

2. Click the ruler near where you want to zoom in. Drag to the bottom of the screen to increase the zoom, and drag horizontally to either edge to move left or right. Release the mouse when you've zoomed in close enough to see your selection (**Figure 9.10**).

3. Position the Range Selection tool at the border of the selection. It will turn into a pair of opposing horizontal arrows. Use this pointer to drag the selection border to where you want the range to begin (**Figure 9.11**).

4. Zoom out by clicking the ruler and dragging up; then zoom back in at the end of the selected range and repeat until you get the exact range that you want.

Navigating with the Locators

Cubase includes a huge range of options for navigation within projects. Anyone doing detailed audio editing should learn some of the key combinations and shortcuts for moving around in events, parts, and selections. These will save you a great deal of time in zooming in and out to find places to edit. For example, you could accomplish the sample extraction described in the previous section with much less zooming by moving the locators and using them as guides for viewing the selection, as you'll learn here.

To use the locators to view a selection:

1. In the Project window, zoom in and set the selection starting point as in Figure 9.11.

   Now you need to set the end point, using the same tools you used to set the start of the selection. Zoom in and use the Range tool to set the end of the selection at the precise point where the sample should end.

2. Right-click (or click) and select Transport > Locators to Selection (**Figure 9.12**).

   This sets the left locator to the start of the current selected range and the right locator to the end of the selected range. Or you could simply press the P key on your keyboard to set both the right and left locators.

Figure 9.12 This menu choice sets the locators as bookends around the current selection.

Figure 9.13 It's easy to get the selection ending right when you can jump to it with the keypad.

✔ Tip

- You can use the numeric keypad to navigate through a project. The numeric 1 key always moves the cursor to the left locator, and the numeric 2 key always moves it to the right locator. **Figure 9.13** shows how, after pressing the 2 key on the numeric keypad, the cursor jumps to the end of the selection range, which makes it easier for you to move it to a new location.

Figure 9.14 The event before it is reversed.

Figure 9.15 Choosing Reverse as the process to be performed on the event.

Figure 9.16 Cubase prompts you to be sure that the processing changes only the events you want it to change.

Processing an Event or Part

Cubase supports two primary ways of processing audio. You can use processes included within Cubase such as noise gating, time stretching, and envelope modification, or you can apply third-party VST (Windows and Mac OS) and DirectX (Windows only) audio plug-ins to a selection, event, or part.

There isn't room here to cover all of the Cubase processes and options (much less all of the VST and DX plug-ins). We'll explore a few examples of the more important processes, but you should take some time to experiment with the audio processes bundled with Cubase.

In this task, you will learn how to reverse the audio in an event.

To reverse the audio in an event:

1. Use the Arrow tool to select the event to be reversed.

   Figure 9.14 shows the event before it is processed.

2. Right-click the event and select Process > Reverse (**Figure 9.15**). If you have a one-button mouse, select Audio > Process > Reverse from the main menu.

   If the event you're processing is used more than once, a dialog box opens and asks whether you want the processing to apply to each event that uses that audio, or whether Cubase should create a new event with the processing applied (**Figure 9.16**).

   continues on next page

3. Click Continue or New Version in the message box, depending on your needs.

A status bar shows the progress of the audio processing. When the processing is complete, the new processed event—with the audio waveforms in reverse order—will appear in the Project window (**Figure 9.17**).

Figure 9.17 The event in the Project window after it has been reversed.

✔ Tip

■ For more information about the options for processing audio, and about the processes themselves, read "Audio Processing Functions" in the electronic documentation that comes with Cubase.

Figure 9.18 The blip next to the cursor will be decreased in volume.

Figure 9.19 Use this panel to set the increase or decrease in gain.

Figure 9.20 The Project window shows the change that results from the processing.

Adjusting Gain in an Event

Often you may want to selectively boost or cut the volume of a section of audio. For example, one note may stick out in a performance, or the sound of the singer taking a breath before singing may be too prominent. There are multiple ways to tackle such a problem, but one of the easier approaches is to process the audio by changing the gain at the level of the event.

To change the gain of a selection in an event:

1. Zoom in until you can easily see the section you want to change.

   In this example, the note just to the right of the cursor is too loud (**Figure 9.18**).

2. Turn off Snap.

3. Use the Range Selection tool to select only the section that needs to be changed.

4. Right-click and select Process > Gain. If you have a one-button mouse, select Audio > Process > Gain.

   The Gain panel opens (**Figure 9.19**).

5. Select an amount of gain reduction by using the slider or the arrow buttons; Figure 9.19 is set to reduce the gain of the selection by four decibels. Click the Preview button to hear the effect.

6. When the selection sounds right, click the Process button.

   When the audio has been processed, you will be returned to the Project window, where you can see the change in the event (**Figure 9.20**).

ADJUSTING GAIN IN AN EVENT

Pitch Shifting an Event

Anyone who has ever used samples or loops has encountered a situation where a piece of audio sounds great, except that it's not quite in tune. Cubase includes a full-featured pitch-shifting process that can be applied to events, parts, or selections of an event or part. Using pitch shifting, you can change the global pitch of an event or surgically alter a note or two that does not sound right. In the following task, you will see how to pitch shift an entire event to match the key of the project.

To change the pitch of an event:

1. Using the Arrow tool, select the event that needs to have its pitch altered.

2. Select Audio > Process > Pitch Shift.

   The Pitch Shift dialog box opens (**Figure 9.21**). This dialog box contains many parameters, but we will discuss only some of them here.

   You can set the amount of pitch shift by entering a number of semitones in the Pitch Shift Settings section, as you will do here, or by using the keyboard.

3. In the Pitch Shift Settings area, click the up arrow on the Transpose box twice to specify two semitones (**Figure 9.22**).

   Cubase plays back a root tone and then a second tone that shows how far the event will be pitch shifted. Pitch shifting cannot be previewed.

4. Click the Process button.

   A status bar shows the progress of the processing (**Figure 9.23**). When processing is complete, you will be returned to the Project window.

Figure 9.21 The Pitch Shift dialog box.

Figure 9.22 This setting will pitch shift the event by two semitones.

Figure 9.23 You can monitor processing by watching this status bar.

Figure 9.24 Selecting the note that needs to be pitch corrected.

Figure 9.25 Use the Fine Tune arrows or the Cents slider (where the pointer is) to adjust the pitch.

Correcting a Mistake Using Pitch Shift

Pitch shifting is often used to correct small tuning mistakes in a live musician's performance. Most often, it is used with vocals, but any performance with a small pitch mistake on a monophonic instrument can be corrected in this way. This pitch-correction process is usually called tuning and can be done in many ways. In the Dark Ages, before about 1998, people used hardware samplers as the preferred tool for correcting pitch mistakes, with the retuned words or syllables fired back to tape or disk via MIDI. One of the most famous VST plug-ins, Auto-tune, automated the pitch-correction process, forever relieving vocalists of the pesky responsibility of singing in tune. All of these tools still work, but using only your ears and Cubase you can single out a note and tune a performance.

To correct pitch mistakes in a performance:

1. Turn off Snap, unless your performer made mistakes for precisely one bar or beat.

2. Listen to the event in question to determine which note is incorrect. Then use the Range Selection tool to select just the note you want to change (**Figure 9.24**).

3. Select Audio > Process > Pitch Shift to open the Pitch Shift window.

   Now comes the tricky part. When tuning a performance, usually the pitch changes are very minor.

4. Use the Cents slider or Fine Tune arrows to pitch shift the selection slightly sharp or flat, as needed. **Figure 9.25** shows a setting that will raise the pitch 20 cents.

   continues on next page

5. When the pitch-shifted audio sounds right (often it's a good idea to use a correctly tuned piano or guitar as a reference), click the Process button to apply the changes.

You may be asked it you want to create a new event with the processed audio (**Figure 9.26**). Under most circumstances, you will, and you should select New Version.

Figure 9.26 The dialog box asks if you want to create a new event with the pitch-shifted audio. Usually, you will want to select New Version.

Figure 9.27 Choosing the audio to be pitch shifted.

Figure 9.28 The Envelope panel allows you to apply pitch shifting according to user-specified curves.

Pitch Shifting with an Envelope

Cubase has a large number of options available for pitch shifting; we will cover only a few of them here. One pitch-shifting option worth noting is the envelope, which you can use as a guide to change the amount of pitch shifting over time.

Envelopes are commonly used in synthesizers to create curves to control parameters automatically, and if you understand a synth envelope, you'll have no trouble using the Cubase pitch-shifting envelope. If you are not familiar with synthesizers, just remember that the envelopes for pitch shifting let you create a smooth curve that changes the amount of pitch shifting over time.

When are envelopes useful? Often live musicians will begin off-pitch and slowly drift back to pitch as their ears lead them back into tune. A singer may start out flat and swoop up to the right pitch, or a saxophone player may be too aggressive and play sharp for a few notes before drifting back down into tune. In situations like this, the envelope can be a very effective tool for tuning the performance.

To pitch shift using an envelope:

1. Turn off Snap.

2. Listen to the event and find the section that needs to be tuned.

3. Using the Range Selection tool, select the range of the performance that needs to be pitch shifted (**Figure 9.27**).

4. Open the contextual menu and select Process > Pitch Shift.

5. In the Pitch Shift panel, select the Envelope tab (**Figure 9.28**).

continues on next page

6. Drag a point to edit the curve; double-click to create any new points needed on the curve.

You can edit envelopes here just like you can edit fades in the Fade-in and Fade-out editors.

The Range setting determines the overall pitch-shifting capability of the editor. The value of this parameter is set in semi-tones, or half steps on a piano keyboard. **Figure 9.29** shows a fairly wide range of two semitones for pitch shifting. The breakpoints create a curve where the first two notes are pitched up signifi-cantly, the second note a little less, and the last two notes unchanged.

7. When you have the curve set as you wish, click the Process button to apply the changes to the audio.

Figure 9.29 A curve has been created with three breakpoints; each horizontal line in the waveform display represents a semitone of possible pitch shifting. In this figure, the range is set to one semitone, so there is one line above and below the waveform.

Figure 9.30 Opening the Phaser plug-in that comes with Cubase.

Figure 9.31 The editor panel for the phase-shifter plug-in.

Processing Audio with VST Effects

VST stands for virtual studio technology. In a virtual studio, the entire processing, recording, and mixing process occurs inside a computer. Among the key components that make a virtual studio possible are effects such as delays, flangers, reverbs, and compressors. Cubase ships with a nice complement of built-in VST plug-ins, but Steinberg also opened its plug-in specification so that third parties could make plug-ins that would work in Cubase.

VST plug-ins can be used in many different ways. Most often, they are used in the VST mixer. You will learn more about them in the chapters about the Cubase Mixer and in Chapter 14, "Audio Effect Plug-ins." In the following task, you will see how to apply a Phaser plug-in, included with Cubase, to an audio event (in this case, a drum loop).

To process an event with a VST effect:

1. Use the Arrow tool to select the event to be processed.

2. Select Audio > Plug-ins > Modulation > Phaser from the contextual menu (**Figure 9.30**).

   The VST plug-in window for that effect opens (**Figure 9.31**).

3. Click the Preview button to hear the event with the effect.

4. Adjust the parameters until the effect sounds the way you want.

5. When you are satisfied with the effect, click the Process button.

   The audio will be processed with the effect, and you will be returned to the Project window.

✔ Tip

■ If you are unfamiliar with the way that a phase shifter works, consult Chapter 8, "Audio Effects," in the Cubase manual.

Additional Settings for Processing Audio

Many of the VST plug-ins and the built-in Cubase audio processes have additional parameters that may be useful depending on the kind of effect you are using and what you doing with it. Many of the panels used to set up processing have a More button on the bottom that, when clicked, opens another set of options that control the use of the plug-in. In many cases, you will not need to use these parameters, but you still should know about them so you can use them to make changes when necessary.

Click the More button on the plug-in's panel to display additional parameters for audio processing (**Figure 9.32**). In this case, we'll look at the ModDelay panel.

◆ **Wet Mix** or **Dry Mix:** These settings control the percentage of the output that is modified by the effect. At 100 percent wet, the entire signal is changed by the effect; at 100 percent dry, none of the signal is modified by the effect. The sliders are ganged, meaning that when you move one, the other moves automatically, so the total of the two is always 100 percent (**Figure 9.33**).

◆ **Tail:** Some effects (notably delays and reverbs) create additional audio that needs to be tacked on to the end of the processed selection or event. If you select the Tail check box, Cubase will make the event longer to allow the effect to die away as it is designed. The slider controls the amount of audio added to the processed event or selection, in milliseconds.

Figure 9.32 Extra buttons lurk beneath the main VST plug-in processing window.

Figure 9.33 The Wet Mix and Dry Mix controls move in opposition to each other.

◆ **Pre-CrossFade:** Selecting this option mixes the effect-altered signal with the dry signal. The slider determines how long the crossfade lasts.

◆ **Post-CrossFade:** If you select this option, the plug-in will be faded out before the end of the selection or event. The slider sets the duration of the crossfade. For example, you might want a delay to fade out so it is inaudible by the end of the selection, and checking the Post-CrossFade button would do just that.

✔ Tip

■ Keep in mind that on a Windows machine, DirectX plug-in effects are used in exactly the same way as VST effects.

ADDITIONAL SETTINGS FOR PROCESSING AUDIO

Removing Audio Processing

Sometimes you will want to remove an effect after processing your audio. Cubase has a powerful set of tools for undoing changes made to a project or file. Some undo features are global, but Cubase also includes some more specialized tools for managing changes made in audio processing. Of course, the most recent action can always be undone by pressing Control-Z (Windows) or Command-Z (Macintosh). However, Cubase also keeps a list of every edit made to a project, and you can continue to undo actions all the way to the state of the project when it was opened. You can also choose from the Edit menu to undo and redo the most recent change to a project (**Figure 9.34**).

Although many audio applications have this level of undo and redo at the project level, Cubase's specialized tools for modifying and undoing audio processes are pretty amazing. It's possible to remove, reorder, and modify all processing done to an audio event or part. For example, you can remove only one process after a series of modifications have been made to an event. You can decide later in a project that you would rather have a slower chorus sound, or less delay, or stronger compression. These changes, amazingly, can be made at any time, even after a project has been saved. You have complete control over the history of processed audio in Cubase.

Figure 9.34 Undo and Redo options on the Edit menu of Cubase; the program keeps all edits since the last time the project was opened.

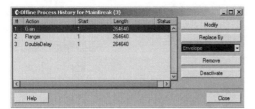

Figure 9.35 This history list shows all processes that have been performed on an event.

Figure 9.36 Cubase prompts you before making changes.

To remove audio processing from an event:

1. Use the Arrow tool to select the event.

2. Select Audio > Offline Process History or right-click to access this selection from the contextual menu.

3. The Offline Process History dialog box lists every process that has been applied to a file (**Figure 9.35**).

   In this example, the first process, Gain, is selected.

4. Select the process you want to delete and click the Remove button.

   A dialog box opens asking for confirmation to remove the process (**Figure 9.36**).

5. Click Remove to delete the process.

   The event will be processed again and placed in the Project window with the new version.

Modifying Effects on Processed Audio

Just as you can undo effects that you've applied to your audio, you can modify a process that you've applied to an event or range. For example, you might notice—after processing—that a Flanger effect is too pronounced. You can edit this effect, even at this point, by using Offline Process History.

To change the processing settings for an event or range:

1. Use the Arrow tool to select the event that you want to change.

2. Select Audio > Offline Process History from the main or the contextual menu.

3. When the Offline Process History dialog box opens, select the process that you want to edit (**Figure 9.37**). Then click the Modify button.

   The editor for that process opens, displaying the same settings used when the audio was processed (**Figure 9.38**).

4. Change the parameters as you like and then click the Process button.

   Cubase reprocesses the audio with the new settings (status bars will show the progress) and replaces the event in the Project window.

5. Click the Close button to dismiss the Offline Process History window.

Figure 9.37 The Flanger will be edited, so it is selected in the list.

Figure 9.38 When you choose to make changes to a process, the original editor will open.

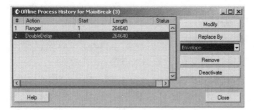

Figure 9.39 The DoubleDelay effect will be replaced with a different effect.

Figure 9.40 Selecting the new plug-in (ModDelay) to use in place of the original delay.

Figure 9.41 The editor for the replacement plug-in.

Replacing One Process with Another

Cubase offers so much flexibility in its audio processing that you can even replace one process with another. For example, you might process a file using a simple delay plug-in, but later you decide that a more complex delay with modulation would sound better. Making this swap is not only possible, but quite easy, using the Offline Process History window.

To replace processing already performed on an event:

1. Use the Arrow tool to select the event that you want to change.

2. Select Audio > Offline Process History.

3. In the Offline Process History dialog box, select the process you want to replace (**Figure 9.39**).

4. Click the pull-down menu in the right panel to select a new process or plug-in to replace the original process. For example, as shown here, choose Plug-ins > Delay > ModDelay (**Figure 9.40**).

5. Click Replace By. A dialog box will open to confirm that you want to replace the process. After you click Replace, the editor for the new process or plug-in opens in a new window (**Figure 9.41**).

6. Change the parameters for that plug-in as you wish.

7. Click the Process button.

   The event is reprocessed, as indicated by the activity in the status bars. When processing is complete, you are returned to the Offline Process History window.

8. Click Close to dismiss this window and return to the Project window.

The Sample Editor

It has been said more than once in this book that Cubase lets you do most of your editing from the Project window, including your audio editing and processing, while still offering the widest view of audio, MIDI, and automation in a project. This comprehensive view is preferred for many operations.

However, Cubase has always included a Sample editor (**Figure 9.42**), and there are still compelling reasons to use it. The Sample editor provides a large-scale, high-resolution view of a single audio file, which makes sample-level editing easy—for example, you can easily create regions in the Sample editor. Also, the Sample editor is the only place where you can use the Draw tool to manually change the actual audio data.

By default, the Sample editor opens to the full size of the Cubase screen. It's designed to give the most complete, high-resolution view possible at a single piece of mono or stereo audio. For the figures that follow, I resized the editor smaller to show more in the illustrations. You should *not* do the same, however; leave the Sample editor windows big and proud.

Figure 9.42 The Sample editor.

Figure 9.43 When positioned over the top half of the thumbnail display, the pointer will be an arrow.

Figure 9.44 Drag over the part of the event that you want to see in the waveform display.

Figure 9.45 The waveform display now shows only the section selected in the thumbnail display.

Zooming in the Sample Editor

The Sample editor has a Zoom tool that works just like the Zoom tool in the Project window. You can also click the ruler and drag vertically to zoom in or out and then navigate in your sample with more precision by using the thumbnail display at the top of the Sample editor's window.

To select a view in the waveform display:

1. Position the pointer over the top half of the thumbnail display at the top of the Sample editor.

   Regardless of the tool that you've selected, the pointer will be an arrow (**Figure 9.43**).

2. Drag over the section of the audio that you want to see in detail in the waveform display (**Figure 9.44**).

   After you release the mouse, just that section will be visible in the waveform display (**Figure 9.45**).

To resize your view in the waveform display:

1. To resize the selected region, position the Pointer over the bottom half of the thumbnail display, at the beginning or end of the area being viewed.

   Regardless of what tool is selected, the Pointer will turn into a pair of opposing arrows (**Figure 9.46**).

2. Drag anywhere on the thumbnail display to resize the selected area (**Figure 9.47**).

   The newly selected area will appear in the waveform display (**Figure 9.48**).

✔ Tip

- The Sample editor is particularly easy to navigate because it shows a great deal of detail for a single piece of audio. However, other windows also have thumbnail displays, including the Project window.

Figure 9.46 The pointer turns into a double-headed arrow when it is over the bottom half of the thumbnail display.

Figure 9.47 Resizing the selection in the thumbnail display by dragging the border.

Figure 9.48 The waveform display now shifts to show the newly selected area.

Figure 9.49 Clicking the Scrub tool to select it.

Figure 9.50 Moving the pointer over the area that is to be played.

Figure 9.51 The cursor will chase the pointer, scrubbing the audio at different speeds.

Using Scrub in the Sample Editor

Scrubbing is a term that comes from the era when editing was done with analog tape. To find the correct place for an edit, tape was manually shuttled back and forth—or scrubbed—over the tape head. Scrubbing is a very intuitive way to find exact locations for edit actions, and Cubase has an excellent digital scrub system built into the Sample editor.

To navigate audio by scrubbing:

1. In the Sample editor, click the Scrub tool on the toolbar (**Figure 9.49**).

2. Click the waveform display near the section you want to hear (**Figure 9.50**) and drag to the left or right.

    The cursor will catch up to the pointer, playing the audio as it moves (**Figure 9.51**).

    Moving the pointer to the left and right and more quickly or more slowly plays the audio forward, backward, and at varying pitches. This is precisely the way real scrubbing works.

✔ Tip

■ If you really dig the Scrub tool, there is also one in the Project window. You can use it in the same way if you wish.

Creating Regions with the Sample Editor

One of the primary uses of the Sample editor is in creating, editing, and otherwise working with regions. A region is simply a section of an audio clip. Regions were discussed in Chapter 4 as they related to cycle recording of audio. One way to cycle record is to record a single clip but have each pass of the loop create a new region. Regions can be converted to events and also exported as discrete audio files if you wish.

To create a region:

1. On the toolbar in the Sample editor, click the Show Regions button (**Figure 9.52**).

2. Use the Range Selection tool to select part of the clip in the waveform display (**Figure 9.53**).

3. In the Regions display at the right side of the Sample Editor window, click the Add button.

   This converts your selection to a new region (**Figure 9.54**). The region is shown both in the waveform display and in the regions list.

✔ Tip

■ If you do much intense editing with regions, the list of regions can grow fast and become confusing. If you name your regions, they'll be much easier to locate and manage. Double-click a region in the list in the Description column and then give it a useful name.

Figure 9.52 Click the Show Regions button to display a list of regions on the right.

Figure 9.53 This selection of the waveform display will be converted to a region.

Figure 9.54 Click the Add Region button to create a new region from the selection.

Figure 9.55 You must click to the far left of the region name for this process to work.

Figure 9.56 As you drag over the Project window; the outline and numeric display show where the region will be dropped.

Figure 9.57 The event after it has been created and placed in the Project window.

Creating an Event from a Region

You can easily drop regions into the Project window to create new events. This is a very simple way to grab the right take from within a larger clip that was cycle recorded, or to place single sounds, samples, or hits somewhere in a project. Any region in the Regions list can be moved into the Project window as an event.

To convert a region to an event:

1. Move the pointer to the Regions list.

   Regardless of the tool being used in the Sample editor, if you move the pointer to the Regions list, it will turn into an arrow.

2. Click to the left of the region name (**Figure 9.55**) and drag over the Events display in the Project window.

   In the Project window, a blue outline shows where the event will be created if the region is dropped at the current mouse position (**Figure 9.56**).

3. Release the mouse to create the event in that location.

   The new event appears in the Project window (**Figure 9.57**).

✔ Tip

- The Snap value is important when you drop a region in the Project window. You may need to adjust your Snap value to get your newly converted event into the right location.

Additional Processing Functions

Envelope: Functions similarly to a fade-in or fade-out, but changing the envelope of an event allows you to draw in a volume curve for the entire event, not just the beginning or end. Use an envelope for breakpoint editing when a fade-in or fade-out is not precise enough.

Fade-In: Identical in sound and function to the fade described in Chapter 8. The difference is that the fade will be applied to the event offline, and not as a real-time playback parameter.

Fade-Out: The reverse of a fade-in.

Gain: Processes an event to change the overall volume of the entire event.

Merge Clipboard: Mixes audio that was copied to the clipboard (usually from the Sample editor) with the selected event and creates a new event using both parts.

Noise Gate: Allows you to set a volume below which Cubase will mute the part. Often used as a noise-reduction tool.

Normalize: Raises the volume of the audio in an event to the highest level possible with no clipping.

Phase Reverse: Swaps the phase of the audio, so that where the waveform goes up, it will instead go down. Sometimes when an instrument is recorded with more than one microphone, one part may cancel out another, and reversing the phase of one of the tracks sometimes helps fix this problem.

Pitch Shift: Changes the pitch of audio and is edited in the same panel as the Time Stretch process.

Remove DC Offset: In some circumstances, audio will be recorded incorrectly with too large a DC current. If this happens, the waveform will not look centered, and clicks and pops will often occur when events are snipped. Using this process fixes these problems.

Reverse: Changes the audio so that it plays backward.

Silence: Reduces the output of the selected event or selection in an event to zero. It has the same result as muting the audio, but it works as a process.

Stereo Flip: Swaps the left and right channels in an audio file.

Time Stretch: Changes the duration of an audio file using the same tools as for pitch shifting.

A Stylistic Warning

I have carefully avoided telling you how your music should sound, or what is musically "right" or "wrong." However, I have a cautionary tale.

On March 18 and 19, 1963, jazz saxophone virtuoso Stan Getz was in New York City with Brazilian legends Joao Gilberto and Antonio Carlos Jobim recording an album that eventually received the understated name of *Getz/Gilberto*. One of Jobim's songs, written in Portuguese, was called "The Girl from Ipanema." The first version was in Portuguese, but the decision was made to include a version with the lyrics translated into English. That created a problem: Brazilian singer Joao Gilberto was not comfortable singing English. Over the objections of nearly everyone, Getz had Gilberto's wife Astrud (who could sing English) brought to the studio to give the song a try. Astrud was not a professional musician and had little previous performance experience. Instead of the train wreck some expected, the exquisite "The Girl from Ipanema" we know was the result. For 5 minutes and 22 seconds, the music of three continents sang in rare harmony.

However, it also sang flat. Astrud gave a staggering performance, but it was certainly not on pitch. But it was precisely that flatness that gave the vocals the languorous, tropical feel of the beaches of Rio. Brazilian vocalists to this day reference that wonderfully flat vocal in their own singing, and it's become a stylistic signature. Even so, I'm sure if that performance were recorded today, someone at some point would demand that the vocals be tuned and run through five limiters and slathered with reverb, thus depriving the world of one of the sublime moments in recording history.

The moral of this story? If every vocal were tuned, and if every take were made perfect, much of what we consider the best recorded music would not exist. Don't automatically airbrush every sound in a project, unless you're making beer commercials.

EDITING MIDI

MIDI is more than just notes—it's a powerful tool that's fantastic for experimentation, because MIDI data is almost infinitely editable. After you record or enter MIDI, you can instantly change the pitch, timing, key, duration, and nearly any other parameter, with no loss in sound quality. And you can also use MIDI to control effects processors, synthesizers, samplers, and, in some instances, mixers or even lights.

Cubase includes very advanced tools for editing and transforming MIDI once it has been recorded. In this chapter, you will learn some of the differences between editing audio and editing MIDI. You will learn much more about the Key editor, including how to modify MIDI notes and how to view and modify MIDI continuous controller (CC) data. You will learn about quantizing, which you can use to make detailed and exacting edits to the timing of a MIDI part. At the end of this chapter, you will learn to use the List editor, which offers an extremely detailed look at all MIDI data in a project and enables precision editing of MIDI.

Audio Editing Versus MIDI Editing

Audio and MIDI are very different elements, so it follows that editing and changing one is not much like editing and changing the other. For example, when you work with audio, you can edit at the level of a single sample, whereas MIDI does not have such fine timing resolution. With audio, you can modify the timbre of a sound—its equalization, for example—through processing. In contrast, when you edit MIDI, you generally use the sound generator triggered by the MIDI notes, usually a sampler or synth, to change the EQ of a sound.

Another major difference between editing MIDI and editing audio in Cubase is that you can do much less MIDI editing in the Project window. When you edit audio, you can see and edit both events and parts directly in the Project window. With MIDI, the events are the notes and data, and these cannot be edited in the Project window. For example, you cannot use the Draw tool to add a MIDI note to a part in the Project window—the tool is supposed to be used in the MIDI editors. If you drag with the Draw tool in the Project window, you'll simply create a new part (**Figure 10.1**). So while you'll learn some MIDI editing tasks that you can do in the Project window, most of this chapter concentrates on the MIDI editors.

Figure 10.1 You cannot use the Draw tool in the Project window to create or change MIDI notes. You can use it only to create new MIDI parts.

Figure 10.2 A MIDI part as it is being moved: The (+4) indicates that the part has been moved four measures forward.

Figure 10.3 A different MIDI part is being copied. At this point, it is two bars forward in time from where it started.

Figure 10.4 The MIDI part after it has been copied.

✔ **Tip**

■ You can also move or copy multiple parts simply by holding down the Shift key and selecting more than one part before making the edit.

Moving and Copying MIDI Parts

You can perform a few large-scale editing operations in the Project window, such as moving and copying MIDI parts. You perform these operations essentially the same way as you perform them for audio parts.

To move a MIDI part:

1. Select the Arrow tool.

2. Click the part that you want to move and drag it.

   As you drag, the current location of the part will be displayed next to the pointer, along with the distance that the part has been moved (**Figure 10.2**). This information tells you exactly where a part will wind up as it is moved.

3. When the part is where you want it, release the mouse.

✔ **Tip**

■ Snap matters when moving parts; if it's on, parts will move only in the increments set in the Snap menu. In this example, Snap is on and set to Beat.

To copy a MIDI part:

1. Select the Arrow tool.

2. Turn Snap on or off.

   Snap also matters when copying parts.

3. While holding down Alt (Windows) or Option (Mac OS), click the part you want to copy and drag to the place where you want the part pasted (**Figure 10.3**).

4. Release the mouse.

   The copy will be at its new location in the Project window (**Figure 10.4**).

Muting and Splitting MIDI Parts

The actions used to mute and split MIDI parts are similar to those used for working with audio parts. You might split a phrase into multiple parts to be used in different parts of a song, or you might want to take only a small piece of a larger performance and change or edit just that small piece of MIDI.

To mute a MIDI part:

1. Select the Mute tool from the toolbar.
   The pointer will change into an X to indicate that the tool has been selected.

2. Click the part or parts you want to mute.
   The muted parts will become dimmed (**Figure 10.5**).

3. To unmute a part, click it again.

To split a MIDI part:

1. Select the Split tool.

2. Turn Snap on to make a tempo-restricted split or turn it off to split anywhere in the part.

3. Position the Split (scissors) tool at the location where you want to make the split.
   You'll see a thin line across the part and a numerical display that shows where the split will be made (**Figure 10.6**).

4. Click the mouse to split the MIDI part into two new parts (**Figure 10.7**).

✔ Tip

■ If a MIDI note spans a part that is split in two, only the section of the note in the first part will play. In other words, the note will not be triggered again in the second part.

Figure 10.5 The dimmed parts are muted and will not play.

Figure 10.6 The thin vertical line on the MIDI part is a guide to where the part will be snipped.

Figure 10.7 After the mouse is clicked, two piano parts are created from the original part. Notes that span a split part, however, will not be triggered in the second part.

Figure 10.8 Use this button to show and hide the Track inspector.

Figure 10.9 Clicking the small plus sign next to the Track Parameters tab will open that tab for editing.

Figure 10.10 This slider controls transposition for the entire track. All notes on the track will be transposed by the amount set here in the Track inspector.

Transposing a MIDI Track with the Inspector

The MIDI Track inspector was introduced in Chapter 5, "Recording MIDI." The Track inspector can be used for more than just selecting MIDI inputs and outputs, however, because it offers control over a number of parameters, such as volume, pan, and timing offset. The inspector for a MIDI track also offers an option to transpose all notes on the track by a specified amount. This can be very useful when a song written in one key needs to be changed later to another key to make it easier for a performer to work with. Transposing can also come in handy to match a pitched audio sample that isn't in the key of the song.

To transpose a MIDI track using the Track inspector:

1. If the Track inspector is not visible, open it by clicking the Show Inspector button on the Project window toolbar (**Figure 10.8**).

2. Click a MIDI track. The Inspector for a MIDI track has six tabs that show different information about the track. Click the small plus sign next to the Track Parameters tab to display it (**Figure 10.9**).

3. On the Track Parameters tab, select Transpose. Then do one of the following:
   ▲ Click the up and down arrows to transpose up or down in increments of one semitone.
   ▲ Click the numeric value in the Transpose field and enter a new value directly.
   ▲ Click below the number to open a slider (**Figure 10.10**) to change the amount of transposition.

✔ Tips

■ Remember that, unlike with audio notes, you can change the pitch and tempo of MIDI notes with no loss of quality.

■ The Track inspector will change the pitch of all notes and parts on the entire track. If you want to transpose only one part, you should use a MIDI editor.

Dissolving One Part into Multiple Parts

You can also use the Project window to break a MIDI part into multiple parts. This capability comes in handy in two situations. First, some MIDI files that play back more than one instrument sound have each instrument assigned to its own channel: channel 1 will play a piano sound, channel 2 will play a bass sound, and so on. In this case, it is easier to place a part for each instrument on its own track so you can assign sounds to each track individually and so the MIDI file will play back correctly. Second, when you're working with drum parts, it is often convenient to have each drum on its own track. Even if the tracks trigger the same instrument, it's great to have individual control over the volume and pan of the kick, snare, hi-hat, and other drums.

The following example shows how to dissolve a drumbeat (**Figure 10.11**) into multiple parts: one for each drum sound and with each part on its own track.

Figure 10.11 This drum part uses only four notes: one for each drum sound that is triggered.

Figure 10.12 In the Dissolve Part dialog box, specify how the part should be dissolved. Here, the part will be dissolved according to pitch.

Figure 10.13 After the part is broken into multiple parts, each is visible in the Project window, and the original is muted.

To dissolve a MIDI part:

1. Right-click (Windows) on the part, and in the contextual menu, select MIDI > Dissolve Part. On the Mac, click the part and choose MIDI > Dissolve Part from the main menu.

2. When the Dissolve Part dialog box opens, choose whether to dissolve each channel into a part or dissolve each pitch into a part. Multitimbral MIDI files will usually be dissolved with the channel options; dissolving a drum part to individual drum hits will normally use the pitch option. Then click OK.

   In **Figure 10.12**, only the Separate Pitches option is available because the MIDI part has only one channel. Cubase will extract all of the notes of each pitch and create a new MIDI part for each one. It will also mute the MIDI part that was dissolved (**Figure 10.13**).

✔ Tip

■ This example explains splitting and dissolving a single-channel MIDI part according to the pitches involved. If you have a multichannel MIDI part (the most common situation for this is if you are importing a standard MIDI file, or SMF, exported from another application), you can also dissolve it into individual parts. In that situation, the other check box in Figure 10.12 will be available, and the MIDI data for each channel will be extracted to a new MIDI part in Cubase.

Editing Multiple Parts in the Key Editor

The Key editor (**Figure 10.14**) is the default editor that opens when you double-click a MIDI file in the Project window. If you have a mouse with a right button, you can also access any of the editors by selecting MIDI from the contextual menu that opens from a MIDI part.

Often it is useful to see more than one part at a time in the Key editor. For example, having both a keyboard and a drum part open in the same editor makes it easy to see when notes might be getting in the way of each other. The following task shows how to open three MIDI parts in the Key editor.

To view multiple parts in the Key editor:

1. In the Project window, hold down the Shift key and click all parts that you want opened in the Key editor.

   Holding the Shift key allows you to select multiple, noncontiguous parts.

2. Double-click one of the selected parts, or click it once and select MIDI > Open Key Editor (**Figure 10.15**).

Figure 10.14 The MIDI Key editor.

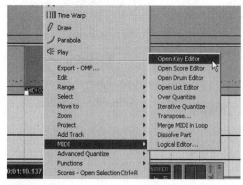

Figure 10.15 One way to open the Key editor is from the contextual menu.

More About the Key Editor

You will often use the Key editor to edit MIDI notes and continuous controller data because it offers many more editing options than does the Project window, and it is much more intuitive and musical than the List editor. If you're working with drum parts, you're likely to prefer the Drum editor.

However, because this section is about what you can do in the Key editor, you might want to quickly review Chapter 6, "Entering MIDI Manually," to refresh your memory of such elements as the Note display, the Controller lane, and the tools on the Key editor toolbar.

Figure 10.16 Multiple parts are opened in a single Key editor.

Figure 10.17 Clicking a MIDI note from another part makes it active, and the velocity stalks in the Controller lane make this obvious.

The MIDI Key editor opens, and the notes from both parts will be shown (**Figure 10.16**). Unlike in the first version of Cubase SX, all notes are visible, and none are dimmed. Although all notes are visible, elements like the Controller lane, which shows velocity, show information for only one part at a time. For example, the velocity for the keyboard notes is shown in Figure 10.16, but clicking a note from the drum part will display the velocity for notes in that part (**Figure 10.17**).

Copying Notes in the Key Editor

You can use the Key editor to copy a MIDI note or a group of notes. The following task shows you how to copy all notes in one measure to the next measure while using Snap to drop the copied notes precisely at the start of the next measure.

To copy MIDI notes:

1. Turn on Snap and set the Quantize value to a 1/4 note or so, to make the move easier.

2. Select the Arrow tool if it is not already selected and drag over the notes that you want copied (**Figure 10.18**).

3. With the notes selected, hold down Alt (Windows) or Option (Mac OS) and click one of the selected notes.

4. Drag the mouse to where you want to copy the notes.

   A numeric display will show how far you have moved the copy from the original (**Figure 10.19**).

5. When the copied notes are where you want them, release the mouse and then the Alt or Option key.

✔ Tips

- If you want to copy notes and also to restrict movement to the vertical or horizontal axis, hold down Ctrl-Shift-Alt (Windows) or Command-Shift-Option (Mac OS). This allows you to copy the notes to a new song position, but forces the pitch to remain the same. If you copy notes on the vertical axis using this technique, the notes will stay at the same song position but change pitch.

Figure 10.18 Selecting a group of MIDI notes.

Figure 10.19 Copying the notes: The original notes are outlined, and the copied notes are solid bars. Note that Snap is on while the notes are copied.

- If you accidentally release the Alt or Option key before releasing the mouse, you will move the notes instead of copying them. Just undo the change and try again.

Figure 10.20 The D# note is about to be changed with the Draw tool.

Figure 10.21 Clicking the note with the Draw tool allows it to be resized.

Figure 10.22 If multiple notes are selected, resizing actions resize all notes simultaneously.

Changing the Duration of MIDI Notes

A very common MIDI operation is changing the duration of a note. Notes can be easily lengthened or shortened by using the Draw tool in the Key editor.

To change the duration of a MIDI note:

1. Turn off Snap and select the Draw tool. The pointer will change to a pencil.

2. Move the pointer over the note that you want to change (**Figure 10.20**) and drag until the note is the duration that you want (**Figure 10.21**).

✔ Tips

- Multiple notes can also be changed using the Draw tool. In Figures 10.20 and 10.21, only one note is changed. **Figure 10.22** shows a group of three notes that have all been shortened after being selected simultaneously.

- You can also change the starting point of a note using the Draw tool. Hold down Ctrl (Windows) or Command (Mac OS), and the Draw tool will change the starting point of the note instead of the ending point of the note, without changing the note's duration.

Editing Notes with Identical Pitch

In many situations, you'll need to edit all notes of a particular pitch. If a phrase was difficult to play, the resulting part may contain multiple incorrect notes with the same pitch. A part may also contain a good performance, but you might decide that a particular chord sounds better without one of the notes.

If you are creating drum parts, each pitch plays a different sound; a C note might play a snare drum, and a C# note might play a snare drum with a hi-hat. Editing all notes on one pitch is very handy in this situation, because when you change the note, you will change the drum sound that is triggered. The following task shows you how to do precisely that: move the notes triggering one drum sound so that they trigger another drum sound.

To change all notes of the same pitch:

1. In the Project window, double-click a drum part to open it in the Key editor.

2. Hold down Ctrl (Windows) or Command (Mac OS) and click the note that you want to select on the keyboard at the left of the editor window (**Figure 10.23**). This selects all of the notes with that pitch in the Key editor window.

3. Keeping the notes selected, press the Up Arrow key on the keyboard twice. This transposes the selected notes up two semitones and constrains them to only vertical movement (**Figure 10.24**).

✔ Tips

- While multiple notes are selected, you can also edit other parameters, such as note length. **Figure 10.25** shows the same MIDI part after changing length with multiple notes selected.

Figure 10.23 Clicking the keyboard with Ctrl or Command held down will select all notes in the editor with that pitch.

Figure 10.24 Simply pressing the up arrow key twice moves these notes to new pitches.

Figure 10.25 Another example of resizing more than one note at a time: all of the B4 notes were selected and then resized together.

- You can also use the mouse to drag the selected notes. Just remember that Snap matters when you make a change in this way, and that holding down the Ctrl or Command key allows you to move the notes vertically (pitch) without changing their horizontal (song position) location.

Figure 10.26 This contextual menu option opens a new Controller lane.

Figure 10.27 The new Controller lane, in this case showing the same parameter a second time.

Figure 10.28 Selecting a different parameter to be viewed in the new Controller lane—in this case, Pan.

Viewing Continuous Controller Lanes

Some basic continuous controller (CC) concepts were introduced in Chapter 6, "Entering MIDI Manually." We'll cover some of the more advanced options and tools for CC editing in the next few pages, but there is more to CC editing than can be covered here. For more information about continuous controller data and how to edit it, see the section about the Key editor in Chapter 23, "The MIDI Editors," in the electronic documentation that came with Cubase.

One of the first things you should know about editing CC data is that you can view more than one Controller lane in the Key editor at the same time. Two of the MIDI values most commonly edited in the Key editor are Velocity and Pan. Here is how to see them both simultaneously.

To see multiple Controller lanes in the Key editor:

1. Right-click and select Create New Controller Lane (**Figure 10.26**) or click the plus (+) sign next to the Controller Lane.

   A new Controller lane is created, and the Key editor will look something like **Figure 10.27**. The precise sizes and parameters of the two lanes may be different.

2. Click the pop-up menu at the left of the Controller lane to select the CC displayed in that particular lane. Most likely, your Controller lane displays the default parameter, which is Velocity.

3. From the pop-up menu, select Pan as the visible parameter in the new lane (**Figure 10.28**).

   Each Controller lane now displays a distinct parameter that you can edit and modify.

✔ Tip

- Controller lanes can be resized by moving the borders between lanes up and down, just as tracks can be resized in the track list.

Viewing Any CC Message

The menu in Figure 10.28 shows only some of the more common CC messages that you can create and edit in Cubase. In fact, there are 128 CC messages, and there are situations in which you might want to use any one of them.

One of the most commonly used parameters is Modulation. Nearly every keyboard synth made, and most other MIDI controllers, have two wheel controllers on them somewhere. One is called the pitchbend wheel and is used to bend the pitch of the notes being produced. The other, called the modulation wheel—or mod wheel—sends CC data that is usually connected to one or more parameters on the presets in the keyboard. The mod wheel is invaluable for controlling both hardware synths and VST instruments because almost every keyboard has this tactile controller. The following example demonstrates how to show modulation data in a Controller lane in the Key editor.

To view additional CC messages:

1. Click the pop-up menu at the left of the Controller lane and select Setup (**Figure 10.29**).

   The Controllers Menu Setup dialog box opens (**Figure 10.30**). The CCs on the left side of the pane, in the In Menu list, are available in the pop-up menu for the Controller lanes in the Key editor. The CCs in the right half of the dialog box, in the Hidden list, are not on that menu.

2. Click one of the CCs in the Hidden list. Choose Modulation if it's there.

3. Below the Hidden list is a button marked <<<. With a CC selected, click that button to move the CC to the In Menu list (**Figure 10.31**).

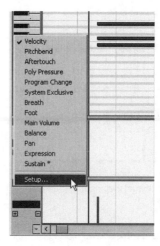

Figure 10.29
Choose Setup to open the dialog box and customize the list of CCs that can be viewed in Controller lanes.

Figure 10.30 The Controllers Menu Setup dialog box.

Figure 10.31 Clicking the button at the bottom of the Hidden list will add the Modulation CC to the CCs available in the Controller lanes.

Figure 10.32 Selecting the newly added Modulation parameter for a Controller lane.

Figure 10.33 A few of the generic CCs: any CC can be viewed in a Controller lane.

4. In the Controllers Menu Setup panel, click OK to save the change and close the panel.

Now when you click the pop-up menu for a Controller lane, Modulation will be available for viewing in the Controller lane (**Figure 10.32**).

✔ Tip

■ If you want to get an idea of just how many parameters MIDI can control, take a look at all of the available options in the Controllers Menu Setup panel. You can use all of these normally hidden parameters, and there are many general CC messages that you can use for nearly anything (**Figure 10.33**). Live sound people even use MIDI for things like lighting cues. Your MIDI devices and MIDI-aware effects should come with lists indicating what CC message controls what parameter, and Cubase gives you graphic control over those parameters.

Creating Tempo-Based CC Data

One of the really fun and very musical things that you can do with CC data in Cubase is creating tempo-based effects with MIDI instruments and MIDI-addressable effects processors. Nearly all MIDI instruments have most of their internal parameters mapped to one CC or another, and you can do a lot of creative things by changing these parameters with CC messages synched to the current tempo of the project. The Cubase Draw tool has multiple modes that make creating such tempo-based data simple.

It's up to you which parameter you want to affect, but some common ones are the cut-off frequency on a synth filter, the amount of feedback on a delay unit, and the amount of reverb applied from an effects processor. To find out which CC message changes what parameter, you need to consult the documentation that came with your MIDI device.

In the following task, you create tempo-based CC data using the Cubase Snap settings and drawing tools. Nearly all MIDI devices, and many VST instruments, map something important to the Modulation CC message, so this next task is a good place to start.

Figure 10.34 The Line tool has more than one mode. The Triangle mode allows you to draw triangle-shaped curves in the Controller lanes.

Figure 10.35 In Triangle mode, the pointer changes to this shape in a Controller lane.

Figure 10.36 Drawing controller data using Triangle mode.

Figure 10.37 After you draw the shape, Cubase enters these values automatically.

To create tempo-based CC data:

1. In the Key Editor, select the Line tool on the toolbar. Click the small triangle to open the tool-selection menu; then select Triangle (**Figure 10.34**).

2. Turn on Snap, set Quantize to 1/4 or 1/2 note, and set Length Quantize to 1/64 note.

3. Set the Controller lane to Modulation and position the mouse pointer in or near the Controller lane.

   The pointer will change shape to show that it is in Triangle mode (**Figure 10.35**).

4. Drag to the right and slightly down or up. A line with a triangle shape shows the values that will be created for the CC message (**Figure 10.36**).

5. Release the mouse button when you have a curve that looks right. You can also play back the MIDI part to hear the change the CC data creates in the MIDI device and adjust the curve audibly and in real time.

   The new CC data is perfectly synched to the tempo, and it's visible in the Controller lane (**Figure 10.37**).

About Snap and CC Editing

You don't have to turn on Snap to create every type of CC data, but you must turn it on if you want to create CC data using the project tempo as a reference. Once Snap is on, the quantize setting determines the way CC data is created and visually displayed by the curves in the Controller lanes. Smaller Snap settings will create CC data that follows shorter meter divisions. The smaller the Snap value is for a CC that controls pan, the faster the sound will be panned left and right.

Another example would be if you are drawing a triangle wave. The Quantize setting determines the number of triangle shapes that are drawn in each measure. **Figure 10.38** shows one measure being drawn with the triangle set to 1/4-note quantize. One triangle is created for each quarter-note.

Length Quantize controls the density of the CC events that are created. Shorter note values create more finely grained CC data. For example, consider **Figure 10.39** and **Figure 10.40**, which use the Triangle tool again. To make things clear, the Quantize setting is 1/1, or a whole note, so only one triangle is drawn for the whole measure. In Figure 10.39, Length Quantize is set to 1/16, and in Figure 10.40, Length Quantize is set to 1/128. The higher Length Quantize value in Figure 10.40 creates 128 steps of MIDI data, while in Figure 10.39 the same overall change in MIDI value is accomplished with only 16 steps. It's not hard to see that the CC data in Figure 10.40 has a much smoother curve, and under most circumstances the change will be audibly smoother.

Figure 10.38 With Quantize set to 1/4, one measure will have four triangles drawn in it.

Figure 10.39 This triangle was drawn with Quantize set to 1/1 and Length Quantize set to 1/16.

Figure 10.40 With Length Quantize set to 1/128, a much smoother curve is drawn.

✔ Tip

- If you are a bit of a synth geek, you may notice that these edits mimic a triangle-wave low-frequency oscillator (LFO). Indeed; using these drawing tools to create CC messages is very much like using an LFO on a synth.

Figure 10.41 The freehand Draw tool.

Figure 10.42 The result of using the Line tool.

Figure 10.43 You can use the Parabola tool to draw curves.

Figure 10.44 Controller data drawn by the Square tool.

Other Curves for CC Messages

The Line tool has more than one option for creating MIDI CC messages, and CC data can also be created with the Draw tool. Here is a short explanation of the other Draw tool modes and their uses for creating tempo-based CC data.

Draw: Use this tool instead of the Line tool to create freehand curves; you can create pretty much any shape you want with the Draw tool. With Snap off, you can create very fine curves (**Figure 10.41**).

Line: Use this tool to create CC data as if it were drawn with a ruler (**Figure 10.42**). Just like the Draw tool, with Snap off, the Line tool creates a lot of finely grained MIDI data.

Parabola: Use this tool to create smooth curves of MIDI data as in **Figure 10.43**. If Snap is on, the CC data curve ends on a particular beat.

Sine: Sine creates a smooth, curved wave that can be used easily for tempo-based effects.

Triangle: This tool creates the triangle or sawtooth waveform shown in Figure 10.37.

Square: Use this tool to create jagged values (**Figure 10.44**) with no curve as they rise and fall. The Snap and Quantize settings determine the number of teeth created per measure.

Paint: When working with CC messages, the Line tool in Paint mode works just like the Draw tool.

Deleting, Moving, and Copying CC Messages

You can move CC data freely within a project or within a part. You can delete CC events with the Eraser tool, select them with the Arrow tool, and move them with the standard Cut, Copy, and Paste commands. The following task describes how to perform one of the more complex operations: copying a triangle curve to a new location.

To copy CC data in a Controller lane:

1. Using the Arrow tool, draw a box around the CC messages that you want to copy (**Figure 10.45**).

2. Turn on Snap.

   Snap can be on or off, but turning Snap on makes it easier to copy CC data to a new measure or beat.

3. Hold down Alt (Windows) or Option (Mac OS) and click the selected CC data.

4. Drag the CC data to the new location.

   An outline shows you where the data is being moved (**Figure 10.46**).

5. Release the mouse when the copy is where you want it.

   The CC data is copied to the new location in the Controller lane, and the original CC data remains in its original location (**Figure 10.47**).

Figure 10.45 Selecting CC data to be copied.

Figure 10.46 The thin outline shows that the copy is taking place.

Figure 10.47 After the copy operation is completed.

Figure 10.48 Setting the meter division to be used when quantizing.

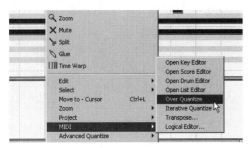

Figure 10.49 This command will quantize the selected notes.

Figure 10.50 After quantizing is applied, each MIDI note starts on an eighth-note.

Quantizing

In previous sections of this book, the term *quantize* referred to the Quantize setting or Length Quantize setting of Snap. These settings determine the influence of Snap on the precise movement or copying of MIDI data.

However, MIDI data can also be quantized—that is, by quantizing MIDI data, you change its timing. The changes can be subtle or dramatic, but whenever a MIDI part or note is quantized, the rhythm changes. The simplest kind of quantizing in Cubase is used to clean up notes so that each note begins at a specific meter division. In other words, each note is moved so that it begins on the nearest eighth, sixteenth, or other user-defined note.

To quantize MIDI notes:

1. Use the Arrow tool to select the notes to be quantized.

2. Set Quantize to the tempo value that you want Cubase to use for placing the MIDI notes.

   In this example, a setting of 1/8 note is used (**Figure 10.48**).

3. Select MIDI > Over Quantize (**Figure 10.49**).

   Cubase moves all selected notes according to the Quantize setting. In this case, all notes will begin on an eighth-note (**Figure 10.50**).

✔ Tip

■ All quantizing can apply either to particular notes selected in a MIDI editor or to an entire MIDI part or parts. Anything selected when the quantize action is applied will be quantized.

QUANTIZING

Adjusting the Quantize Grid

Many musicians think that anything quantized is automatically "bad." It is true that quantized MIDI can sound very machinelike and robotic, and depending on the kind of music, that can be very bad. Like most MIDI applications, Cubase has many options for quantizing MIDI that are designed to make the result sound natural and not quantized. In Cubase, most of these options are on the Quantize Setup panel (**Figure 10.51**).

One of the most important options on the Quantize Setup panel is the option to create user-defined grids to use for quantizing. For example, instead of quantizing to straight robotic eighth-notes as in the previous example, you might want robotic sixteenth notes, or you might want to quantize using a sixteenth-note grid but with a swing feel. The following tasks introduce you to the quantizing options available on the Quantize Setup panel.

Figure 10.51 The Quantize Setup panel.

Figure 10.52 The Quantize Setup dialog box is available only from the MIDI menu.

Figure 10.53 The quantize grid has been changed from Figure 10.51 to a triplet grid.

To customize the quantize grid:

1. Select the notes you want to quantize.

2. From the main Project window menus, select MIDI > Quantize Setup (**Figure 10.52**).

3. In the Quantize Setup dialog box, select 1/8 for the grid setting and Triplet for the Type setting to create an eighth-note triplet grid.

   As the settings are changed for the grid and type, the grid display changes to reflect the current quantize settings (**Figure 10.53**). Compare this grid display to the one in Figure 10.51.

4. To use the setting, click the Apply button; the selected MIDI notes will be quantized using the current grid. To leave the Quantize Setup in its current state without quantizing the selected notes, click the close box in the upper corner of the panel to close the window.

Controlling Which Notes Are Quantized

Cubase provides a useful way to exclude and include only some of the notes in the quantize setup. Quantizing all the notes in a part often produces a more sweeping effect than you need. You might want to tighten up only the timing of notes that fall near a beat grid if some of the other notes were played quite intentionally away from the beat. Normally, all notes will be moved when a part is quantized, unless you specify otherwise. In this next task, you'll quantize notes close to the grid and at the same time leave other notes alone.

To quantize only some MIDI notes:

1. Select the notes, part, or parts to be quantized.

2. Open the Quantize Setup dialog box by clicking the MIDI menu and selecting Quantize Setup.

3. Set the grid as you want it.

   In this example (again, so it is a bit easier to see), the panel has a straight eighth-note grid (**Figure 10.54**).

4. Use the Magnetic Area slider to set limits on what is quantized.

   As the slider is moved, an area on either side of each point in the grid is highlighted (**Figure 10.55**). Only notes within this range will be affected by quantizing.

5. Click Apply to quantize according to the current setting, or click the close box to close the panel without quantizing.

Figure 10.54 The Quantize Setup dialog box starts with a plain eighth-note grid.

Figure 10.55 The Magnetic Area slider adjusts the range in which notes will be quantized, indicated by the lightly colored area next to the grid markers. Notes outside the gray range will be ignored.

Figure 10.56 The MIDI notes before being quantized.

Figure 10.57 This setting determines how strong or weak the iterative quantize effect is.

Making Quantized MIDI Sound More Natural

A method for making quantized MIDI parts sound less robotic and more similar to "live" sound is to use what Cubase calls Iterative Quantize. The dictionary definition of *iterative* is "characterized by repetition or repetitiousness." In fact, iterative quantize is actually used to avoid quantizing MIDI to overly exact, robotic, repetitious timing values. Instead of moving MIDI notes to the nearest, most exact grid location, iterative quantize moves MIDI notes by a percentage of the distance to the nearest grid location. This approach is often the best way to quantize a MIDI part to make it sound realistic—the timing is tighter than the original performance but retains enough slop to sound like it was played by a person.

To apply iterative quantize to MIDI notes:

1. Select the MIDI notes or parts to be quantized.

   To give you a good view of what iterative quantize does, **Figure 10.56** shows a few MIDI notes zoomed in quite close.

2. Open the Quantize Setup dialog box by clicking the MIDI menu and selecting Quantize Setup.

3. Near the bottom of this panel, enter the iterative strength. Start with a setting of 50% (**Figure 10.57**).

   The higher the value, the more the MIDI is quantized by iterative quantizing. At 0%, iterative quantize does nothing; at 100%, it acts just like Over Quantize.

4. Close this window without clicking Apply.

continues on next page

MAKING QUANTIZED MIDI SOUND MORE NATURAL

5. With the notes still selected, right-click (Windows) or Control-click (Mac OS) and select MIDI > Iterative Quantize.

The notes are moved with 50 percent of the quantize strength of Over Quantizing. **Figure 10.58** shows the result. Compare this figure to Figure 10.50, in which all notes started precisely on an eighth-note. You may want to experiment by moving the value up and down to understand how these changes affect the rhythmic feel of the section.

✔ Tip

■ The discussion here only scratches the surface of what can be done with quantizing in Cubase. If you edit a lot of MIDI parts, dig deep into the Cubase documentation to find out more.

Figure 10.58 The notes after iterative quantize is applied: Compare them to the other quantize results described in this chapter.

About Groove Quantizing

One of the glaring omissions in the first version of Cubase SX was the lack of groove quantizing. Cubase VST (and nearly every other sequencer) supported groove quantizing, which uses one MIDI part as the timing grid for another MIDI part. This was accomplished by extracting the "groove" from a MIDI part, or sometimes an audio file, which would then create a complex timing grid that could be used as a quantize source.

Groove quantizing opens up a ton of interesting musical possibilities. A MIDI drum beat can be used to quantize a piano part, which will tighten the groove between the two without any of the robotic feel that is generally part of quantizing. Combining this with other advanced quantizing tools like iterative strength and iterative quantizing creates a very powerful tool for working with MIDI parts.

The next few pages will cover groove quantizing between MIDI parts. Cubase also includes the ability to extract a groove from an audio file by using hit points, but this operation is a bit beyond what this book can cover. If you want to know more about how to do this, check page 407 of Cubase's electronic operation manual. In addition, Propellerheads (www.propellerheads.se) offers a very useful program called ReCycle, which can be used to automatically chop up drum beats and create MIDI files from them. ReCycle MIDI parts can be fabulous groove quantize sources.

Extracting a Groove from a MIDI Part

Before you can apply groove quantizing, you need to create a groove that will be used as a quantize source. The easiest way to do this is by using another MIDI part.

As the following exercise shows, Cubase makes extracting a groove very easy. The hard part is finding a good source from which to extract. Often a drum beat or percussion part will have one part that carries the "heart" of the beat. In a bossa nova groove, for example, it's usually the push-pull relationship between the hi-hat and snare drum that provides a lot if its feel. In hip-hop beats, the hi-hats are almost always in perfect time, so the kick or snare drum or another percussion part or the bass will be important.

To extract a groove from a MIDI part:

1. Select the MIDI part you want to use. **Figure 10.59** shows a hi-hat pattern from a bossa nova MIDI file.

2. Open the contextual menu and select Advanced Quantize > Part to Groove (**Figure 10.60**).

Figure 10.59 This hi-hat part will be used to create a groove for quantizing another part.

Figure 10.60 The contextual menu command to extract the groove.

Figure 10.61 Open the Quantize setup for groove quantizing.

Figure 10.62 The just-created groove is available in the Presets menu.

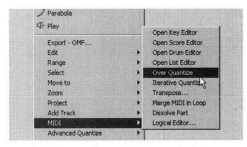

Figure 10.63 Groove quantizing is applied just like any other quantizing, in this case using the contextual menu.

Quantizing with a Groove

After extracting your groove information, using it is almost identical to using any other quantizing operation. You just need to select it as your quantizing source.

To quantize using a groove as the source:

1. Select the notes you want to quantize in a MIDI editor, or select a MIDI part in the Project window.

2. In the MIDI menu, select Quantize Setup (**Figure 10.61**).

3. In the Quantize Setup panel, click the Presets menu and select the groove you have just created (**Figure 10.62**).

4. Close the panel without clicking the Apply Quantize button.

5. Choose the notes or part you want to quantize and select MIDI > Over Quantize to apply the timing of the groove to the selected MIDI part (**Figure 10.63**).

✔ Tip

- You can also use all of the other quantizing options, like the magnetic area and iterative strength described on previous pages, when groove quantizing.

Additional Groove Quantizing Options

Because using a groove as a quantize source is a bit different than using an artificial, abstractly created grid, there are different options for it than for normal quantizing. **Figure 10.64** shows the full Quantize Setup panel when a groove is selected in the Presets menu. The top half of the panel shows the options unique to groove quantizing.

- The **Position** slider is a little like an extra iterative quantize function. It determines how much of the grid information is applied to the quantize destination.

- **Velocity** determines how much, if at all, the velocity or volume of the notes in the groove source is applied to the destination. Often you will want to quantize only the timing, leaving the dynamics of the destination alone, but if you want to include the dynamics, you can use the slider to do so.

- The **Length** slider determines whether the length of the notes being quantized is changed to match the groove quantize source. Again, generally this will be part of the destination you want to keep, but you can quantize lengths if you want.

Figure 10.64 The Quantize Setup panel shows different parameters when using a groove as the quantize source.

The List Editor

Up to now, all of the MIDI editors you've used were comparatively musical. The Key editor uses a keyboard to represent pitch and a grid to represent time. The Drum editor is similar but has some tools specifically for making drum beats. The List editor (**Figure 10.65**), however, offers a very computerish way of working with MIDI. Although it's not the most intuitive editor in Cubase, it offers precise MIDI editing and allows precision placement in the creation of MIDI data. You'll want to use the List editor when you know exactly what you want to change in a MIDI part. It's not something to use for sketching out tunes or figuring out new ways to play a chord. It's for actions like precisely inserting a MIDI command to make a synth change sound at a certain point in a song.

The List editor provides these interface elements:

Toolbar: The List editor toolbar includes familiar tools such as Draw, Mute, and Zoom, as well as List editor–specific tools such as the Insert menu.

Insert menu: You use this menu to select the type of event that you create with the Draw tool.

Filter settings: When the Show Filter View button is clicked, the filter settings check boxes allow you to determine what data is visible and what is not.

List: This pane lists all MIDI events in the part being displayed in the editor.

Event display: This pane provides a visual representation of all of the data in the event list.

Value display: This pane provides a visual representation of the value of each event in the event list.

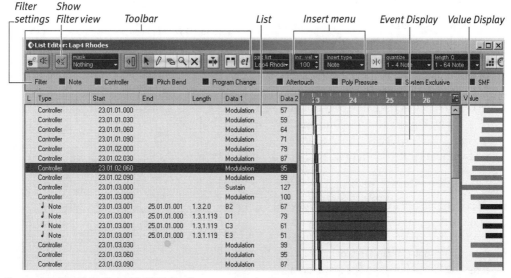

Figure 10.65 The List editor with MIDI data from one part shown.

Filtering Data in the List Editor

One of the most important tools in the List editor lets you specify not what the editor shows, but what it does not show. The List editor can contain thousands of pieces of MIDI data, and finding the information you want can be next to impossible unless some of the data is filtered out of the view. To do this, Cubase uses a clever set of check boxes available via the Filter view. In the following task, you will see how to filter controller information to get a better view of note data. This particular part has a ton of CC messages, but dozens of screens would be needed if all the data were displayed.

To filter MIDI data in the List editor:

1. Open a MIDI part in the List editor, using the MIDI menu or the contextual menu for a MIDI part.

2. Click the Show Filter View button (**Figure 10.66**) if it isn't already selected. The settings for filtering data will be visible directly beneath the toolbar.

3. Select the types of controller data you do not wish to see (**Figure 10.67**).

   In this example, selecting the Controller button will mask out controller data in the editor. With controller data filtered, all of the notes in the MIDI part can be seen easily (**Figure 10.68**). Compare this to Figure 10.65, which shows the same part without controller data filtered.

✔ Tip

■ Of course, all kinds of data can be viewed or hidden, depending on what you check in the boxes for the Filter settings. Just remember that filtering is a negative system. You can't choose to see some data: you can only choose *not* to see some data.

Figure 10.66
This button is used to show the options for filtering visible data in the List editor.

Figure 10.67 Selecting the Controller box will hide all CC data in the list.

Figure 10.68 With only note data visible, you can more easily see what is going on.

Figure 10.69 Selecting the note to be edited.

Figure 10.70 Clicking E3 allows the note value to be edited for this MIDI event.

Figure 10.71 After the value is changed, the note will play C3 instead of E3.

Changing Values in the Event List

The List editor isn't the easiest editor to use, but it offers powerful control for editing MIDI data values. Other editors may be a bit more musical, but nothing can beat the List editor for control. Any of the parameters shown in the event list can be edited. In the following task, you will see how to change the pitch of a note.

To modify MIDI data in the event list:

1. Open the List editor. In the event list, click the MIDI event you want to edit.

   The event will be highlighted (**Figure 10.69**). Note that you can widen this list view by grabbing and moving the line between the Event and Note windows.

2. To edit a value, simply click it and enter a new value.

   For example, clicking E3 (the pitch of the selected note) will select it for editing (**Figure 10.70**).

   You can enter values manually, or you can use the Up and Down Arrow keys on the keyboard to change values.

3. Press the Down Arrow a few times to set the new note value to C3 (**Figure 10.71**).

✔ Tip

- Different kinds of MIDI data have different values that can be edited in the List editor. For MIDI notes, for instance, you can edit the start, end, duration, pitch, and velocity parameters. For a CC message, though, you can edit only the time it starts and the message and the value that is being sent.

Creating a New Event in the Event List

If you need to do a lot of exacting MIDI editing, the List editor is a great tool to know about. A common use for the List editor is to enter a program change at a particular location in a song. Many synthesizers and hardware effects processors can't switch instantly to a new sound or new effects program; they will produce a short glitch, which can sound really awful. This next task shows how to insert a program change message with the List editor so that a synth can change smoothly in time.

Entering a program change in the List editor:

1. In the Event display, find the place where the program change needs to be entered.

   In **Figure 10.72**, the program change should go before the chord is played, at about measure 23.

2. Zoom in close to the location where you want to enter the program change.

3. Select the Draw (or pencil) tool, click the Insert type menu, and select Program Change (**Figure 10.73**).

   The Insert menu determines the kind of event created with the Draw tool.

4. Click the Event display with the Draw tool wherever you want to create a program change.

   This creates a new event, which will be added to the list as well (**Figure 10.74**).

Figure 10.72 The program change needs to be entered before the second note shown here.

Figure 10.73 Selecting Program Change as the type of data to be inserted.

Figure 10.74 Creating the program change with the Draw tool.

MIXING AUDIO

You've recorded, edited, and tweaked each individual sound that makes up a song—now you need to turn the whole track into a cohesive statement. In audio circles, this is called *mixing*, and it is as much an art as is playing an instrument. A good number of audio professionals make a lot of money doing nothing but mixing or remixing tracks already produced by someone else. They rarely, if ever, track an instrument or work with live musicians.

The Cubase mixer is extremely flexible and powerful. As with all digital mixers, all of its settings are saved with the project, meaning that you never have to worry about getting back to where you were the last time you worked on a particular mix. Also, in Cubase, MIDI channels are mixed right next to audio channels (you'll learn about MIDI mixing in the next chapter).

In this chapter, you will learn about the different types of mixer channels you use when mixing audio in Cubase. You'll also learn how to route audio between different kinds of tracks, and how to apply different kinds of effects to your audio.

Why Stereo Mixes?

Hearing is a spatial, as well as an aural, sense. Our ears perceive not only changes in the volume and timbre of a sound, but also the direction from which a sound originated. They can even give us a fairly reliable idea of how far away we are from a sound generator. Presumably, these capabilities evolved as survival tools: We need to know to run when our eyes tell us that a lion is set to pounce, but we also need to be able to read the meaning of sounds so we can react quickly when we hear a few sticks break right behind us.

Although innovations in playback systems continue to appear, a stereo mix with one left speaker and one right speaker can go a very long way toward convincing our ears of a three-dimensional acoustic space. Consider these three basic parameters for creating a stereo mix:

- **Level** is the relative loudness of a sound. Humans tend to notice loud sounds more than soft ones and also to use level to help calculate the distance of a sound source. We know that a full drum kit is louder than an acoustic guitar, so if an acoustic guitar is louder than a drum kit, our ears will guess that the drum kit is far away and the guitar is close.

- **Pan** is the placement of a sound in the left-right field. We perceive a sound played in only the right channel of a stereo mix to be located at our extreme right. We perceive sounds played equally through both speakers to be at the center of the stereo field.

- **Timbre** is the frequency makeup of a sound. The character of the sound generator is the primary factor in determining the timbre of a sound; we know a flute doesn't sound like a shaker, but a sound's

distance and location and the space in which the sound is created also change the timbre of a sound. For example, the sound of a hand clap 20 feet away in a gymnasium is very different from the sound of the same hand clap 2 feet away in a closet.

All of the techniques discussed in this chapter and the next fundamentally involve changing these three parameters to paint a sonic picture in a stereo mix for your listener. You will learn about surround mixing, where more than two speakers are used to create a more complete sound stage, in Chapter 13.

A Practical Example

While my editor and I were working on this chapter (and the next chapter about effects), we decided that practical explanation of some of the techniques discussed would be helpful. It's easier to comprehend some of these concepts with audio and screen shots from a particular track than when you simply read about them in the abstract.

To provide these examples, I've created a tutorial at my Web site. You'll find a few pages with ideas and explanations demonstrated with one of my own tracks. You can download an archive of loops and audio clips, and the full mix created with them, at www.thadbrown.com/cubase if you want to see some of these features in action instead of just on the page. In addition, thanks to magnatune.com, you can download a source file from one of their most popular artists, Emma's Mini, and deconstruct the original mix or my remixed version to see how it's done. See Appendix B of this book for details.

Channels in the Cubase Mixer

Figure 11.1 shows a mixer for a typical Cubase project. As you can see, this one screen contains a great deal of information. Each of the mixer's components is covered in detail later in this chapter. For now, simply note the variety of channels available in the Cubase mixer and the variety of views available for each track. (Not all types of tracks are shown in Figure 11.1.)

Input channel   *FX channel*   *MIDI channel*
   Audio channel   *Group channels*   *VSTi channels*   *Output channel*

Figure 11.1 Mixer window.

MIDI channel: Each MIDI track in a project has a MIDI channel in the mixer. Cubase uses a lot of audio-style tools for mixing MIDI.

Audio channel: Just like MIDI tracks, each audio track in a project has a channel in the mixer. You can also use this mixer channel for processing, applying EQ settings, adding effects, and routing audio for that track.

ReWire channel: ReWire is a protocol for transferring audio, MIDI, and synchronization information between ReWire-aware applications running on the same computer. In Cubase, ReWire is most often used to route audio from another application (such as Reason or Live) to the Cubase mixer.

VSTi channels: Each VST instrument in use also has at least one channel in the Cubase mixer. Some VST instruments may use more than one channel, depending on their configuration. Both the ReWire and VSTi channels have the same controls as audio channels.

FX channel: Effect channels replace the effects sends rack in previous versions of Cubase. An effect channel can include up to eight insert effects, EQ, and automation, just like an audio track. The FX channel also includes a fader to control the overall level of the effected signal in the final mix.

Group channel: A group channel is an audio channel that is not wired directly to any particular audio track. Group channels are used to route audio to a specific source, such as headphones, or to apply effects to multiple tracks or to apply multiple effects in a series.

Input channel: Each input configured on the VST Connections panel has a channel in the mixer. Use input channels to watch the level of incoming audio or to rout incoming audio to effects and groups.

Output channel: Every output configured on the VST Connections panel also has its own fader and full mixing channel in the Cubase mixer. Usually, these output channels are used for the master stereo output of your mix, but they also can include multi-channel surround outputs or access to the hardware outputs on your sound card for purposes such as headphone mixes.

Figure 11.2 Each button shows or hides all of one kind of channel.

Hide input channels
Hide audio channels
Hide group channels
Hide ReWire channels
Hide MIDI channels
Hide VST instrument channels
Hide FX channels
Hide output channels
Hide channels set to "can hide"

Figure 11.3 With all buttons unselected, the Cubase mixer is empty. Clicking any button displays all channels of that type.

Hiding Mixer Channels

The mixer includes knobs, sliders, and buttons for every track in your composition and can quickly overwhelm the screen of your computer. A single project can easily contain dozens, or even hundreds, of tracks. Most users won't break that century mark, but even a project with 24 audio tracks, a few VST instruments, and some group channels for effects can get hard to manage in a reasonable amount of screen space.

Luckily, Cubase provides a number of ways for you to adjust your view—one channel at a time; by the panel, for an individual effect; or for the full mix—so that you can fine-tune your work. One of the simplest ways to manipulate your screen space is to use the buttons at the lower left of the Cubase mixer (**Figure 11.2**). These buttons let you hide entire groups of tracks. Clicking one of the channel types changes its icon to red and hides all channels of that type. Unselecting all of these buttons yields an empty mixer (**Figure 11.3**). The buttons in Figure 11.3 hide, from top to bottom, input, audio, group, ReWire, MIDI, VSTi, FX, and output channels.

Viewing Channel Parameters

In addition to selecting the tracks that you want visible, you'll often toggle back and forth between the normal and extended (or expanded) views to see the effects. In normal view (**Figure 11.4**), you'll see controls that you've worked with before—such as faders and buttons for solo/mute and pan—for each individual track.

The extended view uses an area above the fader and buttons on a channel to show additional information and settings. **Figure 11.5** shows an audio channel with the EQ settings and output routings visible. You can control what is shown in the mixer by selecting the small icon at the lower left of the Cubase mixer (**Figure 11.6**); click the different sections of this control to hide up to two of the three sections of the mixer.

◆ The top section shows or hides the input-output routing section of the mixer. You can use it to select any input configured on the VST Connections panel as an input for that channel and to select any VST Connections output or group channel. In Figure 11.5, the input is set to Left - IN 1, and the output is set to BUS 1.

◆ The middle section of the icon shows or hides the extended mixer section. This section can be configured to show EQs, insert and send effects, a VU meter, or other settings. In Figure 11.5, it shows knobs that are used to change the EQ settings.

◆ The bottom section represents the normal view of the mixer and cannot be turned off; it's always visible.

Figure 11.4 Normal view.

Figure 11.5 The extended view shows crucial information, but makes the mixer much larger.

Figure 11.6 You can click this small icon to show more or less information in the Cubase mixer.

Figure 11.7 The channel on the left is in narrow mode, while the channel on the right is wide.

Figure 11.8 Click this button to change the channel from narrow to wide and back.

Figure 11.9 Click the buttons here to make all channels in the mixer either narrow or wide.

Narrow vs. Wide Channels

It's already been noted that the number of mixer channels can increase dramatically as a track grows. The more tracks you have in a project, the harder it gets to see most or all of your mix at once. The Cubase mixer gives you the option of seeing more detail for fewer tracks, or seeing less detail and many more tracks. You make your choice by making a channel narrow or wide.

Figure 11.7 shows two channels with the extended mixer displayed for both. The channel on the right is wide and shows the EQ settings for that channel; the channel on the left is narrow and shows less. You can switch between the narrow and wide views for each channel by clicking the small opposing arrows above each channel (**Figure 11.8**).

✔ Tip

- You can also change the narrow/wide setting globally for every channel in the mixer. At the far left of the mixer, in the global section, click the button to change all channels to narrow or all channels to wide (**Figure 11.9**).

Changing Categories for All Channels

Another handy set of controls lets you change the visibility of the parameters in the extended mixer so that a common category is displayed in each channel. This provides a quick way for you to see one part of a mix for every channel in the mixer. For example, you can instantly look at the send effects for all visible channels or see the EQ settings for each channel in a mix.

◆ The common buttons next to the extended view force each channel to show the same category of information in that view. Clicking the Inserts button (the top button on the left), for example, displays inserts for all channels (**Figure 11.10**).

You can use these controls to make very quick display changes in the mixer. In **Figure 11.11**, for example, the extended mixer shows the meters for all tracks, spotlighting the levels of different tracks in a mix. One click in the global section, and the same mixer shows all insert effects (**Figure 11.12**).

Show EQs as curves
Show EQs as dials
Show all EQs
Show all sends
Show sends 1–4
Show sends 5–8

Show All Inserts

Figure 11.10 Selecting all inserts for viewing.

Figure 11.11 The mixer showing VU meters for all channels.

Choose Your View

Personally, I tend to use the normal view and then the Edit window for the track I want to modify. The Edit window displays many parameters for an individual track and is described later in this chapter. Many people prefer the extended view because it looks and feels more like a hardware mixer, with EQ, send, and insert controls above each channel fader. Use either or both views, according to what works best for you.

Figure 11.12 The same mixer showing insert effects for all channels in the extended view.

Figure 11.13 Clicking this button solos the channel.

Figure 11.14 More than one track can be soloed at the same time.

Soloing and Muting Mixer Channels

Mixer channels can be soloed and muted just like tracks in the Project window. In fact, wherever you click the button to solo or mute a track, the effect is the same. The following example shows how to solo two adjacent audio tracks.

To solo a mixer channel:

1. In the mixer channel you want to solo, click the S button (**Figure 11.13**).

   When a channel is soloed, the Solo button becomes red, and all other tracks are muted. The X (Mute) button becomes yellow. Only the soloed track will play back.

2. To hear another track, click its Solo button (**Figure 11.14**).

   Now only these two soloed tracks will be heard.

3. To return to hearing the entire mix, click the selected Solo buttons again to deselect them.

   When all of the Solo buttons are deselected, the entire mix is audible again.

✔ Tips

- Of course, you can individually mute channels by clicking the Mute button for a channel. In truth, soloing a channel mutes every other channel automatically.

- You can also rename mixer channels by double-clicking them and typing a new name, just as with tracks in the Project window.

Working with Audio Channels

Figure 11.15 shows a generic audio channel. It's particularly important to understand audio channels for two reasons. First, most of the features in audio channels are also found in VSTi, ReWire, FX, and group channels. Second, nearly every project you create will contain at least a few audio channels.

Audio channels have a few basic parts:

Level meter: This meter provides a graphic representation of the volume of the audio track.

Level fader: This slider controls the volume of the track. The track is silent when the fader is pulled to the bottom, and it gets progressively louder as the fader control is moved higher.

Channel name field: This field is where the name of the channel appears. You can edit the name here or in the Project window.

Record and Monitor buttons: These buttons control whether a track is in record or monitor mode.

Insert/EQ/Send buttons: These buttons show the current status of insert effects, EQ settings, and send effects for the track. If they are in use—that is, if an effect has been applied—the button turns blue. You can also click these buttons to bypass each type of processing. If you've bypassed the processing, the button will be orange.

Automation Read/Write buttons: Use these two buttons to turn automation on and off. Automation is covered in Chapter 16, "Automating a Mix."

Extended view area
Channel view menu
Pan control
Level meter
Solo/Mute buttons
Level fader
Automation buttons
Edit button
Insert/EQ/Send buttons
Monitor and Record buttons
Channel name field

Figure 11.15 An audio channel.

Solo/Mute buttons: Use these buttons to solo or mute the current track in the mix.

Pan control: This setting controls the relative placement of the track in the stereo field. When the pan control is at the far left, the track is audible only in the left speaker; when it is at the far right, the track is audible only in the right speaker; when it is in the middle, the track is equally loud in both speakers.

Channel view menu: Use this menu to change the look and the visible parameters for the individual track.

Extended view area: If extended view is selected, this area displays additional information about the audio channel, such as EQ settings, insert effects, and send effects.

WORKING WITH AUDIO CHANNELS

Choosing an Output for an Audio Channel

By default, audio channels are routed to the master channel and then to the stereo hardware output on the soundcard that is connected to your speakers or headphones. This is a good approach, and it generally routes the audio to where it should be, but Cubase provides great flexibility for routing audio tracks to other locations.

Here are some common situations where you may want to route an audio channel to somewhere other than the master channel:

◆ You may want to route the entire channel to an external effect connected to your sound card.

◆ You may want to route the entire channel to an individual performer in a headphone mix.

◆ You may want to route multiple channels to a group bus so you can add effects or control them using a single fader.

To choose an audio track output:

1. If the Input/Output settings are not visible in the mixer, click the icon in the lower left corner to display them (**Figure 11.16**).

2. Click the output setting for the channel to be routed.

   A pop-up menu opens showing all available hardware outputs and group channels (**Figure 11.17**).

3. From the menu, select the correct output for the audio channel.

   The channel will show where the track is being routed (**Figure 11.18**).

Figure 11.16 Click this icon to display the Input/Output settings in the mixer.

Figure 11.17 This pop-up menu shows all available outputs and groups.

Figure 11.18 The channel is now routed to a group called Epiano.

Figure 11.19 Changing the pan setting with the mouse.

Figure 11.20 The same channel with slightly different settings.

Adjusting Level and Pan

The two absolutely fundamental properties of an audio mixer channel are controls for level and pan. Level is the overall loudness of the channel, and pan is the location of the channel in the left/right stereo field. Both also fundamentally relate to the master channel, because the level and pan of all channels in a mix are what the final master channel level and pan settings control.

If you have used a hardware mixer, you will find the Cubase mixer interface familiar. Nevertheless, you should be aware of some features unique to a digital mixer. And if you are new to mixers, this overview will introduce you to the basic mixer functions.

- The fader is used to increase and decrease volume; the pan control places the channel in the left/right mix. **Figure 11.19** shows the fader at its lowest level, effectively muting the track, and the pan setting is at the farthest left point. **Figure 11.20** shows the same channel with the fader raised and the pan control set to send the channel more to the right of the master channel than the left.

- Cubase SX 2 finally rids us of pan values expressed as binary values. Previous versions of Cubase showed pan values from L64 to R64, but now pan is sensibly shown from C (for center) to 100 percent right or left.

- Clicking either the pan control or the level fader while holding down the Ctrl (Windows) or Command (Mac OS) key resets the controls to their default values.

Panning Conventions

There is a somewhat famous story from a very famous record producer about the beginning of stereo. For many years, all playback formats were monaural; a record had only one channel, and every instrument and vocal had to be crammed into that single speaker. When stereo mixing first came along, nobody really knew what to do with it. According to the famous producer, for his first stereo mix he prepared a complete mono mix, as he normally did, and then he put only the tambourine in the other speaker. Imagine driving down the highway and a song comes on the radio with the entire band and all of the singers playing through the right speaker and the tambourine alone playing through the right.

No rule is unbreakable, but in almost all music mixed for stereo, the kick drum, snare drum, and lead vocal are panned dead center. The rest of the drums are usually panned according to some logical spatial rule: either the way the drummer would hear them or the way a person standing in front of the kit would hear them. The bass is generally also in the middle or close to it. Backing vocals are usually panned to a greater or lesser degree away from the stereo center but to both sides of the mix. Other mono instruments, such as guitars, percussion, and samples, are usually placed somewhere in the stereo field away from the center. Another common trick is to double a part—to play the same acoustic guitar part twice, for example—and then pan one track fully left and one track fully right. Adjusting the pan of each doubled part can create some interesting soundscapes.

All of these rules can be broken if doing so makes the mix sound better, but they provide a good place to start.

EQs Curve   Sends   VU Meter   EQs +   Inserts

Figure 11.21 Extended view for five adjacent audio channels.

Figure 11.22 These are all of the options for the extended mixer.

Working with the Extended View

Figure 11.21 shows the extended view section for five adjacent audio channels. Each channel has the extended view set to one of the possible options, so all of the possible settings are visible in the illustration. Here's a quick explanation of each view and how it is used. To view the options for a channel, click the arrow beneath the extended mixer to open the pop-up menu (**Figure 11.22**) for that channel.

Inserts: This setting displays all insert effects used in that audio channel. Insert effects operate in serial, with each successive insert processing the output of the last one, usually processing the entire audio signal. If you have used a guitar pedal or something similar, you have used an insert effect. Distortion, filters, compression, and sometimes phasers and flangers are used for insert effects.

EQs: Cubase includes four bands of equalization, commonly called EQ, for each audio channel. EQ is used to boost or attenuate particular frequencies in the track being played. The bass and treble controls on a stereo home amplifier provide very simple EQ effects. The EQs option displays all four bands, with sliders and buttons to control the parameters for each of the four EQ bands.

EQs+: This view shows the same EQ options for the same four bands as EQs, but it provides knobs instead of sliders for those who prefer to set EQ that way.

EQs Curve: Instead of displaying EQ settings controllers as knobs or sliders, the EQs Curve extended mixer displays a graphic of the EQ settings, as well as buttons and settings for each band of EQ. The channel on the far left of Figure 11.21 displays EQs Curve.

continues on next page

Sends: Send effects operate in parallel. In other words, the channel plays back the audio without effects, but splits off part of the audio and routes it to an effect for processing as well. The most common uses for send effects are reverb and delay, where the send effect enhances the dry sound.

Sends+: Like EQ+, this option displays the parameters for send effects, but with knobs instead of sliders.

Sends 1–4: This setting shows only the first four sends, but with larger, easier-to-edit buttons and sliders.

Sends 5–8: Like Sends 1–4 but for the last four sends on a channel.

Surround Pan: This option is useful only if you created a surround output in your VST Connection setup and the audio channel is routed to that surround output.

VU Meter: This option displays a large, easy-to-read volume-level meter in the extended mixer area.

Overview: This setting displays all active insert and send effects, as well as each active EQ band, so you can quickly see what is happening overall for the channel.

Understanding EQ

EQ, or equalization, is used to change the frequency characteristics of an audio signal. Software-based EQ did not have an easy youth. For years, most digital audio programs had EQ that sounded almost fingernails-on-the-chalkboard bad. To get around this, many people used expensive and CPU-hungry third-party plug-ins or outboard hardware to do the job. Luckily for you, Cubase now includes flexible, good-sounding EQ on every audio channel.

Working with EQ is an art and a long-time learning experience that can't be immediately explained. All EQ boosts or attenuates sound, which means that EQ can also properly be called filtering. Cubase includes three filters:

◆ **Peak filters** (usually called parametric filters) boost or attenuate sound at a particular frequency. Peak filters have three main parameters. First, you can set the center frequency for the boost or cut. Second, you can set the amount by which the filter boosts or cuts. Third, you can set how far above and below the center frequency the filter is active—in other words, how wide the filter is. Peak filters are very flexible and can be used for broad changes or for very limited corrective EQ.

◆ **Shelving filters** boost or cut everything above or below a certain frequency by the amount that you specify and at a starting point that you define. Shelving filters are not as versatile or precise as peak filters, but many of the most famous, sought-after, vintage EQs are shelving filters. They can be very effective at sweetening tracks with a broad stroke because they usually affect a wider frequency spectrum than peak filters do. Shelving filters are sometimes used on full mixes.

◆ **High/low-pass filters** attenuate audio above or below the specified frequency. They are usually described in terms of how much they cut per octave. For instance, a low-pass filter might decrease audio by 6 dB per octave, meaning that one octave above the frequency set for the filter, the signal will be down 6 dB; two octaves above, it will be down 12 dB; and so on. These filters are very useful for removing low-end rumble and high-end hiss from individual tracks.

The Cubase EQ section is designed with four bands of EQ. The middle two bands are always peak filters, and the high and low bands can be used as peak filters, shelving filters, or high/low pass filters.

Applying EQ in the Channel Settings Window

There is more than one way to set EQ in Cubase. Although you can use the extended view, virtual knobs, or numeric values to set EQ parameters, the best approach is to use the Channel Settings window. The Cubase Channel Settings window is one of the most powerful features of the mixer. It organizes all settings for an audio channel in a single window, from routing to EQ to inserts and sends. You will hear about using the Channel Settings window for a variety of purposes in the rest of this chapter, but it is particularly useful for adjusting EQ because it offers an intuitive, graphical way to see EQ settings. All discussions and examples of EQ here will use this window.

In the following task, you will use the Channel Settings window to add a small peak filter in the high midrange. You might do this in any number of musical situations, such as to add more presence to a guitar sound or to tweak a snare sample to make it more prominent in a mix without raising its overall level.

Figure 11.23 This button opens the Channel Settings window.

Figure 11.24 Click this button to turn on a band of EQ.

Figure 11.25 Dragging the breakpoint creates a small boost for the third EQ band.

To apply EQ to a channel with a peak filter:

1. In the channel to which you want to apply EQ, click the *e* (Edit) button (**Figure 11.23**).

   This opens the Channel Settings window for that channel. The EQ settings appear in the center of the window, displayed as knobs, and are also shown in the display above the knobs.

2. Click the virtual power button (**Figure 11.24**) to activate that band of EQ.

   Each active EQ band appears in the breakpoint display above the EQ knobs. The breakpoints are numbered: the point marked 1 will adjust the first band of EQ, 2 will adjust the second band, and so on. This display provides an easy way to adjust the EQ settings.

3. To adjust the EQ settings, click the breakpoint in the display for the band you want to adjust and move it with the mouse.

   Figure 11.25 shows a slight boost in the midrange, around 2 kilohertz.

4. Use the knobs to make finer adjustments to the EQ settings as needed.

   Pay particular attention to the bottom knob for each band. This knob adjusts the width of the band, referred to as the Q of the band. The higher the setting, the narrower the EQ band will be.

Using a Shelving Filter

Shelving filters boost or cut all sounds above or below a frequency you set. They are great for gently adding or subtracting bass or treble from a track that doesn't sound quite the way you want it to. For example, a shelving filter would be a good choice for removing unwanted low-end sound from an acoustic guitar, boosting high-end sound in cymbals or percussion, or adding low-end sound to a singer with a slightly thin voice. This task shows you how to cut out unnecessary low-end sound from a track with low-shelf EQ.

Figure 11.26 The first EQ band is now turned on.

Figure 11.27 The display shows the effect of the shelving EQ.

To boost or cut with a shelving filter:

1. Click the *e* (Edit) button in the channel that you want to adjust to open its Channel Settings window.

   Only EQ bands 1 and 4 can act as shelving filters; the two middle EQ bands are parametric (peak) filters only.

2. Turn on the bottom EQ band by clicking its power button (**Figure 11.26**).

3. Turn the bottom knob (the Q setting) all the way to the left (counterclockwise).

   The display below the knob says "Low S," which stands for *low shelf* and refers to the type of filter.

4. In the EQ display above the knobs, click the breakpoint for the first EQ band and drag it to set the EQ.

   The display will show you what the filter is doing, and your ears will guide you to the right settings. In **Figure 11.27**, the shelving filter is set for a significant cut, with its center frequency set at 341 Hz.

✔ Tip

- You can also click any of the EQ parameters and enter values using the keyboard or the up and down arrow keys. These methods are convenient when you know precisely the frequency you want to use.

Using a High- or Low-Pass Filter

High- and low-pass filters are most often used to remove unwanted sounds from individual tracks. When recording, it's easy to wind up with low-frequency hum and rumble or high-frequency noise and hiss. The low-end junk might be traffic noise, nearby appliances, or ground loops; the high-end noise might be tape hiss or an air conditioner. A high-pass filter can also help when an instrument was recorded near a drum kit; a carefully set high-pass filter can remove most of the unwanted leaked sound from the simultaneous recording of a nearby kick drum.

This next task shows you how to deal with another common scenario. High-frequency noise and hiss can easily work their way into a recorded track. You can use a low-pass filter to get rid of much of this high-frequency content.

When in Doubt, Cut It Out

Too much boosting with EQ pegs a mix as hopelessly amateur. It's tempting to crank up every value on every track so that each one sounds wicked loud—but usually the song turns to mush instead. Pick your spots for EQ boosting, and don't get carried away. Often the only places that need EQ boosts are the parts that should be most prominent in the mix, like the main vocal, an instrument solo, or the snare drum.

On the other hand, you can probably use a lot more subtractive, or cutting, EQ than you realize. If you read the music production magazines, you've read about producers using 128-track mixes and 60 tracks of backing vocals. The only way to keep that many tracks from trampling all over each other is to use a *ton* of subtractive EQ. Producers and engineers use EQ to carve away everything but the smallest part of the audio spectrum for each track. If two instruments seem to occupy the same sonic space, instead of boosting the one you want to make it more prominent, try cutting the other one. Often this will make a mix sound a lot better.

To use a high- or low-pass filter:

1. Activate the fourth EQ band for use as a low-pass filter (**Figure 11.28**).

   Remember that only the top EQ band can be used as a low-pass filter, and only the bottom EQ band can be used as a high-pass filter.

2. Click the Q knob and drag it all the way to the right (clockwise).

   At this extreme position, the band will become a low-pass filter. The Q display will show "Low P" to indicate this (**Figure 11.29**).

3. Click the breakpoint to adjust the location where the filter begins to take effect. You can also use the knob or enter a frequency manually.

✔ Tip

- Don't be afraid to experiment with low- and high-pass filters on most tracks. Getting rid of excess high- and low-end sound on most tracks can really clean up a mix.

Figure 11.28 Click this button to turn on the top EQ band, which can be a low-pass filter.

Figure 11.29 Use the Q knob (the bottom knob for each band) to set a filter as a low-pass filter; the result is visible in the EQ display.

Figure 11.30 The Magneto plug-in along with all of the other installed effects plug-ins.

Figure 11.31 The editor window for Magneto.

Figure 11.32 You can also use the Channel Settings window for insert effects.

Insert Effects Basics

An insert effect is the simplest kind of effect. The entire audio signal from a channel is fed into the effect, the audio is modified in some way, and the audio with the effect replaces the original track in the mix. The following task uses the Magneto plug-in included with Cubase as an insert for an audio channel. This particular plug-in emulates the saturation, overdrive, and compression of an analog tape machine.

To use an insert effect:

1. Use the extended view drop-down menu (click the downward-pointing arrow on the left side of the mixer) to display inserts in the extended view area.

2. Click the top effect slot, marked "No Effect."

   A drop-down menu opens showing all installed VST effects and any installed DirectX effects (**Figure 11.30**).

3. From this drop-down menu, choose Dynamics; then select Magneto.

   Selecting this plug-in automatically opens its editor window (**Figure 11.31**).

4. Adjust the settings to get the sound you want.

✔ Tips

- You can also access inserts in the Channel Settings window. **Figure 11.32** shows the inserts for the audio channel in Figures 11.30 and 11.31. Note that the top slot has the Magneto plug-in selected and turned on.

- Insert Effects are discussed in depth in Chapter 14, "Audio Effect Plug-Ins."

Bypassing EQ and Effects for a Channel

As a mix progresses, you'll often want to check to see if your changes are working. For instance, EQ on a bass track might sound great when it's soloed, but not so good in the context of a mix. It's also easy to add so many effects to a sound that the sound gets lost. Cubase offers a quick and easy way to keep track of the effects in use in a channel and to bypass groups of effects. Huddled together next to the channel fader are three buttons with particularly obscure-looking hieroglyphics (**Figure 11.33**). These buttons can bypass all of the EQ settings, insert effects, or send effects for that channel. These three buttons also do more than just bypass EQ effects; they indicate whether any EQ bands, insert effects, or send effects are active on that channel, and they provide important information about the channel no matter what their active status.

Insert Effects button
EQ button
Send Effects button

Figure 11.33 An audio channel, with each button marked to show its function.

Figure 11.34 For this channel, the send and EQ buttons are lighted.

Figure 11.35 If effects are bypassed with these buttons, the buttons turn yellow.

The buttons can be white (or clear), blue, green, or yellow, depending on the status:

◆ A white (or clear) button indicates that none of the represented effects are on. In other words, if the EQ button is white, none of the EQ bands for that channel are on.

◆ Blue is used for the send and insert effects. When a send or insert effect is turned on, the appropriate button for the audio channel turns blue, showing you at a glance whether any effects are active for that channel.

◆ Green is used only for the EQ button. When one or more bands of EQ are active for a channel, the button turns green. **Figure 11.34** shows an audio channel with both the send effect and EQ button active.

◆ Yellow indicates bypassed effects. If a button is blue or green (indicating that EQ or effects are in use), clicking that button bypasses those effects, and the button then turns yellow (**Figure 11.35**).

These buttons are very useful elements of the Cubase mixer. They let you know what is active within an audio channel, and they provide a one-click method for bypassing all of the EQ and other effects for that channel. This capability can be extremely useful, because it's easy to go overboard with effects and EQ. For example, after spending a long time working on a sound, it's good to be able to check the original to see if all of the effects and EQ really are improving things.

About FX Channels

All previous versions of Cubase (both SX and VST) used a special-effects rack called the Sends rack for send effects. Thankfully, SX 2 dispenses with that convention and replaces it with FX channels in the Cubase mixer. FX channels are a huge improvement over the Sends rack, giving you more routing flexibility and processing options than the Sends rack ever did.

The easiest way to understand a send effect is to contrast it with an insert effect. Insert effects are serial: the sound from the audio track goes into each insert effect, one after the other, and then out to the channel fader. Send effects are parallel, meaning that part of the audio from a channel is split off and routed to the send effect for processing and then is sent to the master output, where it's combined with the original signal, so you hear both the dry and effected signals.

In SX 2, instead of using the Send rack, you create your own send effect destinations called FX channels. An FX channel (**Figure 11.36**) looks and acts almost exactly like an audio channel. Each FX channel can have up to eight insert effects and its own fader and pan control and four-band EQ and can be automated and modified just like an audio channel.

Figure 11.36 An FX channel showing insert effects in the extended area.

Figure 11.37 Adding an FX channel using the Project menu.

Figure 11.38 Inserts are selected for display in the extended mixer.

Figure 11.39 This FX channel chains together two effects plug-ins: a delay and a flanger.

Configuring an FX Channel

Just as when you use audio, ReWire, and VST instrument channels, you have to create a new FX channel for each effects send you want to use. For example, suppose that you want to create a send effect that has a delay routed through a flanger. The following task shows you what to do.

To create and configure an FX channel:

1. From the Project menu, select Add Track > FX Channel (**Figure 11.37**). You can also create FX channels using the contextual menu in the Project window.

2. Find the newly created FX channel in the mixer. FX channels appear pink in the Cubase mixer.

3. Open the extended mixer menu for the FX channel and select Inserts to display inserts in the extended view (**Figure 11.38**).

4. Add any effects you want to the insert slots. **Figure 11.39** shows an FX channel (renamed DelayFlange) with a delay plug-in and a flanger plug-in.

After an FX channel is set up, you can route audio to it from any audio, VSTi, or ReWire track. Also, remember that you can always add more effects and EQ to FX channels.

CONFIGURING AN FX CHANNEL

275

Sending Audio to FX Channels

After you've set up the FX channel, you can send audio to it from any audio channel in the Cubase mixer. There are many reasons to do this. First, using a reverb plug-in as a send effect for six channels is a whole lot easier on the CPU than using a reverb as an insert on each of six different channels. Send effects can also be very useful for putting a group of instruments together in a mix. Say, for example, that you combine four acoustic guitar parts and a shaker to form a rhythm track. Creating an effects send with a chorus or delay part and feeding just a tiny bit of each track to the effects send can pull the tracks together by creating a common sonic space for the individual instruments. These are just two situations where send effects are very useful.

To send audio to an FX channel:

1. Create and configure your FX channel as described in the previous example.

2. Find an audio channel you want to use as a source for the send and set it to display sends in the extended mixer.

3. Click one of the effects slots on the audio channel that will be source for the send. All groups, output busses, and FX channels will be available.

   Figure 11.40 shows the DelayFlange FX channel being selected.

4. Click the power button for the send effect (**Figure 11.41**).

5. Use the slider below the name of the send effect to adjust the level of the audio sent to the FX channel (**Figure 11.42**).

6. Repeat steps 2 through 5 for all the channels that you want to send audio to the FX channel.

Figure 11.40 Selecting the FX channel as the destination for the effects send.

Figure 11.41 This button turns on the effect send.

Figure 11.42 The slider controls the level of the audio sent to the FX channel.

Figure 11.43 A VSTi channel (left), an audio channel (middle), and a ReWire channel (right).

VST Instrument and ReWire Channels

VST instruments were explained in Chapter 7, "Using Virtual Instruments," and ReWire will be covered in Chapter 15, but in brief, ReWire is a protocol that lets audio applications on the same computer exchange MIDI, audio, and synchronization information.

VST instruments and ReWire applications usually create channels in the mixer, where the audio they produce together can be folded into a project. **Figure 11.43** shows three mixer channels: from left to right, a VSTi channel, an audio channel, and a ReWire channel.

If you say to yourself that these three channels look an awful lot alike, you will be right. In fact, the only difference between an audio channel and a VSTi or ReWire channel is the source of the audio. ReWire and VSTi channels use the same effects, EQ, and mixer settings as described earlier in this chapter for audio channels.

The only situation in which you might trip up with these two types of channels is when they are soloed or muted. Remember that most VST instruments (and many ReWire channels) are triggered by a MIDI channel in the Cubase mixer. It's easy to inadvertently mute the MIDI source for a VST instrument and then wonder why it isn't sending audio to its mixer channel.

Using Output Busses

If you have a sound or audio card with multiple outputs, you can activate the additional outputs on the VST Connections
panel to make them available for routing
audio in Cubase. These are called output
busses and are used to send audio directly to
the sound card outputs configured as VST
connections, instead of to the main mixer.
You can use output busses in many ways.
For instance, you can send tracks to output
busses to create individual headphone mixes
for each performer, or you can send tracks to
external effects or processing devices connected to the sound card in the computer.
You may want to run a kick drum sound
through a special compressor, for example,
or you may have an external effect that you
want to use on a guitar track.

Figure 11.44 All VST connections
are available in the Output settings
pop-up menu.

To view and activate output busses:

1. If you need to create any VST connections,
   choose Devices > VST Connections
   (**Figure 11.44**) to make any configuration changes necessary.

2. Set the Cubase mixer to show the
   Input/Output settings.

3. Find the mixer channel you want to
   route to an output bus. Click the Output
   setting, and a pop-up menu will show all
   available output busses and group channels (**Figure 11.45**). Select the output
   bus you want for that channel.
   Figure 11.45 shows an external effect
   being selected.

Figure 11.45 Busses
can also be used as
destinations for send
effects.

✔ Tip

■ You can also use output busses as send
effects. The send slots for audio channels
show both FX channels and output busses.

Figure 11.46 Giving a group channel a descriptive name makes it much easier to figure out what should be routed to it.

Assigning Group Channels

The final channels in the Cubase mixer are the group channels. A group channel (**Figure 11.46**) is like an audio metachannel. A group channel plays back audio only when another channel (such as an audio, VSTi, or ReWire channel) is configured to send audio to it. Group channels do the same thing that audio bus channels do on more complex hardware mixers, but because they are part of a digital mixer, group channels offer additional flexibility for routing and effects.

One of the main uses for a group channel (or a mixer bus, in hardware mixer language) is to control multiple channels with one fader. A carefully recorded acoustic drum kit may have 12 channels or more, with multiple microphones on each drum and many more for cymbals and room ambience. After each channel gets its own tweaks and modifications, usually the full drum mix is sent to a group channel. At this point, it may get additional EQ and effects before being sent to the final stereo output of the mix. You may also use a group channel when you overdub multiple guitar tracks playing the same part to get a thicker sound. You can send all of those tracks to one group for additional mixing before sending the channel to the final stereo output.

To route multiple channels to a group:

1. Create the group channel by choosing Project > Add Track > Group Channel and give it a name as shown in Figure 11.46.

2. Set the other audio (or VSTi or ReWire) channels that should be routed to this group to show Input/Output settings in the extended mixer. Click the Output setting to open the pop-up menu and assign the channel to the group (**Figure 11.47**).

3. Repeat step 2 for each channel that you want to route to the group.

   Figure 11.48 shows multiple channels of a drum kit routed to the same group.

Figure 11.47 Using the Output settings pop-up menu to send an audio channel to a group.

✔ Tips

- When tracks are routed in this way, they are sent to the group channel at the very end of the signal chain. All insert effects, EQ settings, and pan settings for each individual channel will be reflected in the group channel.

- Remember that group channels themselves can be routed to other group channels or to output buses. This capability can be useful when routing audio to external effects, creating headphone mixes, and performing many other mixing tasks.

Figure 11.48 Five channels in a drum mix, all routed to the same group for more convenient mixing and control.

- Group channels have one additional, very important property when the channels are soloed. When a channel routed to a group is soloed, the group to which it is routed is soloed as well. In addition, when a group is soloed, all channels that are routed to it are soloed along with the group.

- If you have more than one group channel, you can route a group channel to another group channel, but only in ascending order. That is, you can route group channel 1 to group channel 4, but you can't route group channel 11 to group channel 9.

- Group channels cannot be monaural.

- Group channels contain all the insert and send effects and EQ capabilities of audio channels. The only difference is the source of the sound.

- You create group channels in a project exactly like you create any other kind of channel: by using the contextual menu in the Project window or by choosing Project > Add Track > Group Channel. You can add more group channels to a project whenever you need them.

ASSIGNING GROUP CHANNELS

Linking Mixer Channels

Another common approach when working with multiple tracks is to link channels. Two channels that are linked will synchronize their fader moves with each other. If you move the fader on one channel, the level of the other channel will change as well. In fact, the two channels will change levels proportionally, allowing them to be treated as one fader.

One situation in which linked channels are very useful is when you are working with multiple sounds from the same instrument. For instance, a bass might be recorded on two tracks: one with a microphone on an amplifier and one plugged into the sound card after a direct box or a preamplifier. After you set the relationship between the two tracks to achieve the sound you want, you can link the channels together and edit them as a group.

What Should Your Listener Hear?

Much of the art of mixing involves leading your listener to the parts you want heard. A song can have dozens of instruments and hundreds of tracks, with each one being important to the final mix, but a complex mix can easily become confusing.

Assume that you are mixing a song completely on your own and can make all of the decisions. When starting to mix the song, try to identify the two or three most important and highest-quality parts of the song (and hope that they are the same). If you are mixing a hip-hop tune, for instance, the bass line and the vocal may be what matter most. For an acoustic jazz record, you might decide that the soloists and the ride cymbal are most crucial. With a singer-songwriter recording, you might have only a guitar and a vocal, so you don't have much of a decision to make.

After you've identified the crucial elements of a song, check yourself every now and then while you are mixing to see whether you have made changes that enhance or detract from these critical parts.

To link mixer channels:

1. Set the relative levels of the two tracks so they sound correct to you (**Figure 11.49**).

2. Click the bar, just above the name, at the bottom of one channel (**Figure 11.50**) and hold down the Shift key while clicking the other channel.

   This will select the channels to be linked.

3. Right-click (Windows) or Ctrl-click (Mac) any selected channel to open the contextual menu and select Link Channels (**Figure 11.51**).

4. Click either fader to change the level of one channel, and the other will follow (**Figure 11.52**).

✔ Tip

- To unlink channels, select them and choose Unlink Channels from the same contextual menu as shown in Figure 11.51.

Figure 11.49 Two channels that together create a single bass sound. The main bass amp sound is supplemented by the direct (or DI) sound.

Figure 11.50 Selecting one of the bass channels.

Figure 11.51 Selecting Link Channels from the pop-up menu.

Figure 11.52 With the channels linked, moving the fader on the left forces the fader on the right to follow.

Learning from Masters

One of the best ways to learn about mixing is to listen to great mixes. Don't listen as a fan or a musician, but try to figure out what kind of panning, level, EQ, and effects techniques were used to create the mix. Try to figure out what the mixer did to make the mix sound good. And don't listen only to types of music that you like, but try to learn from a variety of styles.

Here is a purely subjective list of albums that I find provide insight into mixing techniques and that you might want to listen to to get ideas.

Rock/Pop

AC/DC—Back in Black: An extremely simple approach to a two-guitar rock band with bass, vocals, and drums. Drums are in stereo, guitars are panned fairly hard right and left, and vocals and bass are right up the middle.

Ministry—Filth Pig: Nobody crams sonic information into a track like Ministry. Every single slice of the frequency spectrum is used, often as abrasively and aggressively as possible.

Verve—Urban Hymns: An expertly mixed, lush pop record. The vocals are always prominent, but other instruments are still present and forceful.

Acoustic

Buena Vista Social Club: An expertly recorded and mixed record of rediscovered Cuban music legends. Producer/engineer/guitar genius/legend Ry Cooder creates a very believable space with a stereo mix.

Grant Green—Idle Moments, RVG Edition: RVG stands for Rudy van Gelder, the engineer behind the classic Blue Note records from the 1950s forward. He remastered this eerily present and real-sounding 60s classic.

Electronic

Madonna—Ray of Light: Pop superstar gives big-budget access to dream shopping list of British/European dance music producers.

Thievery Corporation—Richest Man in Babylon: American downtempo duo brings mixing techniques from hip-hop, dub, pop, and R&B to a single record. Expert use of effects.

MIXING MIDI

MIDI mixing in Cubase is about as close to audio mixing as two such different procedures can be. Steinberg went out of its way to copy the familiar look and feel of an audio mixer for its MIDI mixing setup. If you are comfortable with the audio mixer, you won't have much trouble getting up to speed with Cubase MIDI mixing. That said, there are differences between audio and MIDI mixing, and there are some real treasures buried in the MIDI mixer if you are willing to learn where they are. Knowing how to mix MIDI well will help your projects sound the best that they can.

In this chapter, you'll learn about the channel strips in the Cubase mixer that are used to mix MIDI tracks. You'll also learn about some of the MIDI plug-ins that you can use as send and insert effects. For more powerful MIDI mixing, you'll also learn how to use the MIDI mixer for continuous controller (CC) messages and how to save your mixed MIDI as new and distinct parts.

Basic MIDI Mixing

As mentioned previously, MIDI mixing controls in Cubase are very similar to audio mixing controls. This means that many of your audio mixing skills will translate easily to MIDI.

For example, you control both pan and volume for MIDI channels precisely the same way you do for audio channels. **Figure 12.1** shows a MIDI channel with the fader pulled down a bit and the track panned to the right in the stereo field. Keep in mind, though, that what the channel fader really does here is proportionally decrease the velocity of the MIDI notes, and the pan control sends a CC message to the MIDI device.

You also solo and mute MIDI channels in the same way as audio channels. **Figure 12.2** shows two adjacent MIDI channels with the one on the left soloed. It's hard to see in the illustration, but just as with audio channels, when one MIDI channel is soloed, all other tracks are muted.

Finally, Cubase also has a Channel Settings window for MIDI channels (**Figure 12.3**), just as it has one for audio channels. Click the *e* (Edit) button for a MIDI channel to open this window. Most of the examples in the following pages use this Channel Settings window.

Figure 12.1 Simple velocity and pan settings are obvious in this MIDI channel.

Figure 12.2 Solo and mute controls for MIDI channels work just like those for audio channels.

Figure 12.3 The MIDI Channel Settings window is much like the Channel Settings window for an audio channel.

BASIC MIDI MIXING

Mixing MIDI Versus Audio

Though MIDI and audio are very different, Steinberg went out of its way to make MIDI mixing feel, as much as possible, like audio mixing. A MIDI mixer channel looks in many ways like an audio channel. It has a fader and a pan control, as well as mute, solo, and automation buttons and other buttons and controls.

As much as MIDI channels look like audio channels, the fact remains that they do not deal with the same kind of information. An audio channel plays back files created by Cubase, and those files are stored on a local hard drive. MIDI channels are often used to send instructions and data to hardware and software such as synths, samplers, effects devices, and controllers that may or may not behave as expected. For example, the pan control for an audio channel will work flawlessly every time. With a MIDI channel, the pan control actually sends a MIDI continuous controller message; most devices will respond correctly to this CC, but an older synth or a synth that is filtering CCs will not respond correctly to the pan control in the Cubase mixer.

A second level of complexity is introduced by the fact that often MIDI parameters can be set in two places: in the Cubase mixer or in the device receiving the MIDI data. For most synths, the pan location can be stored as part of the sound preset, but it can also be set in the Cubase mixer. Neither approach is necessarily better, but keep these alternatives in mind if the MIDI channel parameters aren't functioning as you expect; the problem may be related to settings on the device that is receiving the MIDI data.

MIDI Insert Effects

One of the ways in which Cubase is different from many other MIDI applications is in the way it processes MIDI. Most applications—including Cubase—process MIDI data in an interface like the Project window or the Key editor. However, the MIDI channels in Cubase's mixer also have their own specialized effects.

MIDI insert effects are much like audio inserts. The MIDI data goes into the effect, where it's processed or changed in some way, and then continues through the channel to the fader and output. Again, remember that MIDI isn't audio, so many more parameters, such as note pitch and duration, can be changed with insert effects. The next few pages describe some of the important effects that ship with Cubase and offer ideas for using them in your own music.

What's a Tick?

You can edit MIDI effects plug-ins with different kinds of values. You can use note values as parameters, such as 8T for tied eighth note or 4th for a quarter note, when you want musically obvious time settings. However, you can also set most parameters to a certain number of *ticks*, which are the smallest time divisions that MIDI uses. Internally, MIDI has a timing resolution of 480 ticks per quarter note, and you can set most tempo-based parameters in MIDI effects to a particular number of ticks. This feature is useful for creating non-tempo-based settings or for creating settings that modulate another parameter slightly. For example, you could set a delay that becomes a few ticks longer with each successive delayed note.

Figure 12.4 Choosing Inserts to display MIDI inserts in the extended mixer.

Figure 12.5 Selecting the MidiEcho effect.

To create and edit a MIDI insert effect:

1. Open the extended view drop-down menu and choose Wide.

2. Open the extended mixer and select Inserts (**Figure 12.4**) to display these effects, or open the Channel Settings window.

   You will see four slots that can be used for MIDI insert effects.

3. Click the top slot, where "No Effect" is displayed, to open the pop-up menu (**Figure 12.5**); then choose an effect.

   For this example, select the MidiEcho effect; this both turns on the effect and opens its editor window (**Figure 12.6**). MidiEcho and its parameters are described later in this chapter.

4. Close the effect window when you are finished setting the parameters.

   You can reopen the editor by clicking the *e* (Edit) button, shown above the MidiEcho slot at the top left of the Figure 12.5.

Figure 12.6 The editor window for MidiEcho.

MIDI INSERT EFFECTS

MIDI Effect Presets

Many MIDI effects include preprogrammed settings to help you get started with the effect. When you first use a particular effect, you should check for presets to learn more about how the effect works.

We've already discussed how to save presets for VST instruments, and we'll discuss the use of presets with audio plug-ins later. But MIDI effect presets work a bit differently than either of these. The biggest difference is that a MIDI effect preset is saved within the plug-in, not as a discrete file on your hard disk.

To save a MIDI preset:

1. Open the Effects editor window (click the *e* button). In this window, set the effects parameters exactly as you want them saved. Click the drop-down Presets menu if you want to view the list of current MIDI effect presets.

2. To add a new preset to this list, click the Add button (the button with the plus sign; see **Figure 12.7**).

   A dialog box for naming the preset opens.

3. Type a name (**Figure 12.8**) and click OK. After the preset is saved, you can select it from the drop-down menu (**Figure 12.9**).

✔ Tips

■ To delete a MIDI effect preset, select it in the list and then click the Remove button (the button with the minus sign), located just to the right of the button for adding a preset. Be careful, though—you won't get a dialog box that asks if you really want to delete the preset. Once you click Delete, the preset is gone.

■ Although you can't save presets as discrete files, you can use your MIDI effect presets in other projects. You can save a preset in one song and use it in another one.

Figure 12.7 Opening the MIDI effect presets menu; click the button with the plus sign to save the current settings as a preset.

Figure 12.8 Naming the preset in the Type In Preset Name dialog box.

Figure 12.9 The new preset appears in the Presets menu for that effect.

Figure 12.10 Use this window to modify settings for MidiEcho.

MidiEcho

Cubase includes a number of MIDI effects. The next few paragraphs should help you become familiar with them and learn how to modify them to make the sounds you want.

The MidiEcho insert effect (**Figure 12.10**) is a delay effect that acts a lot like an audio delay effect and uses some of the same parameters. As a MIDI effect, though, it also does some things that would be impossible for an audio delay effect, such as changing the length and pitch of the delayed sounds. Keep in mind, too, that the MidiEcho effect works differently than an audio delay. The MidiEcho effect sends additional notes to a synth or sampler, whereas an audio delay repeats a sound after a specified amount of time.

Four MidiEcho parameters are grouped at the top left of the Effects editor:

◆ **Quantize** controls the time of the delay effect. Usually, you will set this to a musical value by clicking the arrows next to the setting, or with the slider below the numerical field.

◆ **Length** determines the duration of the delayed notes. If you set this parameter to its minimum value, each delayed note will be exactly as long as the original. If you set it to another value, you can use this parameter to shorten or lengthen delayed notes.

◆ **Repeat** controls the number of times that a delayed note repeats. This parameter is similar to the feedback control on an audio delay effect.

◆ **Echo-Quant** forces all delayed notes to fall on a quantize grid. Even if the original or delayed note is off of the grid, you can set a note value with Echo-Quant to force all delays to be quantized.

MidiEcho also has controls to change or transform the delayed MIDI notes:

◆ **Velo Decay** modifies the velocity of the notes generated by the effect. If the number is negative, each successive note will have a lower velocity and will be quieter. If the number is positive, the delayed notes will have a higher velocity than the original.

◆ **Pitch Decay** changes the pitch of the delayed notes over time, similar to the way Velo Decay changes the velocity. Setting this parameter to –1 will, for example, decrease the pitch of each repeat by one semitone.

◆ **Echo Decay** modifies the length of time between repeats. You can use this control to slightly (or dramatically) speed up or slow down the repeated notes.

◆ **Length Decay** modifies the duration of repeated notes. You can set the repeats so that they are longer or shorter than the original notes.

Figure 12.11 You can use the Arpache effect to create arpeggios.

Figure 12.12 The Playmode controls determine the order in which notes are played in the arpeggio.

Figure 12.13 These settings control the nature of the notes in the arpeggio.

Arpache 5

The Arpache effect (**Figure 12.11**) is a powerful arpeggiator for transforming MIDI tracks. An arpeggiator is fundamentally a simple effect; it takes a group of notes played simultaneously and transforms them into an arpeggio (notes played in rapid succession). An arpeggiator has many uses, but most often it is used on synth bass or synth lead lines to create note patterns out of chords. You can use this effect on tracks you have already recorded or to create arpeggios in real time.

Arpache has two main sets of controls. The Playmode set controls the way that the effect orders the notes in the arpeggio (**Figure 12.12**), and the other window controls parameters related to the notes themselves (**Figure 12.13**).

To navigate the Playmode area:

◆ Click the up arrow to create an arpeggio that plays from low to high pitch.

◆ Click the down arrow to create an arpeggio that starts at the highest pitch and proceeds to the lowest pitch.

◆ Click the button on the top row with both up and down arrows to create an arpeggio that ramps up and down in pitch.

◆ Click the question mark button to order pitches in the arpeggio randomly.

◆ Toggle the Order On button to turn on the Play Order section of the effect, which lets you set the pitch order of the arpeggio manually.

Creating a Simple Arpeggio

The Arpache effect is difficult to understand in theory, but pretty easy to use in practice. The following shows you how to create a simple effect for a MIDI track that has already been recorded. Remember that the effect can also be used on live MIDI coming from a MIDI controller.

Figure 12.14 Setting the arpeggio to ramp up.

Figure 12.15 Setting Quantize to 8 creates an arpeggio with a note played every eighth note.

To create an arpeggio effect with Arpache:

1. Choose a MIDI track with some kind of chord material. Select Inserts from the extended view pop-up menu (on the left side of the Mixer window).

2. Select an insert slot and, from the pull-down menu, choose the Arpache 5 effect for that MIDI channel.

3. Click the up arrow button (**Figure 12.14**) to create an arpeggio that moves from low to high pitches.

4. Click the arrow in the Quantize setting to set the number of notes in the arpeggio.

   In this example, the value is set to 8 (**Figure 12.15**). With this setting, the effect will play a note in the arpeggio every eighth-note.

CREATING A SIMPLE ARPEGGIO

Figure 12.16 If you set Length to 32, the effect will play only short notes, creating a very staccato sound.

5. Use the Semi-Range value to set the low and high boundaries of the arpeggio.

This value is set in semitones. For example, set the value to 24, and all notes created in the arpeggio will be within a two-octave range.

6. Set the Length parameter to determine the length of the notes in the arpeggio.

If you set this value higher than the Quantize value, more than one note will play back simultaneously; a lower setting will create progressively more staccato arpeggios. A setting of 32, as shown in **Figure 12.16**, creates a very short note length.

7. Start playback in Cubase to hear the effect.

The track with chords will now play a staccato, ascending arpeggio.

AutoPan

If any MIDI effect in Cubase is poorly named, it's AutoPan (**Figure 12.17**). Anyone seeing the name would sensibly assume that the effect is used to modulate the pan setting for a MIDI device. Although AutoPan certainly can do this, it actually does much more and can be used to generate a huge variety of MIDI continuous controller information. For example, an AutoPan-generated controller can be used to generate controller data for nearly any parameter on any MIDI device, such as volume, filter cutoff, and delay time.

AutoPan generates controller data according to the shape you choose for it. Use the buttons at the top of the effect window to make this choice (**Figure 12.18**). You can understand most of them just by looking at the curve shape on the button. The other main parameters in the AutoPan window are as follows:

◆ **Period** specifies how quickly the controller curve changes. You can set the period in ticks or rhythmic values. For example, if you set the period to 4th, the controller will complete its curve every quarter note.

◆ **Density** specifies how often a new controller message is sent; like the period, it is set in ticks or note values. A very small value, such as 30 ticks (the equivalent of a sixty-fourth note), will send a new controller message every 30 ticks. This will create a very smooth curve, but it can pump out so much MIDI data that a synth may have trouble handling it.

◆ **Max** and **Min** set the boundaries for the controller values that are sent.

AutoPan comes with many presets (**Figure 12.19**) to get you started. However, it's a complex effect; it will require—and reward—time spent learning it.

Figure 12.17 The AutoPan editor.

Figure 12.18 These buttons set the shape of the controller.

Figure 12.19 Cubase includes a large number of AutoPan presets.

Figure 12.20 A square wave shape will create a strong, pulsing effect.

Figure 12.21 Set the controller to Main Volume to create a tremolo effect.

Creating a Tremolo Effect with AutoPan

To see the versatility of AutoPan, we will use it to create a tremolo effect, changing only a few parameters from the defaults. Remember that you can use this effect to modify any continuous controller message.

To create a MIDI tremolo effect with AutoPan:

1. Using a track with some sustained notes or chords (electric piano sounds work great for this), click an insert slot and select the AutoPan effect as an insert on the mixer channel for the track.

2. Select the square wave (**Figure 12.20**).

   Any of the controller shapes will work for a tremolo sound, but we will use the square wave to achieve a somewhat choppy effect.

3. Click the handle below the Controller setting and use the slider to set the value for the Main Volume controller field (**Figure 12.21**).

   Tremolo is nothing more than modulation of the output volume.

4. Set Density to 32 (it probably will default to that value).

continues on next page

5. Set the period to determine how rapidly the controller cycles. In this case, click the arrows next to the Period value to set it to 2th (**Figure 12.22**), which translates to a half note.

With this setting, the waveform will cycle through its complete range every two beats, creating a fairly slow tremolo effect.

6. Set the Max and Min values to specify the range of the controller values sent.

The settings in Figure 12.22 will create a fairly subtle effect, varying the output velocity between 90 and 105. A larger range would create a more pronounced effect.

7. Start playback in Cubase to hear the effect.

You can change the parameters in real time to get a better understanding how they work.

Figure 12.22 With Period set to 2th, the pulse controller waveform will finish once every half note.

Figure 12.23 The MIDIControl effect is a Swiss Army Knife tool for changing any controller parameter.

Other MIDI Effects

The past few sections discussed a few of the MIDI effects that come with Cubase. Here is a quick description of the other MIDI effects you can use. If you want to find out more about them (and you probably should), check the electronic documentation that accompanies Cubase.

Chorder triggers whole chords with a single note from a controller. This effect is useful for one-finger keyboard playing and can be used to create some interesting MIDI parts.

Compress is a simple effect that reduces the range of MIDI velocity values. You can use it to reduce the dynamic range of a MIDI part, much the same way that you can use an audio compressor effect to change the dynamic range of audio.

Density thins excessive MIDI data. Some old (and, sadly, some not so old) synths have trouble processing large streams of MIDI data. Symptoms of problems include missing and delayed notes, as well as full lockup of the device. You can use the Density effect to filter out data so the device stops choking on MIDI.

Micro Tuner allows you to change the tuning of any MIDI instrument that supports it. If you are interested in microtuning and alternate scales, this effect allows you to use both external devices and VST instruments with altered tuning parameters.

MIDIControl can change up to eight MIDI controllers for a MIDI channel (**Figure 12.23**). You can choose the controllers and values that are sent.

continues on next page

OTHER MIDI EFFECTS

Note 2 CC is a simple effect that lets you play notes on a MIDI keyboard to control any controller message. A higher note played on the keyboard translates as a higher controller value. By converting note values to controller values, this plug-in provides another way to send CC data.

Quantizer allows real-time quantizing of MIDI data. Though it lacks some of the quantizing options of the Key editor, it has the advantages of being simple and easy to use.

Step Designer is more than just a MIDI effect. In fact, it blocks note data when it is used as an insert in a MIDI channel. Step Designer is a very powerful step sequencer (**Figure 12.24**). You can use it to program note, velocity, gate, and up to two controller messages at the same time. Step sequencers were the first sequencers created, and they're used to create patterns of MIDI data. If you are interested in electronic music, particularly techno or electro, take extra time to learn this MIDI effect.

Track Control gives users of GS and XG synthesizers (you know who you are) graphical control over the specialized parameters for those synths.

Track FX mirrors the Track Parameters section of the Project window's Track inspector for a MIDI track. Use this effect if you prefer it to the Track inspector.

Transformer can do nearly anything imaginable to MIDI data. It's a lot like the logical editor that was part of Cubase VST, and you can use it to modify MIDI data by building rules to insert, delete, or modify notes and controllers. It's pretty geeky, and using it feels more like computer programming than playing an instrument, but it's extremely powerful and accurate.

Figure 12.24 Step Designer, for serious step sequencing in MIDI.

MIDI Send Effects

So far, we've explored MIDI effects for insert processing. An insert effect takes incoming MIDI, routes it through the effect or effects, and takes the output and routes it to the VST instrument or MIDI output for that channel. Send effects operate differently. When you use a send effect, part of the incoming data is split off from the main data stream and processed in parallel with the original signal. Essentially, the MIDI data is sent to the send effect and also to any insert effects and to the MIDI output for that channel.

Some effects, such as MidiEcho, lend themselves easily to send effects. Others, such as Density, don't necessarily make sense as send effects, because there's no benefit from thinning MIDI data using only part of the data stream.

One very cool feature of MIDI send effects is that they can be sent to their own outputs. This gives rise to some interesting creative possibilities. For instance, the delay from a MIDI track can trigger a different sound than the original MIDI notes.

To use MIDI send effects:

1. Open the pop-up menu for the channel to which you want to apply the effect and select Sends to display these effects in the extended mixer (**Figure 12.25**).

2. In the extended view area, click the first send effect slot, which will default to No Effect, and select MidiEcho (**Figure 12.26**).

3. Set the parameters of the plug-in as you want and close the editor when you are finished.

4. Click below the name of the selected effect to access a menu that allows you to specify where the output of the effect is routed. In this case, specify where to route the MIDI echoes.

   In **Figure 12.27**, the output of the send effect is routed to a third-party VST instrument called Atmosphere.

5. Start playback of the project to hear the original MIDI sound and the echoes.

Figure 12.25 Opening send effects in the extended view area.

Figure 12.26 Selecting MidiEcho as a send effect.

Figure 12.27 A MIDI send effect can route its output to any MIDI device— in this case, to a VST instrument.

MIDI SEND EFFECTS

Saving MIDI with Effects

When mixing a project, different people will want to use MIDI effects in different ways. Some people will always want to use the mixer and effects live, with all effects running at the same time. Other people will want to freeze the effects into a distinct MIDI part, so they can play it back later without need for the effects.

If you are familiar with traditional audio mixing, freezing is akin to what is called printing effects when recording audio. Some engineers like to add all effects at mixdown so that every sonic decision can be considered and reconsidered. Some prefer to record the effects along with the original signal to tape (or disk) and thereby commit to the sound with the effects. Many people use both approaches. You might want to commit your MIDI effects to new parts for convenience or to have a copy of one attempt to get a good sound, avoiding the trouble of saving and recalling presets later.

To save parts with MIDI effects:

1. Use the mixer, insert effects, and send effects to set up all MIDI channels precisely as you want them. You can do this for one channel or multiple channels.

2. Solo all channels that you want to print to a new part.

   Figure 12.28 shows three channels, with insert and send effects, soloed and ready to go.

3. In the Project window, set the left and right locators to include the area you want to save to a new MIDI part.

4. Still in the Project window, select an empty MIDI track as the location to which you want to save.

5. From the MIDI menu, choose Merge Midi in Loop (**Figure 12.29**).

   A dialog box opens (**Figure 12.30**).

6. If you want to print the effects, check Include Inserts and Include Sends.

7. Click OK.

Figure 12.28 Three tracks, all soloed, with MIDI send and insert effects.

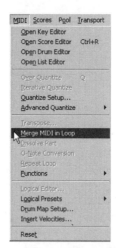

Figure 12.29 This command, Merge MIDI in Loop, makes Cubase bounce MIDI to a new part.

Figure 12.30 Select both of these options to include all MIDI effects in the new part.

13

MIXING SURROUND

For almost 30 years, nearly all music has been mixed in two-channel stereo. There have been exceptions, of course, and flirtations with various schemes to put more than two speakers around the listener, but stereo has remained king of the castle. In contrast to the stereo-centric world of music, Hollywood has been mixing movies in surround for years.

Very slowly, music mixers are also becoming surround aware. With more consumers owning decent-quality home theater setups, there is a ready market for those willing to release their music in surround. Luckily, you as a Cubase user have some of the best surround mixing tools available.

In this chapter, you'll learn how to configure Cubase to route sound to your multichannel speaker setup, as well as your options—such as sound placement and frequency distribution—for those speakers. You'll also learn how to pan tracks in a surround mix and how to automate your surround mixes, as well as a little about your options for releasing your own surround mixes.

Surround Defined

Surround is the general term used to describe a wide range of speaker configurations that all have one point in common: they all use more than two speakers to allow sounds to be located in a wider spatial range than simple stereo mixes allow. The most common surround format is the one used for home theater, which is a six-channel system usually called 5.1. A 5.1 setup has left- and right-front speakers, a center channel located in between the two main front speakers, left and right speakers behind the listener, and a subwoofer for low-end enhancement, which is represented by the .1.

But 5.1 is not the only option; you can mix to everything from four to nine (or even more) speakers, and you'll explore a few of these options as you learn how to set up your VST connections for surround.

Getting two speakers set up correctly and sounding great in a room is not easy, and configuring a surround setup is much more difficult. Your setup will depend a lot on your room and speakers. For a super introduction to surround in general and speakers in particular, go to the Web site for Wendy Carlos (yes, *that* Wendy Carlos, of *Switched-On Bach* fame) at www.wendycarlos.com/surround.

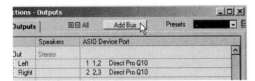

Figure 13.1 Click this button to create a new output bus.

Figure 13.2 Selecting 5.1 as the type of bus to be created.

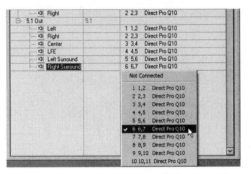

Figure 13.3 For 5.1 output, six of the hardware outputs on your sound card will be used.

Configuring Surround Outputs

When you set up your outputs for surround, you use the same section of Cubase as when you set up your stereo or effects outputs: VST connections. The exact setup you have will determine the kind of busses you use, but the basics will be the same. The following example shows how to configure a 5.1 setup.

To configure surround outputs:

1. From the Devices menu, select VST Connections.

2. In the VST Connections panel that opens, click the Outputs tab.

3. Click the Add Bus button (**Figure 13.1**).

4. In the Add Bus panel, select 5.1 as the type of bus (**Figure 13.2**) and click OK.

5. In the VST Connections panel, the new bus will be visible. Click each of the six outputs and select the hardware output on your sound card for the correct speaker (**Figure 13.3**).

6. If you like, click the name of the bus to rename it.

About Child Busses

It's common when working with a surround mix to want to route a track or tracks to only specific speakers in the surround configuration. For example, in film mixing, the center channel is used almost exclusively for dialogue by on-screen characters, so it's useful to be able to route a track directly to that speaker without having to spend time panning it. Similarly, you may have a stereo delay or reverb effect that you want to use only in the rear surrounds and in no other speakers.

You can do this with Cubase by using a child bus. A child bus is simply a subset of the main bus, used so you can select a specific part of the surround setup for routing your audio. The following example creates a child bus for the rear surround speakers only.

To create a child bus:

1. From the Devices menu, select VST Connections, and in the panel that opens select the Outputs tab.

2. Find the surround bus to which you want to add the child bus. Click on it to select it.

3. Open the contextual menu for the surround bus by right-clicking or Control-clicking (Mac). In the contextual menu, select Add Child Bus > Stereo (Ls Rs) (**Figure 13.4**).

4. Child busses are much easier to manage with names. Click the newly created child bus twice (click slowly) to highlight it (**Figure 13.5**) and give it a more obvious name (**Figure 13.6**).

Figure 13.4 This menu option creates a child bus, or a subset of the main surround bus.

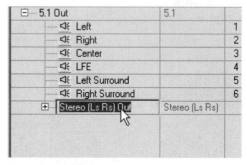

Figure 13.5 Clicking the child bus to rename it.

Figure 13.6 The child bus, completely configured.

Figure 13.7 All of the options for a surround bus in Cubase.

Surround Formats

In these first few examples, you've been working with stereo or 5.1 surround configurations. **Figure 13.7** shows the full menu on the Add Bus panel of VST Connections. Here's a quick rundown of the surround options.

LRCS stands for Left, Right, Center, and Surround. In this configuration the surround speaker is positioned behind the listener. This setup was used in the early home theater market by Dolby ProLogic.

5.1 is the most common surround setup for consumers—DVDs generally use it. The 5.1 setup uses stereo front speakers, stereo surround speakers, a center channel, and a subwoofer or LFE (low-frequency enhancement) channel.

5.0 is 5.1 without the subwoofer.

LRC is the same as LRCS but without the surround.

LRS stands for Left Right Surround.

LRC+LFE is LRC but with an added subwoofer.

LRS+LFE is LRS but with an added subwoofer.

Quadro uses four speakers: stereo front speakers, and stereo surround speakers. This was the configuration for the '70s-era quadraphonic vinyl records and still has some use for music mixing.

LRCS+LFE is the same as LRCS but with a subwoofer channel as well.

Quadro+LFE uses the four-speaker Quadro setup with a subwoofer.

6.0 Cine uses three front speakers—left, right, and center—and three surrounds—also left, right, and center.

6.0 Music uses stereo front speakers, stereo surrounds, and two side channels, located to the left and right of the listener.

Routing Tracks in Surround

Once you have your surround outputs configured, you can easily route any kind of audio to them. This includes, of course, not just audio tracks, but VST instrument and ReWire tracks. The following task routes an audio track to a 5.1 output.

To send an audio track to a surround output:

1. Open the VST mixer and click the icon at the lower left of the mixer to display input and output settings (**Figure 13.8**).

2. For the channel you want to route, click to open the Output Routing menu (**Figure 13.9**).

3. Select the surround output from the list.

✔ Tips

■ You can also always select outputs in the Project window in the Track inspector for an audio track (**Figure 13.10**).

■ Note in Figure 13.9 that the child bus Stereo Surrounds is also an option. You can always route tracks to any child busses you've created using the same menus.

Figure 13.8 Making the input and output routing visible in the mixer.

Figure 13.9 Selecting the 5.1 output bus.

Figure 13.10 You can also select surround bus in the Project window.

Figure 13.11 The channel on the right is stereo, and the channel on the left is surround; note the difference in the pan controls.

Figure 13.12 SurroundPan, used in Cubase for all panning to a surround output.

Figure 13.13 SurroundPan after the signal has been moved in the surround sound field.

Panning Tracks in Surround

Once you've routed a mono or stereo track to a surround output, you'll need to be able to place it in the surround field. Naturally, the familiar stereo-style pan slider in the Cubase mixer isn't going to do the job. **Figure 13.11** shows two audio channels: one routed to a stereo output, and one to a 5.1 output. Note that the pan controls for each track are different; the surround track has a small square with a dot inside instead of the pan slider.

If you double-click that box, the Cubase SurroundPan panel opens (**Figure 13.12**). In the default mode, you can drag the ball around the box to move the sound in the surround field (**Figure 13.13**). This is about as intuitive as surround panning gets, believe it or not, and you should take some time to experiment. Here are a few of the features you might want to note:

◆ Clicking any of the speaker icons while holding down the Alt (Windows) or Option (Mac OS) key will turn off that speaker, routing no audio to it.

◆ You can use the LFE knob to turn down the subwoofer channel. By default, the LFE knob is set to maximum output; turning the knob to the right decreases the amount of the signal that goes to the LFE channel.

◆ The Center knob does something similar for the center channel. By default, the center channel provides 100 percent of the center information, but you may want to reserve the center channel for dialogue or just not use it at all. As you turn the Center knob to the left, the left and right speakers provide progressively more of the center information, as is normally true in a stereo setup. When the knob is fully to the left, at 0 percent, the center channel is effectively turned off.

Effects and Surround

There are comparatively few true surround effects, or effects that process six or more channels independently. There are a few third-party surround effects, and Steinberg makes a set of surround effects for Nuendo, the company's other main audio application, but true surround effects are still largely a thing of the future.

A more common way to use effects in a surround mix is to route stereo effects completely or partially to the surround speakers to add ambience and space to the mix. The following example does just that, routing a reverb to a surround.

To use a stereo effect in surround:

1. Create an FX channel by opening the contextual menu or the Project menu and choosing Add Track > FX Channel.

2. In the Cubase mixer, click the output setting and choose your surround output for the FX channel (**Figure 13.14**).

3. Select Inserts to display inserts in the extended mixer, and select a reverb effect for one of the inserts.

4. Double-click the pan setting for the track to open SurroundPan and drag the panning ball back, toward the bottom of the panning area, so the signal will come out of both the front speakers and the surrounds (**Figure 13.15**).

Figure 13.14
Selecting the 5.1 output bus for the FX channel.

Figure 13.15 Moving the reverb closer to the middle of the sound field.

Figure 13.16 Turning on the send effect for an audio channel.

Figure 13.17 With the power turned on, you can use the slider to send more of the track to the effect.

5. To choose an audio channel that you want to feed the surround effect to, select Sends to view sends in the extended mixer. Click one of the slots in the mixer and select the effect you just created (**Figure 13.16**).

6. Turn on the send effect and use the greenish slider to send some of the signal to the surround effect (**Figure 13.17**).

7. Go back to the FX channel and adjust the SurroundPan settings to change the location of the effect in the surround mix.

EFFECTS AND SURROUND

Surround Mixing Conventions

Over 30 years of mixing in stereo has led to a rough set of rules, or at least guidelines, for stereo mixing. For example, the snare and lead vocal are almost always placed at dead center in the mix. Surround mixing, especially for music, has no such guidelines, but it's useful to consider some practices that have been used in film mixing for some time.

The center channel is usually reserved for dialogue and voice-over—what the people on the screen at the moment are saying. The left- and right-front speakers are used for the musical score of the film, some off-screen dialogue, and special effects. The left and right surrounds are used for ambience, special effects, and directional events. The subwoofer covers the not-very-directional low frequencies and helps shake the walls during explosions.

When mixing music only, instead of mixing audio for a film, the glaring difference is that music doesn't have dialogue. A big question for a music surround mix, therefore, is what to do with the center channel? Some mixers just turn it off, meaning that they mix in a Quadro+LFE type of setup. Some mixers use the center channel only for special effects, while others use it liberally as part of the mix. There still are no real rules for this, but pay attention to your center channel as you build a mix; it might offer as big a mind shift for you as the rear speakers.

Surround Delivery Formats

After you're created a surround mix, you need some way to get it to people. A stereo mix can easily go to a CD, tape, or MP3, but surround mixes are different creatures. Luckily, DVD players are ubiquitous, so most people have at least some ability to play back surround mixes if they have a home theater. Here are some of the options for getting your surround mix out to the public:

◆ **DVD Audio**, or DVD-A discs, are DVDs in which the full storage capacity of the DVD is used just for audio. DVD-A has the most options for the creator: you can have a super-high-bandwidth stereo mix, 24-bit full bandwidth 5.1, or a combination of both. The downside is that very few DVD players can play DVD-A, so fewer people will be able to listen to your discs.

◆ **Super Audio CD**, or SACD, is a proprietary format by Sony/Phillips, the people who first created the CD itself. SACDs are audio-only discs that, once again, have a wide range of options for either high-bandwidth stereo or surround mixes. The downside of SACDs is that, like DVD-A discs, relatively few players can read them. Also, there is no easy, inexpensive way to create one, so if you want to make an SACD, you'll have to take it to a specialized production facility.

continues on next page

◆ **Video DVD**, of course, can play back a surround mix just fine. Most DVD authoring suites include the ability to add Dolby Digital surround to the video. Dolby Digital is a good-sounding, compressed format with a very large market share. Almost every DVD player can decode a Dolby Digital DVD, so you can use blank video along with your audio information.

◆ Finally, you can make a **DTS CD** of your surround mix. DTS is a competitor of Dolby Digital and is generally considered to be a better-quality compressed delivery format. Because it's compressed, you can fit a surround mix on a normal-capacity CD, and if you have a DVD player that can decode a DTS data stream, your surround mix will sound fine.

Just as we don't cover CD burning in this book because Cubase can't burn CDs, surround authoring is beyond this book's scope. However, some good places to look for more information are www.surcode.com, www.discwelder.com, www.dts.com, and www.dolby.com.

AUDIO EFFECT PLUG-INS 14

Audio effects date back to the earliest days of recording, and many different effects are used today in all styles of music. If you have ever recorded in a studio, you have probably used hardware effects, implemented through devices such as compressors and delays.

Steinberg pioneered the use of software effects, usually referred to as plug-ins. Unlike the hardware effects units in the racks of a recording studio, these effects run completely inside the computer. Now, instead of using external hardware or having to learn a whole new application to apply reverb or chorus to a track, you can use effects to accomplish everything within Cubase itself.

In this chapter, you will first learn about the types of plug-ins you can use in Cubase. You will also learn about the basic kinds of audio effects available and about some of the plug-ins included with Cubase. Once you are familiar with some of the tools, you will learn more about routing audio to effects and about creative ways of combining effects using groups.

Supported Plug-in Formats

In an enlightened world, every audio application would work with all effects from every developer. Sadly, this is not the world we live in, and not every plug-in will work with all programs. Steinberg was a pioneer in the software effects arena, and its VST format is probably the most popular on the market, so as a Cubase user you have one of the widest selections of plug-ins from which to choose. Still, it is important to remember that (depending on your platform) only one or two plug-in formats are supported in Cubase.

Cubase supports the following plug-ins formats:

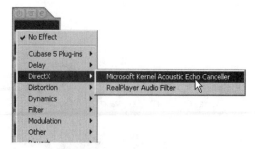

Figure 14.1 A list of installed VST plug-ins, with DirectX plug-ins in a submenu.

◆ **VST** plug-ins naturally are supported by Cubase. Steinberg created the VST format, and one of the greatest attractions of the first VST versions of Cubase was the wide range of effects plug-ins for the program. VST plug-ins are supported on both PCs and Macs.

◆ **DirectX** (usually referred to as DX) is the Microsoft-supported and blessed format for multimedia development in Windows. For years, installing a new version of DX had an effect on computer stability and performance roughly akin to pouring gasoline on the CPU, setting it on fire, and then throwing the machine from a third-story balcony. Luckily, things have improved greatly, and DX on Windows XP works quite well. DX plug-ins are for PCs only. You can select them at the bottom of the drop-down menu in each effect slot (**Figure 14.1**).

Cubase does *not* support the following plug-in formats:

◆ **RTAS** and **TDM** are proprietary formats designed by Digidesign, and they work only within its hardware/software systems.

◆ **Audio Unit** is part of the new system-level multimedia toolkit from Apple. As this is written, Cubase does not support Audio Unit, but Audio Unit plug-ins for use with Cubase may be available in the future.

◆ **MAS**, or the MOTU Audio System, is a proprietary format used only by Digital Performer, a Mac-only digital audio sequencer from Mark of the Unicorn.

Four Kinds of Effects

You probably have heard of dozens of different kinds of effects over the years. It can seem overwhelming at times to keep track of all of the different names and types of effects. However, nearly every effect can be considered a member of one of four groups.

◆ **Filter** effects change the harmonic or timbral content of a sound. The simplest filters to use (such as shelving EQ) modify, mask, or highlight bass or treble frequencies in a sound. If you have ever used an analog or virtual analog synthesizer, you know that synths also have filters, which are often more dramatic and aggressive in their sonic characteristics, but they still are for changing timbre of a sound.

◆ **Dynamics** effects include compressors, limiters, and expanders. These effects modify the volume, or level, of a sound. A compressor, for example, lessens the dynamic range of a sound by reducing the volume of the signal when it passes a defined level. Usually the compressed track is then turned up a bit in the mix to increase its overall perceived volume.

◆ **Delay** effects are used to create repeats of a sound, which is offset in time as the sound is sent through the effect. In some instances, delays are used to mimic sound bouncing off walls, and in some instances, they are used for much less natural effects. Very short delay times can thicken a sound without sounding like an effect at all.

◆ **Modulation** effects are technically a subset of delays but work so differently from delays that they are best considered on their own. Very short delay times (from less than a millisecond to a few milliseconds) are used to create effects like chorus, flanging, and phase shifting. When a slightly delayed sound is mixed back with the dry, nondelayed sound, various comb-filtering, doubling, and phase-shifting effects result. Often the length of the delay is modulated in some way—thus, the general term *modulation* effects.

It helps to keep in mind that all effects are some variation on these four basic sound modifiers. The legendary voltage-controlled filter in a Mini-Moog is just a versatile and great-sounding low-pass filter. A ridiculously expensive vintage Echoplex is simply a great-sounding delay unit that uses magnetic tape to generate the repeats. Even a trippy effect like a vocoder is still just a number of narrow-frequency-band filters that can be modulated.

Insert and Send Effects

An insert effect is the simplest kind of effect. The audio enters the effect, is modified, and then is routed to the fader for that channel and to whatever output that channel feeds.

With send effects, the audio is split and routed to two or more paths. The audio sent to the "normal" path (which can include insert effects and EQs) runs directly to the channel fader. Audio routed to the send path is processed by the effects on an FX channel and then usually sent to the master output. The fader on the FX channel controls the final volume of the effected audio in the master mix. Often an audio channel in the mixer will have both send and insert effects, and some effects lend themselves specifically to use as send or insert effects. Others can work quite nicely in both contexts.

The fundamentals of creating and using insert effects have already been covered in Chapter 11, "Mixing Audio," in the section called Insert Effects Basics. Before you learn about the effects included with Cubase, you ought to know the basics of creating and using send effects. This involves setting up a special channel in the Cubase mixer called an FX channel. Each FX channel can have one or more effects, and any audio, ReWire, or VST instrument channel can use any FX channel as a send effect.

To create a send effect:

1. In the track list in the Project window, open the contextual menu and select Add FX Channel Track (**Figure 14.2**).

2. In the Add FX Channel Track dialog box that opens, select the kind of send effect you will be using (**Figure 14.3**). Most often, send effects are entities like reverbs and delays that will likely be stereo effects. For now, select Stereo for the FX channel and click OK to create it.

Figure 14.2 Use this option on the contextual menu to create a new FX channel.

Figure 14.3 Just like an audio track, an FX channel can be stereo, mono, or surround.

Figure 14.4 Selecting Inserts to view insert effects in the extended mixer area of the FX channel.

Figure 14.5 Selecting the Reverb A effect for the FX channel.

Figure 14.6 Selecting the FX channel for the send effect for the audio channel.

3. Open the Cubase mixer and find the FX channel you just created; it will look like an audio channel but will be purplish and will most likely be called FX 1. Be sure you can see the extended mixer; then click the drop-down menu between the main channel area with the fader and the extended area. Select Inserts for display in the extended area (**Figure 14.4**).

4. In the top insert slot, click the blank field to open the menu of available effects. For this example, select Reverb > Reverb A as the first effect to be applied to the FX channel (**Figure 14.5**). You also might want to give the FX channel a meaningful name, such as MainReverb.

With the FX channel created, you can select any other audio channel, and the reverb send effect will be available as an option for each of the eight send effects slots on every audio channel (**Figure 14.6**).

You can create an almost unlimited number of FX channels, and each audio channel can send part of its signal to up to eight different FX channels. Later in this chapter, you will also learn how to use group channels for some specialized tasks, but most effects situations demand either an insert effect applied to an audio channel or a send effect that can be used by multiple audio channels. The following pages describe the effects included with Cubase; then you will learn how to use effects to create better-sounding mixes.

INSERT AND SEND EFFECTS

DoubleDelay

Delays, as you might guess, are effects that delay and then repeat the incoming audio signal. Delay effects have the following fundamental parameters:

Figure 14.7 The editor panel for DoubleDelay.

◆ The length of time for the delay, usually expressed in milliseconds or in tempo divisions.

◆ The amount of the delayed signal that is fed back into the delay effect. This creates "delays upon delays" of more than one repeat created by the effect and is usually called feedback.

◆ The mix between the unaffected dry signal and the effected "wet" signal.

The DoubleDelay plug-in included with Cubase (**Figure 14.7**) looks fairly simple, but it is actually a quite powerful delay. As its name indicates, it's really two delays in one plug-in, and it has some parameters beyond those mentioned in the preceding list. Each delay can have its own, independent delay time setting, and each also has a pan setting for the delayed audio, but the amount of feedback is set globally for both delays. The following example uses Double-Delay as a send effect.

Figure 14.8 Choosing DoubleDelay from the list of available plug-ins.

To use DoubleDelay:

1. If necessary, create an FX channel as described previously and display insert effects in the extended mixer area.

2. Click the top, empty insert effect slot, and in the drop-down menu that opens, select Delay > DoubleDelay (**Figure 14.8**).

   In the editor for the DoubleDelay plug-in that opens, you will set a number of parameters.

Figure 14.9 Click the white button to set the DelayTime parameter to TempoSync.

Figure 14.10 Use this drop-down menu to select the delay time in note values.

Figure 14.11 The send effect slot set to route audio to the delay effect.

Figure 14.12 Use the slider to determine how much audio is sent to the effect.

3. Set the Mix slider all the way to the top, to 100 percent.

Because send effects run in parallel, you will usually want only the effected signal (without the dry signal) to come out of the effect.

4. Turn on tempo sync for both delays by clicking the white button above each DelayTime knob (**Figure 14.9**).

Most likely, the defaults for the tempo-based delay times will be just as shown in Figure 14.9, where 1/4 means a quarter-note.

5. Click the setting for DelayTime2 and select 1/8 from the menu (**Figure 14.10**). Leave the other parameters at their defaults.

6. Close the DoubleDelay editor and name the FX channel something like Delay1.

7. Find a channel to send to the delay. A percussive sound or drum loop will let you hear the delay clearly. Open the extended mixer for that channel and make send effects visible.

8. In the top send effects slot, click the blank area to open a list of available sends. Select the delay channel you just created (**Figure 14.11**).

9. Turn on the effects send by clicking its power button at the top left of the channel (if the button is not already lighted and activated). Drag the green slider in the send effects slot to add more or less of the signal to the send effect (**Figure 14.12**).

10. Play the project to hear the effect.

DOUBLEDELAY

Using Tempo-Synchronized Delays

DoubleDelay is one of many plug-ins with parameters that can be set to note values that automatically synchronize with the project tempo. Because so many plug-ins have tempo-based parameters, including many third-party plug-ins that are not covered in this book, it's worth looking at these a bit more closely. Most plug-ins use the same basic settings:

◆ Straight, or "normal," settings are simply the note values shown: 1/4 means a quarter-note, 1/8 means an eighth-note, and so on.

◆ Dotted note values add half again to the duration of their note value. That is, a dotted eighth-note sets the parameter value to the duration of an eighth-note with a sixteenth-note tacked on the end of it.

◆ Triplet settings result in a duration that is a third of the note value set. That is, a quarter-note triplet setting will set the parameter value to one-third the duration of a quarter-note.

If you don't read standard musical notation and this is all mumbo-jumbo to you, don't worry; you can hear these changes easily when working with a plug-in. Here is a way for you to hear the tempo-synced parameters using another delay plug-in bundled with Cubase.

Using Delays

Delay is used in nearly every kind of music, for all kinds of effects. If you listen to the original Sun Studios' Elvis Presley tracks, you will often hear a clearly audible, very short single delay on the vocals and guitars. This prominent delay is usually called slapback and is characteristic of lots of early rockabilly and rock'n'roll. Guitar players have used delay effects for years to thicken their guitar sounds, usually less prominently than on the rockabilly tracks, and usually with a few more repeats.

Rock music often uses a combination of delay and modulation effects on snare drums, vocals, and guitars, all with the goal of fattening the sounds of the instruments. Only rarely are the effects obvious enough that average listeners can hear them.

To really hear a delay in a mix, electronic music and Jamaican music are the best places to listen. In fact, a CD by one of the '70s dub pioneers from Jamaica like King Tubby or Lee "Scratch" Perry is almost a master class on creative delay techniques.

Figure 14.13 The ModDelay editor panel.

Figure 14.14 The bundled VST plug-ins all use these buttons to turn on TempoSync.

Figure 14.15 Selecting a tied eighth note as the delay time.

To hear tempo-based delays:

1. Find a track with percussive content. Even a simple snare drum will do. Avoid full drum loops, vocals, or string tracks because delays on these types of tracks can be difficult to hear. In the mixer channel for this track, select Inserts for display in the extended mixer area.

2. In the first insert effect slot, select Delay > ModDelay.

3. In the setting window that appears, set the Mix slider to 25 percent, Feedback to 30 percent, and Delay Mod to zero (**Figure 14.13**).

4. Click the box next to the DelayTime setting to turn on tempo synchronization (**Figure 14.14**).

5. Start project playback and click the DelayTime setting to open the drop-down menu (**Figure 14.15**). Select some of the tempo settings to audition the straight, dotted, and triplet time delay settings.

✔ Tip

■ The TempoSync setting, to the right of the DelayTime setting in Figure 14.14, is a multiplier for the tempo sync. That is, if DelayTime is set to 1/8 and TempoSync is set to 3x, the resulting delay time is the duration of three eighth notes.

Varying Pitch with ModDelay

ModDelay is useful for more than just learning about tempo-based parameters or creating simple repeats. The *Mod* in ModDelay stands for modulation, which plays a significant role in many different kinds of effects. Modulation is the automatic changing of the value of a particular parameter over time. A simple modulator is the speed setting on a tremolo effect: the volume of the signal is changed more slowly or quickly according to that speed setting.

ModDelay uses pitch modulation to add to what the effect can do. Classic delay units, like tape delays and analog chip-based delays, change the pitch of the delayed signal if the delay time changes. This makes sense in the example of a tape delay; one way to change the delay time of a tape delay is to speed up the tape, which, of course, will temporarily increase the pitch of the repeats.

Figure 14.16 The ModDelay plug-in set to allow you to hear how it works.

Figure 14.17 Dragging the Delay Mod knob adds pitch modulation to the delays.

To use ModDelay:

1. Using the same sound as in the previous example with DoubleDelay, open ModDelay as an insert in the channel by selecting Delay > ModDelay in the first insert slot.

2. In the ModDelay window, set the Mix slider at 25 percent, set Feedback to 30 percent, turn on TempoSync with the square button above and to the right of the DelayTime knob, and select 1/16 (**Figure 14.16**).

3. Start playback of the project to hear the delay effect on the channel. You may want to solo the channel as well.

4. Drag the Delay Mod knob to increase the value (**Figure 14.17**).

    You'll hear the pitch of the delays change as you increase this setting.

Figure 14.18 Adding a Reverb A send effect.

Figure 14.19 The Large preset is selected for the Reverb effect.

Reverb

Reverb, of course, is short for reverberation. A sound in an enclosed space will take part of its quality from the space in which it occurs. Reverb is really nothing more than an extremely complex set of delays that simulate the effect of a sound bouncing off the walls, floor, ceiling, and any other objects in the room. These numerous delays (and delays of the delays) are so close together that our ears perceive them as a wash of smeared sound instead of as distinctive sonic events.

The characteristics of reverb vary widely, depending on the room (its size, shape, composition, number of objects inside it, and so on), the position of the sound generator and the listener, and even factors such as the temperature and humidity of the air. Reverb is almost always used as a send effect and is used at least some of the time on every instrument in every type of music, for every style of mix. Cubase includes two distinct-sounding reverb plug-ins.

To use reverb:

1. Create an FX channel to use as the reverb send.

2. In an open insert effects slot on the FX channel, select Reverb > Reverb A (**Figure 14.18**). You may want to name the FX channel Reverb.

3. In the Reverb A window that opens, click the presets menu at the bottom and select Large; then drag the Mix slider all the way to the bottom, to 100 percent wet (**Figure 14.19**).

continues on next page

REVERB

4. In the Cubase mixer, find a track to test the reverb and select Sends for display in the extended mixer area.

5. Click an open effect slot and, from the drop-down list, select the FX channel with the reverb plug-in.

6. Drag the blue-green slider in the effects slot to the right to send part of the signal from that channel to the reverb effect (**Figure 12.20**); then play the project.

7. Go back to the Reverb A editor panel and audition some of the other presets to become more familiar with the way that they modify the sound.

Figure 14.20 Adding the reverb effect for an audio channel via a send slot.

REVERB

Figure 14.21 The Reverb A editor panel.

Reverb A Settings

Cubase's Reverb A plug-in (**Figure 14.21**) includes parameters common to most digital reverb effects. If you take the time to become familiar with how it works and how the parameters change the sound of the reverb, you will have an easier time understanding lots of other reverb effects.

◆ **Predelay** mimics one of the characteristics of reverb in an actual room, where there is usually a slight delay between the sound being created and the start of the reverb. This delay occurs because the sound has to travel to at least one wall or other surface and then travel back to our ears before we hear the start of the reverb. This delay can be anywhere from a couple of milliseconds in a small room to much longer in a big room.

◆ **Filter** changes the timbre of the reverb. The High Cut filter is used to make the "room" sound more or less bright. A room with deep shag carpet on the floor and curtains on one side will sound different than a brick-walled room with a hardwood floor. Using High Cut to filter out the high-end sound will make the reverb sound more like the carpeted, "darker" room. The Low Cut filter is useful for cutting out low-end rumble that usually sounds pretty bad when fed to a reverb.

◆ **Roomsize** controls the character of the reverb by mimicking the timbre differences between larger and smaller acoustic spaces.

◆ **Reverb Time** controls the length of time the reverb lasts. The Reverb A plug-in reverb time can range from very short to very, very long.

✔ Tip

■ Reverb B, the other reverb plug-in included with Cubase, uses many of the same parameters, but with a more knob-oriented interface. It also sounds a bit different and uses somewhat less CPU bandwidth to run.

Using Reverb

Few topics in the audio world create more catfights than reverb. With reverb, beauty is as much in the eye (or ear) of the beholder as it is for anything related to music. The earliest reverb units were what are now called reverb chambers. A fairly small, bright (lots of flat surfaces to reflect sound), enclosed space was set up with a speaker on one side and a microphone on the other side; the reverb send on the mixer routed audio to the speaker in the reverb chamber, and the microphone in the chamber picked up the sound with its added reverb effect and returned it to the mixer. One famous '50s engineer drove around the countryside yelling into empty water tanks until he found one he liked the sound of; then he bought the tank, outfitted it with a speaker and a microphone to create a reverb chamber, and buried it behind his recording studio.

Even in the '50s, not many recording studios could or would go to that trouble, so other methods of artificial reverb were created over time. Usually they used some kind of transducer to translate sound waves into energy that would move a metal spring or plate, and the resulting back-and-forth motion of the metal would produce a reverberating effect on the sound. The reverb tanks in guitar amplifiers and some electric pianos descend from those artificial reverb units. Eventually, effects designers put reverb on computer chips, giving birth to digital reverb.

Reverb can be used on pretty much every instrument in a mix, though this does not mean that it needs to be slathered on everything in sight. As when you overuse EQ, a huge wash of long reverb on every instrument in a mix positively screams "novice mixer." When you are working with a mix, try creating two reverb sends with different sounds and then send very slight amounts of grouped tracks to one or the other. For example, if you have multiple acoustic guitar tracks, applying a little reverb will make them sound like they are from the same acoustic space and can really flesh them out. The same can be done with horns or backup singers or some other part of the mix. Often one or two very prominent parts, like the snare drum or the vocal, will have their own reverb sound parts.

A very personal note: I love digital sound, digital recording, digital synths, and electronic music. My life often seems to be a riot of the digital—but most digital reverb sounds awful to me. Because of this, I tend to use very low-tech, low-fidelity spring reverbs from the '70s and '80s when I use reverb at all. Until my landlords agree to let me tear up the parking lot behind my house and bury a water tank underneath it, that's really my only option. You may find reverb plug-ins that you think sound great, but take a look at some of the hardware units, both digital and analog, to see if one better fits your sonic needs.

Chorus

Chorus is a modulation effect used to add thickness and often audible pitch modulation to a signal. The name is derived from the fact that a chorus of four singers, no matter how skilled and prepared, cannot sing the same part in exactly the same way and at exactly the same pitch. A chorus effect takes the signal, splits off a very short delay line, pitch modulates the delayed signal (or signals, in a stereo chorus), and then mixes the delayed signal with the original. The modulation is from a low-frequency oscillator, or LFO. Like a lot of modulation effects, chorus sounds show up in many places, from very inexpensive stomp boxes, to vintage analog devices, to high-end digital multi-effects hardware boxes.

Chorus can provide a lot of sonic effects. As an insert effect, it can thicken sounds by adding a subtle doubling effect, like two players playing the same part. Because it pitch modulates the delays, it can also offer a good way to add stereo ambience to a mono signal. To do this, chorus needs to be used as a send effect, because applying an insert effect to a mono channel produces only mono output. The following example uses chorus as a send effect.

To use chorus:

1. Create an FX channel and, in one of the insert effect slots, select Modulation > Chorus. If you like, name the FX channel as well.

2. In the Chorus settings editor panel, set the Mix slider to 100 percent and drag the Frequency knob to a setting slightly below 1.00 Hz. Set Delay to about 1.5 ms and set Stages to 2 (**Figure 14.22**).

3. In the mixer, find a channel that you want to send to the chorus effect. Select Sends for display in the extended mixer area.

4. Click the drop-down menu in the top send slot in the channel strip to select Chorus if it isn't already selected. Turn on the power button for the send slot and use the green slider in the settings window to adjust and send audio for the chorus effect (**Figure 14.23**).

5. Play the project to hear the effect.

✔ Tips

- The Stages setting in the settings window controls how thick the chorus sounds. Each progressive stage adds another delay to the effect.

- The Shapes buttons in the settings window control the shape of the LFO that modulates the pitch change in the effect. The default sawtooth waveform is very common for effect modulation, but the other two waveforms produce interesting results as well.

Figure 14.22 The Chorus editor.

Figure 14.23 Adding chorus via a send slot.

CHORUS

Figure 14.24 The Dynamics editor.

Figure 14.25 You can use these buttons to change the order of the three effects in the Dynamics plug-in.

✔ Tip

■ The Routing section (**Figure 14.25**) is used to change the order of the effects. By default, the plug-in routing path is Compressor > Autogate > Limiter, but you can use the Routing buttons to reorder the effects.

Dynamics

Dynamic effects alter the level, or volume, of audio and can perform all manner of tasks. For instance, they can perform compression to reduce the dynamic range of audio, perform expansion to increase the dynamic range of audio, and set limits to establish the absolute maximum level for a signal. Cubase includes plug-ins that can accomplish all of these tasks and a good many more. The main plug-in covered here is the Dynamics plug-in (**Figure 14.24**).

The Dynamics plug-in is actually three plug-ins in one, with distinct sections for three different dynamics control jobs:

◆ **Compress** is the compressor section. A compressor reduces the dynamic range of an audio signal by reducing the level of that signal after it rises above a certain value.

◆ **Autogate** is an audio gate effect. Gates are normally used for noise reduction; a gate silences the channel when the level reaches a specified value. In other words, below a certain volume, a gate mutes the channel. Gates can be useful for controlling tracks with unwanted sounds such as background noise and hiss.

◆ **Limiter** is a little like a compressor but is a more heavy-handed effect. A compressor reduces the signal when it passes a certain level, but a limiter is a brick wall and will not let a signal sound beyond a certain level.

You turn each of the three types of effects on or off by clicking its name at the top of its section of the editor.

DYNAMICS

Compressor

The Compress section (**Figure 14.26**) of the Dynamics plug-in is probably its most used component. The controls and parameters for this effect are pretty standard. If you have used hardware compressors, you should be able to negotiate this section immediately. If you are not familiar with compression, here are the parameters and what they do:

Figure 14.26 The compressor effect in the Dynamics plug-in.

- **Threshold** determines at what level the compressor starts to act on the signal. Audio below the threshold passes through unchanged.

- **Ratio** controls how much the audio above the threshold is compressed. For example, a 3:1 ratio means that for every increase of 3 decibels in the signal, the compressor will increase the level by 1 decibel. The higher the ratio, the more pronounced the compression effect.

- **Attack** is used to change how quickly the compressor takes action once the signal is above the threshold. Short attack times clamp down on the audio quickly, while longer attack times allow more of the front edge of a signal to pass through the compressor before it starts to change levels.

- **Release** is the flipside of attack. It controls how long the compressor takes to stop compressing when the signal drops below the threshold.

- **Mode,** using the RMS and Peak buttons, determines how the compressor looks at the incoming signal. RMS responds to the average level, which is usually best for legato instruments and vocals, and Peak responds more to transients and is generally better for transient-heavy material like percussion.

DYNAMICS

Figure 14.27 The Autogate effect in the Dynamics plug-in.

Autogate

The second section of the Dynamics plug-in is Autogate (**Figure 14.27**). The main use of gates is to mute channels that have excessive noise or hum, so they don't clutter up the sound of a mix. You can also use gates to create dramatic and obvious stuttering audio effects. Autogate is a very complex tool, and a lot of people don't use it much, but it's still good to understand how it works in case you do find the need for the effect. Here's what the settings do:

◆ Three of the bottom four knobs, **Threshold**, **Attack,** and **Release**, act in the same way as in the Compressor section. Threshold sets the level at which the gate is opened and the level below which the channel is silenced. Attack controls how quickly the gate opens when the signal passes the threshold level, and Release controls how quickly the gate closes when the signal goes below the threshold setting.

◆ **Hold** governs how the gate closes, because when you use a gate as a noise-reduction tool, it often makes a sound when it opens and closes, and this sound usually sounds bad. The Hold setting simply holds the gate open for a specified amount of time when the signal gets below the threshold. When that time has passed, the Release parameter takes over. Use Hold if you have a good gate setting that closes a little too often. One example would be a gate that is closing too quickly on a horn player, muting the sound of her breathing. You might want the breath to make the performance more realistic, and changing the Hold setting will cause the gate to close more slowly.

continues on next page

DYNAMICS

- **Trigger Frequency Range** provides an even more advanced approach to noise gating. This setting, modified by the slider, limits the part of the signal that the gate watches to see when it should open. By limiting the frequencies that can open the gate, you can keep out unwanted sounds such as low-frequency rumble or high-frequency tape hiss. **Figure 14.28** shows a very narrow range, and **Figure 14.29** shows the full audio spectrum.

Figure 14.28 A narrow frequency range for triggering the gate.

Figure 14.29 A wide range.

Limiter

The third section of the Dynamics plug-in is the **Limiter** (**Figure 14.30**). Limiters are devices that set an absolute ceiling on how high (loud) the level of an audio signal is allowed to go. Limiters are particularly useful with digital audio, to keep ugly digital distortion from being introduced later in the processing chain.

Figure 14.30 The Limiter section has only a few adjustable parameters.

The parameters for the Limiter in the Dynamics plug-in are very simple. **Threshold** sets the ceiling for the limiter; audio will not be allowed to exceed the level set here. **Release** controls how quickly the limiter lets go of the signal when the level falls below the threshold. You can click the **Auto** button in the Limiter settings window to enable the plug-in to find a setting based on the kind of audio passing through the plug-in. You'll know when the Limiter is engaged and acting on the signal when the red **Limiting** light is on. The light can help you gauge how much the Limiter is changing the signal.

Analog limiters have a very difficult job. Usually a limiter is supposed to grab transients (the beginning, percussive milliseconds of a note produced by some instruments) and pull down their levels, but most transients are short and sudden. It takes a real expert to properly set a hardware limiter to act as a brick wall for audio. For digital audio, though, the limiter can peek ahead to see what is coming down the audio pipe.

Figure 14.31 Selecting Dynamics as an insert plug-in.

Using Dynamics

As with EQ, using compression is an art, and your skills will get better with practice. If you already know a good bit about compression, the controls for the Dynamics plug-in should be transparent. If you're not familiar with compression, spend some time working through the presets, and practice with different kinds of audio material.

Compression is nearly always used as an insert effect. The point of a compressor is to control the dynamics of a sound, and routing only part of a channel to a compressor will not give full control over its dynamics. A compressor used as a send effect and set to reduce the transient pluck part of a bass sound will do so for only part of the signal. Only an insert effect will fully control that part of the sound. The following example shows you how to compress an electric bass track to bring it out more in the mix.

To compress a track with Dynamics:

1. For the channel you want to compress, set the extended mixer area to display inserts.

2. Click the top insert effect slot to open its drop-down menu and then select Dynamics > Dynamics (**Figure 14.31**).

3. Play the project to hear the track.

4. Click the Compress button in the settings editor window to activate compression in the plug-in. The button will turn yellow to indicate that it is active. If either Autogate or Limiter is selected, unselect them.

continues on next page

USING DYNAMICS

5. Drag the Threshold knob until the Gain Reduction meter begins to show that the compression is taking effect (**Figure 14.32**).

   The lower the threshold, the more the signal will be compressed.

6. Adjust the Ratio setting if the compression sounds too strong or not strong enough.

   Higher compression ratios force the level of the sound into a smaller range.

7. Adjust the Attack parameter if the compression is acting too quickly; this will take away the transient of the instrument being compressed.

8. Using the Gain Reduction meter as a guide, increase the MakeUp Gain knob setting (**Figure 14.33**) so that the effect of the plug-in is roughly equal for the overall level of the channel.

Figure 14.32 The meter shows gain reduction of about 4 dB.

Figure 14.33 Adding back the gain that has been taken away by the compressor.

Thinking Compression

Compression is not easy to understand, and the graphical tools for editing the parameters of an effect are not necessarily the easiest to use for an effect. Delay time is a comparatively easy parameter to figure out, but release for a compressor isn't, and editing release with a knob is not terribly intuitive. When learning to work with compressors, think about each sound as having three dynamic parts. The first part is the *transient*: the pluck of a guitar string or the sound of the stick hitting a drum. Next is the *sustain* of the sound: the guitar string in its full resonance moving the wood of the guitar or the sound of the full drum as it resonates. Last is the *decay*: where the string or drum stops moving and where the ambience of the room is heard. If you think of a sound as having these three main parts, it's easier to understand how dynamics control works.

Each of these dynamic components occurs over time, and every instrument is a bit different in how these three dynamic characteristics are manifested. If you think of a sound in terms of these three factors, it becomes easier to work with compression. For instance, the previous task, "To compress a track with Dynamics," discussed how to set a compressor for a bass. **Figure 14.34** shows a quick-and-dirty compressor setting for this bass. I wanted to keep the transient of the bass sound (the finger plucking the string) prominent, so I used a fairly slow attack. I set the threshold low, but I didn't want the ratio too high. The compressor will compress a lot of the bass sound, but it won't compress it too much. I turned off the autorelease and set a fairly long release time, to help smooth the transition from the compressed to the uncompressed part of the signal. In the end, this setting raises the level of the middle, sustained part of the bass line, leaving the transient mostly untouched. There is little decay in the bass sound anyway, so the long release allows the action of the compressor to be very smooth.

Figure 14.34 A setting that I created quickly to compress a bass channel.

Magneto

One of the hidden goodies in SX 2 is the Magneto tape saturation plug-in (**Figure 14.35**). Magneto was previously available only as an add-on plug-in from Steinberg, and at additional cost of course.

Figure 14.35 The editor panel for Magneto.

Magneto mimics one of the most sought-after sounds in analog audio recording: the saturation and compression audible when analog tape is recorded at very high levels. This form of distortion was used for years when recording rock and R&B music to multitrack tape, where "hitting the tape hard" with very hot levels would produce a thicker, stronger sound. Most often used (at least intentionally) on drum and guitar tracks, tape saturation is one of the sounds many people accustomed to analog recording miss when they switch to digital. Magneto lets you emulate tape saturation inside your digital mixes. The plug-in has four main sections:

Figure 14.36 Each meter can show the input level, the output level, or the level driving the tape saturation algorithm.

- The **Metering** section (**Figure 14.36**) allows you to see the level of the audio coming into the plug-in, the level of the signal "on tape" (controlled with the help of the Drive knob), and the level of the output from the plug-in. You use the three buttons to select the options.

Figure 14.37 The main controls for changing how Magneto sounds.

- The **Drive** section (**Figure 14.37**) controls how much the "tape" signal is overdriven. The higher the Drive knob setting, the more compressed and saturated the sound will be. The Characteristics knob changes the timbre of the drive applied, allowing you to emulate different styles of tape saturation.

MAGNETO

Figure 14.38 Additional parameters used to emulate more detailed aspects of some tape decks.

Figure 14.39 The Input Level and Output Level knobs.

Effects Creep

Magneto, along with many other effects, can be easy to overuse. Over time, our ears adjust to the presence of audio effects of any kind, and quite often, after a little bit of an effect is applied, it seems to disappear. It's tempting to crank up the effect higher, assuming that not enough was applied at first, but that isn't always a good idea.

Most people learn about effects creep with reverb. After working on a mix for a few hours, it's easy to have way too much reverb on way too many instruments. Listen to a CD of the final mix the next day, and it sounds like a tinny little band playing inside a canyon.

The best ways to avoid effects creep are first, to be aware that it happens, and second, to turn off effects every now and then to refresh your ears. Also, unless you're a real pro, your ears will get tired after a while, and you'll need to take some breaks. Don't be surprised if, after such a break, a lot of your tracks that have Magneto on them sound a little too saturated.

◆ **HF Adjust** and **Tape Speed** (**Figure 14.38**) allow Magneto to emulate additional tape machine parameters. Tape Speed models the slight timbral difference between tape decks that run at 15 inches per second and those that run at 30 inches per second. HF Adjust lets you add or subtract high frequencies from the effected signal, much like different kinds of tape or differently adjusted tape decks do.

◆ **Input Level** and **Output Level** knobs (**Figure 14.39**) set the volume of the audio going into and out of the plug-in. The Input Level knob lets you boost a signal before it gets to the Drive control if needed, and the Output Level knob lets you boost or cut the signal if the effect changes the level of the track in the mix.

Using Magneto on an audio channel:

1. Select Inserts for display in the extended mixer area of a stereo or mono audio channel. A drum loop is a good source for experimenting with Magneto.

2. Click an empty insert effect slot and select Dynamics > Magneto.

3. Leave all of the plug-in parameters at their defaults and start the project playing. If necessary (it won't be unless you've changed it from the default), set the meters to On Tape (**Figure 14.40**).

4. Watch the meters, and set them so they go into the red—in other words, above 0 dB, at least a little bit (**Figure 14.41**).

5. Adjust the Drive, HF-Adjust, and Tape Speed parameters to hear how Magneto changes the sound of the processed audio.

✔ Tip

■ Mac users: If you're using SX 2.0 and you download the update patch for SX 2.01, be sure to pull the original version of the Magneto plug-in out of your plug-ins folder and store it somewhere else before you install the patch, or else Magneto will be overwritten by a bad file and you'll have to reinstall from scratch.

Figure 14.40 With this setting, you can see how hard the tape saturation is being driven.

Figure 14.41 The farther the signal goes beyond 0 dB, the stronger the tape effect will be. These meters will generate a moderate amount of saturation effect from Magneto.

MAGNETO

Figure 14.42 The StepFilter plug-in combines a synth-style filter and a step sequencer.

Figure 14.43 The bundled Vocoder plug-in.

Other Cubase Audio Plug-ins

The electronic documentation that comes with Cubase includes a PDF file containing parameter lists for the rest of the plug-ins included with the program. Here is a short description of each of the other effects:

◆ **SPL DeEsser** is an effect used to remove or limit harsh *s* sounds from vocals.

◆ **Bitcrusher** reduces the fidelity of the audio that plays back in Cubase. This effect is often used to mimic older, lo-fi samplers.

◆ **DaTube** emulates the saturation and compression characteristics of vacuum tubes.

◆ **StepFilter** combines a multimode resonant filter, as might be found on a virtual analog synthesizer, with a step sequencer. The sequencer can control both the frequency of the filter and the resonance (**Figure 14.42**).

◆ **Ringmodulator** is a classic synthesizer effect, generated by finding the sum and difference of two audio signals.

◆ **Rotary** emulates the sound of a spinning speaker, like the Leslie speakers used with Hammond B3 organs.

◆ **Vocoder** creates incredibly versatile and interesting effects. Vocoder uses two banks of identical filters, one of which modulates the other. A different signal is fed to each filter, and the filters of one of the signals are used to control the filters of the other signal (**Figure 14.43**).

continues on next page

OTHER CUBASE AUDIO PLUG-INS

- **VST Dynamics** adds a few features to the Dynamics plug-in discussed in this chapter. However, it operates at a slightly higher latency and can use more CPU bandwidth.

- **Multiband Compressor (Figure 14.44)** is a different type of compressor than Magneto or VST Dynamics. As its name implies, a multiband compressor splits the audio signal into more than one band, and the compression settings for each band can be different. Multiband compressors are often used on full mixes when mastering, or on very full-range instruments like drums or a piano.

- **QuadraFuzz** is a multiband distortion plug-in. The audio spectrum is divided into four bands that you can modify, so you can change the level of each band before processing with the distortion effect.

- **Flanger** derives its name from the effect produced by running two tape recorders with the same sound in sync and then slowing down or speeding up one recorder by dragging or pushing on the flange of the tape to create a doubling and filtering effect that modifies the sound. This plug-in mimics that effect digitally.

- **Symphonic** is a stereo-enhancement plug-in.

Figure 14.44 The multiband compressor is most useful on material with a wide frequency range.

Figure 14.45 Tranceformer allows any channel to be ring modulated.

◆ **Phaser** is a phase-shifting plug-in used to generate a swirling, filtering effect somewhat like a flanger.

◆ **Overdrive** attempts to emulate the effect of a guitar amplifier and speaker combination.

◆ **Chopper** combines a tremolo effect and an autopanned effect to produce effects from subtle tremolo to stuttering audio.

◆ **Metalizer** is a filtering/modulation plug-in that applies a metallic-sounding band-pass filter that can be modulated to the audio.

◆ **Tranceformer** modulates the audio in the channel with its own, internal, oscillator (**Figure 14.45**).

◆ **Grungelizer** is another lo-fi effect used to mimic the static, pops, clicks, and noise found on old vinyl records.

◆ **Q** is a high-quality, four-band equalizer plug-in.

◆ **Mix6to2**, **SurroundPan**, and **Surround Dither** are all used when mixing to multichannel output. **Mix6to2** is probably the most often used; it easily controls the levels in a six-channel surround mix when mixing a stereo version from a surround version.

Pre-Fader Send Effects

Effects are most often used in the ways described up to now: as either insert effects or as send effects, where a percentage of the signal is sent in parallel to the send effect. There are other options for effects, though, and the last few pages of this chapter will explain some of them. For instance, effects can use a pre-fader.

To understand what a pre-fader is, it's important to remember how send effects work in the default post-fader method. By default, the blue-green slider that controls the level of send effects is actually just a ratio control. If the channel fader is moved up, more signal goes to the send effect, and if the fader is moved down, less signal goes to the send effect. The ratio between the two stays the same. With a pre-fader send effect, the same blue-green slider controls the amount of signal sent to the send effect regardless of where the channel fader is set. It no longer just sets a ratio, but acts almost like a second fader controlling the level of the send effect. The following task lets you hear the difference.

Figure 14.46 The audio channel with the send effect selected and the fader at zero.

To hear a pre-fader send effect:

1. Create a send effect using an FX channel. For this example, use a delay or reverb plug-in, because they are easy to hear as pre-fader send effects. Whatever effect you use, set the mix slider to 100 percent.

2. Choose a channel for testing the effect, solo the channel in the Cubase mixer, and set the channel fader to zero.

3. Select send effects to be viewed in the extended mixer area.

   The channel strip should look something like **Figure 14.46**.

Figure 14.47 Adding the reverb send.

Figure 14.48 Clicking the Pre-Fader button changes the send effect to pre-fader.

4. Play the project and drag the green slider for the send effect slot halfway or so to engage the send effect (**Figure 14.47**).

5. Drag the channel fader up until you hear both the channel and the send effect to be sure everything is working.

6. Drag the fader back to zero.

   You will hear both the dry and effected signal fade out.

7. Click the Pre-Fader button in the send effect slot (**Figure 14.48**) but don't bring up the channel fader.

   The button turns orange when the Pre-fader is selected. After this button is clicked, you will hear the send effect, even though the channel fader is set to zero.

8. Move the green slider left and right to hear the effect change.

When to Use Pre-Fader Send Effects

The most accurate answer to the question of when to use a pre-fader send effect is whenever you need control over the level of the effect independent of the channel fader. Here are a few situations where a pre-fader send effect is useful:

◆ With some effects, such as gates and vocoders, one sound triggers or modifies another sound. If you don't want the dry signal at all, you can use a pre-fader send effect.

◆ For some special effects, you may want the effect louder than the dry signal. For example, you may want a lead vocal to be very dry, with the backing vocals very low but soaked in reverb. A pre-fader send effect lets you control the level of the backing vocals going to the reverb effect.

◆ You can use pre-fader send effects to create headphone mixes for multiple musicians.

These are only a few of the situations where pre-fader send effects can be useful. Keep this capability in mind as you work with the Cubase mixer, and you'll find more places where pre-fader effects work for you.

Group Channels and Effects

Most people use effects mainly as either insert or send effects, but Cubase provides another way to work with effects: using group channels. Chapter 11 includes a brief discussion of how to control the volume of multiple channels by assigning the channels to one group. One common application of group channels is in drum mixes; each individual drum sound can be mixed and effected, and in addition, the whole drum mix can be controlled (and effected) by routing each part of the drum mix to a group. You can also put insert and send effects in the group channel for routing and effects flexibility.

The following task shows how to apply an effect to a group of tracks at the same time. Putting a compressor across the stereo drum mix is standard operating procedure for rock and pop drums, but the same basic approach works in many other situations as well.

Applying an effect to multiple tracks with a group:

1. Create a group using the Project menu; select Add Track > Group Channel.

2. Name the group channel by double-clicking the name in the mixer and typing a new name.

3. Find the channels you want to route to the effect and add any individual effects, EQ, and inserts for the individual channels.

   Figure 14.49 shows a simple five-channel drum mix, which includes mono channels for the kick, snare, and hi-hat, and stereo channels for drum overheads and a pair of room mics.

4. Click the bottom of each channel to open the pop-up menu for routing the channel. Route each channel to the group.

   Figure 14.50 shows a channel being routed to the DrumMix group.

5. After all channels in the drum mix are routed to the group, navigate in the mixer to the group, drag the fader to zero, and make inserts visible in the extended mixer area.

6. Click the first insert effect slot and add the Dynamics plug-in by selecting Dynamics > Dynamics.

7. Play the project; then display the group channel fader and use the Dynamics plug-in on the full stereo drum mix (**Figure 14.51**).

Figure 14.49 A simple five-channel drum mix.

Figure 14.50 Selecting the group channel as the output for one of the tracks in the mix.

Figure 14.51 The DrumMix group and the compressor section of the Dynamics plug-in. This plug-in compresses the whole drum mix, and the single fader can control its level.

Third-Party Plug-ins

Much of the fun of being a Cubase user comes from the ability to choose from the huge list of cool VST plug-ins. As with VST instruments, Cubase users get all of the really cool stuff first, and it usually works best in the Cubase program. There are lots of resources on the Web for obtaining free or shareware plug-ins, some of which are as good as their more expensive commercial counterparts. Here's a list of a few of my favorite plug-ins from the major groups of effects. This selection is purely subjective, but it should give you a start in finding the right stuff for you.

Filters: I actually use the VST EQ a good bit, but the kind of music I do involves fairly little EQ. I also use the Cubase StepFilter on occasion in my own music. For synth-style filtering, I usually use hardware, though the Prosoniq North Pole plug-in (www.prosoniq.com) is a very good free synth-style filter. German hardware synth manufacturer Waldorf (www.waldorf-music.com) also makes D-Pole, a digital multimode filter patterned after its hardware filters. I also use vocoders a good bit, and Orange Vocoder from Prosoniq is one of the finest ever made.

Dynamics: The Universal Audio UAD-1 card (www.uaudio.com) is a hardware/software plug-in combination that works great on both PCs and Macs. The package includes a PCI card that performs the calculations, so adding the amazing sound compressors places almost no hit on the CPU. The plug-ins include fantastic-sounding emulations of the super-famous (and super-expensive) LA-2A limiter, Fairchild, and 1176N compressors. I use the UAD-1 or the PSP Audioware (www.pspaudioware.com) Vintage Warmer for full mixes.

Delay: I'm a delay fanatic, so I use everything, from the Cubase delay plug-ins to old guitar pedals. One of my favorite plug-ins is Ohm Boyz from Ohm Force (www.ohmforce.com) software. It's a really powerful delay with an easy-to-use interface. Another great plug-in is the PSP 84 delay (also from PSP Audioware), which was inspired by a famous early digital Lexicon delay. Both sound great and have a lot of modulation possibilities. A final option is the Karlette plug-in from Steinberg. If it didn't come with your copy of Cubase, you can download this emulated tape delay from the Steinberg Web site (www.steinberg.net). The freeware TempoDelay from Voxengo (www.voxengo.com) is another great option and the price is right.

Modulation: I've spent a lot of money and time collecting a good number of funky old hardware flangers and phasers, and I do a lot of my modulation effects with them, but there are plug-ins that sound great. Mobilohm from Ohm Force is an extremely versatile phaser plug-in, and again the plug-ins included with Cubase are pretty good, too.

A

ReWire and Cubase

Cubase is designed to be a complete audio and MIDI music production system, and you can use it from start to finish for many projects. Even so, there are some situations where additional tools might improve a project or make it easier to finish. Steinberg recognized early, though, that letting other developers create tools to work within Cubase would greatly extend what it can do. Its VST instruments, which you've already learned about, let developers create software-based sound generators that work inside Cubase.

In this chapter, you will learn how to configure Cubase as a ReWire master application and how to configure other ReWire-savvy applications as slaves and then share audio and MIDI with them. To illustrate the use of ReWire with Cubase, this chapter uses two third-party programs—Reason and Live— as examples. The discussion applies equally, however, to other ReWire applications you might use with Cubase.

What Is ReWire?

ReWire is a protocol developed by Propellerheads (www.propellerheads.se), makers of Reason, and Steinberg. While VST instruments work inside of Cubase, ReWire lets other programs run beside it while sharing audio, MIDI, and synchronization information between programs. Its original purpose was to enable Propellerheads' synthesis and sampling applications (such as the very successful Reason and Rebirth) to work seamlessly with other music applications—such as Cubase—and with each other. Today, ReWire is supported by many applications from companies other than Steinberg and Propellerheads.

What Does ReWire Do?

ReWire allows multiple music applications to share audio, MIDI, and tempo information. When two applications are "ReWired" together, they almost act as one big application, leveraging the capabilities of the separate applications into (one hopes) a more creative and productive whole.

Many applications support ReWire in one form or another, but two applications commonly linked to Cubase via ReWire are Propellerheads' Reason (**Figure 15.1**) and Ableton Live (www.ableton.com) (**Figure 15.2**). Reason is an integrated sequencer/sampler/synthesis application, and Live is a performance and recording tool for working with audio loops. This chapter includes examples of these two applications, but the basic rules apply to any ReWire-savvy program.

You may be asking why ReWire would be necessary. Cubase, after all, has its own set of software synthesis and loop tools, so why use anything else? The answer is nothing more than that there is more than one way to skin a cat, and some are quicker, easier (for us of course, but about the same for the cat), and more productive. Reason, for example, includes a boatload of cool pattern-sequencing options that no other program has. And with ReWire, instead of creating tracks in Reason, exporting loops or MIDI files, and then importing them to Cubase, you can run everything together in real time.

Figure 15.1 Reason is an integrated sequencer/sampler/synth application that supports ReWire.

Figure 15.2 Live is a powerful looping and performance application that supports ReWire.

Figure 15.3 ReWire applications are treated like devices and need to be activated in this menu.

Figure 15.4 Clicking any button will activate that audio channel for a ReWire program.

Figure 15.5 Reason now has six channels of audio that can be routed to Cubase.

Enabling a ReWire Application in Cubase

When a ReWire-capable application is installed, it becomes available to Cubase, but you have to activate it in Cubase before Cubase and the ReWire application can work together. When the ReWire application is enabled, Cubase creates ReWire channels in the mixer and allows the ReWire application, like Reason, to connect with Cubase. If the application is not ReWire-enabled in Cubase, it will simply open as a stand-alone application, unaware that it ought to be synced with Cubase and sending MIDI and audio data back and forth.

To enable a ReWire application:

1. With Cubase open but with the ReWire application closed, open the Devices menu in Cubase and select the application you want to configure (**Figure 15.3**). The ReWire configuration panel (**Figure 15.4**) for the selected application opens, showing available and active audio channels.

2. Click the power buttons to activate as many ReWire audio channels as you want (**Figure 15.5**). The buttons on the active channels will turn blue.

3. When you have finished, close the window and open the Cubase mixer to see the ReWire channels.

✔ Tip

■ Up to 64 audio channels can be activated for *each* ReWire application. That's usually more than you'll need, but it's nice to know that you have them. Between 8 and 16 channels is usually enough for me, and selecting a number in this range makes the Cubase mixer less cluttered.

Starting and Closing ReWire Applications

ReWire applications need to be started and stopped in a particular order to work correctly. This is because one ReWire application will always be the master (telling other applications when to play), and all others will always be slaves to that master application. The ReWire slaves get their tempo and synchronization information from the master application, and the first ReWire application opened will always be the master. Most of the time, you will want Cubase to be the master, with the other applications slaves to it, so you should follow this sequence when working on a Cubase/ReWire project:

1. Start Cubase.

2. Start the ReWire applications.

3. When you are finished working, close the ReWire applications.

4. Close Cubase.

If you try to close Cubase with any ReWire applications active, Cubase will display an error window and refuse to quit (**Figure 15.6**).

Some ReWire applications (including Cubase) will work only as a ReWire master, and some will work only as a ReWire slave (Reason, for example). Others (such as Live) will work as either a ReWire master or ReWire slave; Live can be slaved to Cubase, or it can be the master with Reason slaved to it. However, if Live is the master application and Reason is slaved to it, then Cubase can't use ReWire with either of them. This can sometimes get confusing; just remember that only one application can be the master, and all others must be slaves to it.

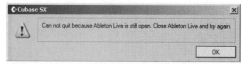

Figure 15.6 This error message appears when ReWire master and slave programs are not closed in the correct order.

Transport Controls and Looping

One very convenient benefit of using ReWire is that when you use it, the Transport bar of any application can be used to control the others. For example, if you are editing a part in a ReWire slave application and move the left and right locators and start playback, the controls will all move transparently in the master application. This feature can save you a whole lot of mouse clicking, window hiding, and general messing around when you're working with ReWire applications.

Figure 15.7 The Cubase and Reason transport panels, set to 87 beats per minute.

Figure 15.8 You can enter a new tempo manually in the tempo track editor by typing a number in the Tempo field.

Figure 15.9 After you change the setting in the tempo track editor, both the ReWire master (Cubase) and the ReWire slave (Reason) show the new tempo.

✔ Tips

- A fair number of ReWire applications have the annoying habit of sending Cubase a tempo change when they start. The result is that the Cubase tempo track is turned off. It's not a huge problem—just click the Master button on the Transport bar and all is well, but it is a drag.

- There's a lot more to the tempo track and its editor than is discussed in this book. If you have music with tempo changes, you should research the tempo track in the Cubase electronic documentation.

Tempo and ReWire

There are two ways to set tempo in Cubase. One is to simply type a setting for the project on the Transport bar. The other way is to use the tempo track in Cubase, which is turned on and off using the Master button on the Cubase Transport bar. The latter is the better way to go when you're working with ReWire applications. (The tempo track was discussed in Chapter 3, "Starting a Project.")

If you are using a tempo track, you should make all tempo changes for your project in Cubase. If you make changes in tempo with a ReWire slave application, it might turn off the tempo track and reset the tempo in Cubase. The following example uses the tempo track to change the tempo for both Reason and Cubase.

To change the tempo for Cubase and ReWire applications:

1. In Cubase, click the Project menu and select Tempo Track.

   You will be changing the tempo for both Cubase and the ReWire application—in this case, Reason. **Figure 15.7** shows the Cubase and Reason Transport bars. Note that the tempo for both is 87 beats per minute.

2. When the Tempo Track editor opens, double-click the Tempo field and type a new tempo (**Figure 15.8**).

   When you check the ReWire slave, you will find that the tempo has changed to match the Cubase master tempo (**Figure 15.9**).

Using Multiple ReWire Applications

Cubase can use more than one ReWire application simultaneously. Using multiple ReWire applications helps you keep everything running together in real time, as long as you don't get confused working with a lot of open windows and applications. There are only a few points to remember:

◆ You need to enable audio inputs for each application (**Figure 15.10**).

◆ If you are using Cubase it must be the ReWire master, so it must be started first, before any of the ReWire slave applications are opened.

◆ Don't forget to open the ReWire applications (and the projects in those applications) the next time you work on the project in Cubase.

Figure 15.10 Two ReWire programs enabled.

Multiple Displays for Multiple Applications

If you use a lot of ReWire applications, you might want to consider upgrading your studio by adding another monitor or two. Many modestly priced video cards have dual outputs and can drive two monitors. Digital videographers and graphic designers have long used multiple monitors to extend their workspaces so they spend less time showing, hiding, and moving application windows.

Using two or more monitors with Cubase provides a lot of flexibility. In Cubase-only projects, the project window can be stretched across both monitors, or one monitor can show the project window while the other displays the mixer. For a project including Reason, one monitor can display the Reason rack while the other shows Cubase. Most people have limited budgets for studio upgrades, but a few hundred dollars for a new or additional video card and monitor can make your time in Cubase a lot more fun and productive.

Figure 15.11 One module in a Reason project: a preset of the legendary Rhodes electric piano.

Figure 15.12 Selecting the Reason Rhodes sampler in Cubase.

Sending MIDI via ReWire

Most, though not all, ReWire programs are synthesis applications. Some include their own sequencers, while others work exclusively with MIDI data sent from a ReWire master application. In either case, it is usually possible to send MIDI to the ReWire sound generators, regardless of whether the ReWire slave includes a sequencer to generate its own MIDI.

Reason, for instance, has a built-in sequencer that is linked via ReWire as a Cubase slave, and it can also receive MIDI directly from Cubase.

To send MIDI from Cubase to a ReWire slave:

1. Open both Cubase and the other application with ReWire enabled; for example, open both Cubase and Reason.

2. Set up the ReWire synth or sampler as you want.

   Figure 15.11 shows a Reason sampler named Rhodes that includes a Reason electric piano preset.

3. Returning to Cubase, click a MIDI file to select it and open the Track Inspector for that track.

4. In the Track Inspector, open the MIDI output drop-down menu and make a selection.

   In addition to the MIDI hardware and VST instruments, all possible Reason MIDI destinations are also visible. **Figure 15.12** shows the Rhodes sampler being selected.

5. Start playback in the project to trigger the ReWire instrument.

✔ Tip

■ Note also that using this method of MIDI routing lets you play a ReWire instrument directly from Cubase, even if it has its own sequencer. You might prefer this approach to working in the sequencer included with the ReWire slave application.

Sending Audio via ReWire

The first two ReWire audio inputs in Cubase are almost always dedicated to the full mix coming from the ReWire application. When you use Live with Cubase, for example, the master two-channel output from the program will be routed by default to ReWire inputs 1 and 2 in Cubase. That's fine for many situations, but part of what makes ReWire so great is its multichannel capability. If you want to apply EQ to one Live loop in Cubase or to bus a synth sound from Reason to a group with other VSTi synth sounds and a delay insert, ReWire lets you. Not every ReWire slave application manages this routing in the same way, but all will work somewhat like the following example, which uses Live.

Saving ReWire Projects

One of the great advantages of a software system like Cubase is that when a project is saved, every element is also saved. This includes not just audio files, but mix settings, plug-ins, software synths, and everything else that makes a project a song. When you start using ReWire applications, you bring an extra layer of power and complexity to your workflow and project file management.

Here are some keys to help you master file management.

- First, always save all ReWire slave projects in the same folder as the Cubase project. This makes finding your files later easier.

- Second, if you import samples or loops to the ReWire slave application, make a folder inside the Cubase project folder and copy all of the imported files into that folder. If you move the project later, you won't miss any of the files if you keep them together with your project.

- Last, include something in the file name of the Cubase project to indicate that it uses a ReWire application. For example, I include an R for Reason in the name, so WhirlingDub.cpr becomes WhirlingDub_R_.cpr.

Figure 15.13
Multiple audio busses activated for Live in Cubase.

Figure 15.14 Selecting a particular output bus in Live.

Figure 15.15 The left ReWire channel has the mix output from Live, but the second stereo pair is playing back the audio from the channel in Figure 15.14.

To route audio from a ReWire slave application:

1. Configure Cubase and Live to work via ReWire and enable more than one pair of ReWire inputs in Cubase (**Figure 15.13**).

2. Switch to Live. Each channel strip in Live has a drop-down menu for routing its output (**Figure 15.14**). Open this menu and select Bus 3/4.

3. Return to Cubase and open the mixer. Start playback of the project.

   The audio from the ReWire slave will play back on the channel selected in the slave application (**Figure 15.15**).

✔ Tip

■ Name your ReWire mixer channels right away, because they don't have even slightly descriptive channel names like VST instruments do.

Stand-alone Versus ReWire Applications

Many ReWire applications can be used either as stand-alone music-creation tools or as ReWire slaves. There are advantages to both, and the two methods are not mutually exclusive. Here are some pros and cons.

Stand-alone application

◆ Usually, stand-alone applications can use ASIO drivers directly, making routing audio to and from external hardware easier than when using Cubase and ReWire.

◆ Stand-alone applications may have some features that are unavailable when they're in ReWire slave mode. Live, for example, can use VST effects when the application is run alone, but it cannot use them when it's slaved via ReWire.

◆ Switching between stand-alone applications can become tiresome.

ReWire application

◆ The Cubase mixer is generally much more powerful and flexible than the mixer that comes with most ReWire applications, such as Live or Reason.

◆ Cubase is a top-quality audio recording and editing platform and is far superior to ReWire applications for adding overdubs and new audio.

◆ Audio from ReWire applications that do not support VST effects can be routed through those effects in Cubase when slaved.

◆ Cubase mixer automation, which is both powerful and easy to use, can be applied to ReWire channels. Many ReWire applications alone do not have the same quality and complexity of mixer automation.

✔ **Tip**

■ Here's one approach to working with ReWire: I often start songs in Live or Reason and then slave them to Cubase only after the first bits are ready. I record new tracks in Cubase and mix in Cubase, leaving the ReWire applications running as slaves. When a song is finished, I always archive all of the ReWire sounds and tracks with the rest of the project.

16

Automating a Mix

One theory of mixing holds that the only proper way to mix is with a board. If sounds are recorded correctly, according to this theory, all you need to do is push the faders up to unity gain and then leave things alone. You might get lucky with a track every now and then, and the board will be enough, but usually when you listen to your song with the levels about right, there will be some parts that you want to change.

Mix automation is the ability to record your mixing moves and have them play back automatically, rather than having to move the controls yourself every time you play the track. Instead of changing the level of the vocal track manually, for example, you can have Cubase record your changes to the fader and play them back automatically.

In this chapter, you will learn the two ways of creating automation in Cubase: by recording your actions in the Cubase mixer, and by creating automation manually in the Project window. You will learn about the tools available for manually creating automation and how to view and edit automation as efficiently as possible.

Why Automate Mixes?

For most of the time that music has been recorded and mixed, actual human beings have had to perform all of the changes to a mix in real time. Mixing, though, is like many areas of endeavor in that human solutions have become less prominent and technological solutions have expanded.

The simplest reason for automating a mix is that it makes mixing easier for you to do by yourself. Before the era of full-featured mixer automation, many studios had a team of mixers to set up and practice a mix and then perform each action at the right time. If one person forgot to mute the shaker after the second chorus, the only options were to live with the mistake or redo the whole mix. Mixer automation allows you to find such a mistake and fix it quickly. Automation also lets you make and set precision changes to your mix, such as fading a track, without having to move the faders yourself each time you play the mix.

One of the great advantages of working with software and digital mixers is that they usually have very deep and powerful mix automation. If you learn the automation features of Cubase and listen carefully, you will be able to add a great deal of polish to your mixes, because the program has world-class automation tools.

Writing Automation with the Mixer

Cubase offers two primary methods for creating automation. One is using the mouse or a remote controller and the Cubase mixer; the other is writing automation directly to automation tracks in the Project window. Most jobs can be accomplished about as well using either method, although you might find you prefer one method to the other. Manually writing automation is a bit less intuitive for some people, though it has the advantage of providing visual access to the audio waveform. You can start learning about automation by using the mixer, which makes automation obvious and graphical.

In the following example, you will automate a fader or two in a project. You'll start writing automation in Cubase and then move channel faders in the mixer. Cubase will be able to make those moves automatically if Read is turned on. Automation can be tricky to understand at first, so you might want to start with an empty project or a backup copy of a recorded project. Of course, you can undo or erase automation after the fact, but it's a bad idea to start learning automation on an important track. Always begin work on a copy.

To write automation with the mixer:

1. Open the Cubase mixer.

2. Click the global Write button to activate it if it isn't active already.

   The Write button is at the far left of the mixer; it is the button marked with a W (**Figure 16.1**).

   With Write turned on, Cubase will write automation.

3. Make sure the Read button is *not* active by clicking it if necessary.

   The Read button appears above the Write button and is labeled with an R.

4. Start the project playing and move a few of the faders in the mixer to create your automation (**Figure 16.2**).

5. Stop the project and rewind to where you began writing automation.

6. Click the R button (**Figure 16.3**) to activate reading of all automation. It's also usually a good idea to deactivate writing automation if you only want to read it.

7. Play the project.

   You will see the faders move just as you moved them when you wrote the automation in step 4.

Figure 16.1 This button turns on write automation for all channels in the mixer.

Figure 16.2 The faders are being moved with write automation enabled.

Figure 16.3 Turning on read automation for all mixer channels.

Figure 16.4 Select this menu to see all automation in a project.

Figure 16.5 Automation as it appears in the Project window.

Figure 16.6 Showing all automation used for a single track.

Viewing Automation

Cubase has top-quality tools for viewing and editing automation in the Project window. You'll learn more about editing and creating automation graphically later in this chapter, but seeing the automation in the Project window is a good way to start getting a better understanding of how automation works.

The easiest way to see automation for a project is to click the Project menu and select Show Used Automation (**Figure 16.4**).

◆ In the track list, all tracks with automation applied to them display a new automation subtrack for each automated parameter.

Figure 16.5 shows two tracks (this is an empty project). Audio 01 has no automation, and Audio 02 has one parameter automated.

◆ The name of the automated parameter appears on the automation subtrack; in Figure 16.5, the parameter is Volume.

◆ A line appears in the Event display showing the value of the automated parameter and any changes in it over time.

✔ Tip

■ You can also show and hide automation on a per-track basis. Right-click (Windows) or Control-click (Mac OS) the track in the track list for which you want to view automation. Select Show Used Automation (**Figure 16.6**).

Mixer Automation Modes

Not every setup or individual will write automation in the same way. Because of this, Cubase writes automation from the mixer in five different modes, which you can select in the Automation Mode pop-up menu in the Project window (**Figure 16.7**). Here is an explanation of each mode, with a few suggestions for using each one:

Figure 16.7 The five modes for writing automation from the mixer.

- ◆ **Touch Fader** mode will start writing automation when you click a control, and it will stop writing when you release the mouse. Touch Fader is usually the best mode for writing automation when using the mouse and the Cubase mixer.

- ◆ **Autolatch** mode will start writing automation when you click a control, and it will continue writing automation until you deactivate it manually or stop the transport. You need to use Autolatch if you're using one of the supported external controllers for Cubase, such as a Steinberg Houston controller, a MIDI fader box, or an external digital mixer that can send MIDI. You should also use Autolatch when you want to write over a large amount of previous automation.

- ◆ **X-Over** mode works like Autolatch mode, except that when you cross a line of previously written automation, writing is turned off. This mode is great for making small tweaks on previously written automation that is not quite as you want it to be.

- ◆ **Overwrite** is used for volume automation only. It works like Autolatch mode, but instead of writing automation only when the fader is touched, in Overwrite mode new automation is written from where playback starts to where it stops. This is useful if you don't like the previous automation and want to start over completely.

- ◆ **Trim** is also a volume-only mode. In Trim mode, the channel fader becomes a relative volume control. All automation moves remain intact, but moving the fader up or down raises or lowers the volume of all recorded automation.

✔ Tip

- ■ Over the course of a mix, you often will use more than one mode. You might write a first pass in Touch Fader mode, then make some tweaks in X-Over mode, and then decide you want to redo everything for one particular track; for that track, you would probably use Autolatch to write over all previous automation.

Figure 16.8 Turning the send effect off before writing automation.

Figure 16.9 Changing parameters for the plug-in while writing automation.

Figure 16.10 The result of the plug-in automation in the Project window.

Writing Plug-in Automation

By now, you might be asking, "What can I automate?" The answer is just about everything in the mixer, including fader level, pan, EQ, send and insert effects, and send/insert effects parameters. A good way to see the options available is to automate the amount of the signal sent to a send effect. This automation can be used to add different amounts of the effect to a track over the course of a song.

To write plug-in automation:

1. Create a send effect using an FX channel and select the send for a track to be automated. For now, click the power button to turn off the send effect on the track (**Figure 16.8**).

2. Activate write automation for all channels by clicking the W button on the left of the Cubase mixer. Deactivate read automation if it is active.

3. Set the automation mode to Touch Fader or Autolatch.

4. Start playing the project; then turn on the effect send and drag the blue-green slider to adjust the amount of the signal that goes to the send effect (**Figure 16.9**).

5. Stop playback to stop writing automation.

6. Turn off write automation and turn on read automation.

7. Rewind the project and play it back to see the automated moves, or look in the Project window to see the automation graphically represented (**Figure 16.10**).

Automating Effects Parameters

While automating the on/off status of an effects send and its level for one track is certainly useful, you can do much more with effects automation. Any parameter in a VST effect can be automated. While mixing, you might want to change the feedback on a delay plug-in, increase the depth of a phase shifter, or change the dry:wet ratio in a vocoder. In the following example, an insert effect is automated on an audio track.

To automate effects parameters:

1. For the channel you want to automate, select and activate an insert effect.

2. Activate write automation for all tracks, and deactivate read automation if necessary.

   Figure 16.11 shows a plug-in ready for automation.

3. Begin playing the project and change the effect parameters as you like; stop the project when you are finished.

4. Turn off write automation and turn on read automation.

5. Rewind the project and play it back to see your automated moves.

   You can also look in the Project window; insert effects automation will be visible in automation subtracks for the track that has been automated (**Figure 16.12**).

✔ Tip

■ Unfortunately, only VST plug-ins can be automated, so PC users with DirectX plug-ins are out of luck. If you use a DX plug-in, you might be able to control some or all of its parameters via MIDI; check the help files or manual for the effect.

Figure 16.11 The Write button is active, so this plug-in will write automation when its parameters are changed.

Figure 16.12 Automated insert plug-in parameters viewed in the Project window.

Figure 16.13
Automation subtracks for an audio channel.

Figure 16.14 A VST instrument, when automated, has its own track and automation subtracks.

Figure 16.15 Automation for inputs and outputs as shown in the Project window.

How Automation Is Displayed

By now, you've probably figured out that to automate anything in Cubase, you need to enable write automation, make whatever moves you want as the track is playing, enable read automation, and play back the project.

You can view all automation data for a project in the Project window, but what is being automated determines where in the Project window the automation data appears.

- ◆ **Channel strip** automation—including automated fader, pan, EQ, insert effects on/off status and parameters, and send effects on/off status and amount—is visible in automation subtracks under the automated track. **Figure 16.13** shows one audio channel with automation subtracks. Automation for MIDI tracks also is visible in subtracks below the track in the Project window.

- ◆ **VST instruments**, when automated, appear on their own automation tracks, with automation subtracks for each automated parameter. **Figure 16.14** shows a VST instrument that has been automated.

- ◆ **FX channels**, when automated, appear almost exactly like audio tracks. Each FX channel effect has its own entry in the track list and automation subtracks below it.

- ◆ **ReWire** automation is just like audio track automation and is viewed on automation subtracks below the ReWire channel on the Project window.

- ◆ **Master automation** is viewed in much the same way as VSTi and send effect automation. The master fader and all active output busses have automation tracks with subtracks. **Figure 16.15** shows master automation active.

Writing Automation for a Single Track

Up to now, all of the examples have involved turning on write automation for the entire project and then turning on read automation for the entire project. This is often the best way to work; when you are creating a first take of a mix, for example, you might want everything you touch to be recorded.

Later in a mix, though, it's common to want to change or write automation for a single track (or a few tracks) instead of for the whole project. A solo part may need to be carefully tweaked while the rest of the mix sounds great, or a part may need to be muted for certain sections of a song. Cubase allows you to turn automation reading and writing on and off on a per-track, per-effect, or per-instrument basis. The following example shows how to write automation for one track while reading previously created automation in the rest of the project.

Write button for a single channel

Figure 16.16 This button turns on write automation for this track only.

Figure 16.17 The track on the right will write new automation, and the other track will read automation.

To write automation for one track:

1. Open the Cubase mixer and find the channel strip you want to automate. Click the Write button for that channel (**Figure 16.16**).

2. Click the global Read button on the far left of the mixer to set all tracks to read automation.

3. You probably want to create all new automation data for your chosen track, so click the Read button for that channel to turn off read automation for it.

   Figure 16.17 shows two adjacent channels: one set to read automation, and the other channel set to write it.

4. Start playing the project and write new automated actions on the channel you want to modify.

5. Stop playback when you are finished.

6. Turn off write automation for the channel you just wrote. Then turn on read automation for that channel.

   Now when the project plays, you will hear the new automation.

Reading and Writing Automation at the Same Time

One of the tricky aspects of working with automation, particularly when changing automation already recorded, is figuring out when to read, when to write, and when to do both. The nice thing about having read and write active at the same time is that you can watch a track that is automated and then grab it whenever you want to try something new. The tricky part is what happens when you let go of that control.

Suppose, for example, that you want a sound that is panned hard left to move toward the center a little bit during a mix. If you enable read and write, you can hear everything happening on that track and then just snag the pan control when you want to move the sound closer to center. If you are in Autolatch mode, once you touch the pan control you will keep writing until you either turn off writing or stop the project. If you are in Touch Fader mode, though, as soon as you let go of the pan control, it will snap back to hard left.

If you find this confusing, the best approach is to use Autolatch mode with read turned off to write new automation for a track. Another option for tweaking an automated track is to make the finer changes using the graphical tools, which are covered next in this chapter.

Writing Automation Manually

Almost any action in Cubase can be done by hand, graphically, in the Project window, including writing automation. Many of the tools used to write automation are like those used in MIDI continuous controller editing, so if you know about them, you already know a good bit about the tools for creating and editing automation. In the next task, you will create a simple ramp-up in volume.

To write automation manually in the Project window:

1. Find the track in the Project window that you want to automate. Display the automation subtrack by clicking the small plus sign at the lower-left corner of the track (**Figure 16.18**).

2. In the automation subtrack, click the drop-down menu (**Figure 16.19**) and select Volume if it is not already selected.

   Your choice in this menu determines what parameter is viewed and edited in that automation subtrack.

3. On the toolbar, on the Draw tool, click the small arrow to open a drop-down menu to select the mode for this tool. Select Line (**Figure 16.20**).

4. Using the Line tool, drag in the automation subtrack, creating a line from low to high (**Figure 16.21**).

   When you release the mouse, a new automation line will be written (**Figure 16.22**).

5. Turn on read automation and play the track to hear the result. The track will ramp up in volume.

✔ Tip

■ The snap setting and value determine the granularity of the data created when writing automation in the Project window.

Figure 16.18 Clicking the small plus sign opens the automation subtracks.

Figure 16.19 This menu sets the parameter to be viewed in the subtrack. In this case, Volume is selected.

Figure 16.20 Selecting the Line tool on the toolbar.

Figure 16.21 Drawing a line of automation to write a volume change.

Figure 16.22 The result after releasing the mouse.

Figure 16.23 Selecting the Eraser tool.

Figure 16.24 Clicking this breakpoint with the Eraser tool will remove it.

Figure 16.25 After you remove the breakpoint, the volume change will begin from the correct value.

Deleting Automation Breakpoints

If you examine the results of the previous task, you can see one of the pitfalls of writing automation manually. You can see in Figure 16.22 that the ramp-up in volume probably isn't going to sound right with the sudden drop before it starts and the drop when it ends. Automation breakpoints indicate a change in direction or a change in value. Figure 16.22 has two breakpoints that need to be deleted for the automation to produce the desired sonic results.

To delete automation breakpoints:

1. Using the toolbar (**Figure 16.23**) or the contextual menu (right-click Windows, Control-click Mac OS), select the Eraser tool.

2. Click the breakpoint you want to delete to remove it (**Figure 16.24**).

✔ Tip

- **Figure 16.25** shows the automation for this track after the first breakpoint is erased. Keep in mind that the first automation breakpoint determines the initial value for the parameter, and the last automation breakpoint for a track sets the value extending to the right for the duration of the project. Sometimes a stray, forgotten breakpoint will cause all kinds of confusing results with automated parameters.

Other Breakpoint Operations

You can move automation breakpoints manually, just as you can move breakpoints and change curves when editing objects such as MIDI controllers. Here are a few operations you can perform on breakpoints using the Object Selection (or arrow) tool:

◆ You can move any breakpoint simply by dragging it (**Figure 16.26**).

◆ You can double-click with the Object Selection tool to create a new breakpoint, which you can move (**Figure 16.27**).

◆ You can use the Object Selection tool to select a group of breakpoints (**Figure 16.28**). You can then use the same tool to move these breakpoints as a group (**Figure 16.29**).

Figure 16.26 You can use the Object Selection tool to manually move automation breakpoints.

Figure 16.27 Moving a newly created breakpoint.

Figure 16.28 Selecting multiple breakpoints with the Object Selection tool.

Figure 16.29 With multiple breakpoints selected, you can move them as a group by dragging any one of them.

Figure 16.30 The blip in the middle of this event needs to be silenced.

Figure 16.31 Selecting the Draw tool.

Figure 16.32 This automation, created with the Draw tool, will effectively remove the section from the song.

✔ **Tip**

■ You can also use the Line tool to draw automation, and it has more than one mode. If you want to explore more drawing automation, try experimenting with the Line tool.

Writing Automation with the Draw Tool

One of the most useful tools for writing automation is the Draw tool (or pencil). It's particularly powerful because it's very visual—you can see the audio as you are making the changes to the mix. There are tons of applications for this tool, but this example and the next one show two of the more common ones.

Musicians often play an extraneous sound or inadvertently hit an instrument or microphone while performing. You can deal with this problem in a couple of ways, but mixer automation is one of the easiest and most visual approaches.

In **Figure 16.30**, the piece of the waveform in the middle of the illustration is the sound of the bass being hit unintentionally. In the Project window, you can see exactly where in the waveform the mistake occurs, so you can fix it right there.

To write automation with the Draw tool:

1. Zoom in so you can easily see the section of the project that you want to automate.

2. Select the parameter to be automated on the automation subtrack. In this example, we are automating Volume.

3. On the toolbar, click the Draw tool to select it (**Figure 16.31**) if it is not already selected.
   The mouse pointer will turn into a pencil.

4. On the track you want to automate, drag around the part of the track that you want to remove (**Figure 16.32**).

5. Turn on read automation for the track and play the project to hear the results of the automation.

Selectively Boosting a Part

Another common use for graphical, manually written automation is to selectively boost a small part of a track. Often mixers refer to this as *pushing* a certain part of a track. A syllable may be a little too quiet in one word, or a particular word may need to be emphasized in a vocal; in either case, you can use manual automation to boost the sound.

To boost part of a track with the Draw tool:

1. Zoom in to see the section of the track that you want to automate (**Figure 16.33**).

2. From the toolbar, select the Draw tool as described in the previous task.

   The mouse pointer will change into a pencil when you have the right tool selected.

3. Drag to create a small volume boost where the word should be more prominent (**Figure 16.34**).

4. Activate read automation for the track and play the project to hear the results of the automation.

✔ Tip

■ Pushing a track like this is very common in rock and pop productions. Often, most tracks will be carefully automated to bring out notes or words that are a bit weak. You may not want to go to that extreme, but if you do, you can use the method described in the preceding task.

Figure 16.33 One word in this phrase needs to be boosted slightly to make it more intelligible.

Figure 16.34 After writing with the Draw tool, only the one word in the phrase will be boosted.

Figure 16.35 The silence in the middle of this vocal can be muted automatically.

Figure 16.36 Select Mute for display on the automation subtrack.

Figure 16.37 The first mute automation breakpoint is created.

Figure 16.38 The completed mute automation.

Automating Mutes

Many people recording or mixing at home don't take advantage of an easy way to improve the sonic quality of their mixes: muting unused parts. Microphone input always has some hiss and room noise, no matter how careful the recording process, and as the number of microphones multiplies, so does the sonic trash.

Cubase has more than one way to get around this problem; the audio events themselves can be edited, for example. A common and simple approach, however, is to automate mutes.

To automate mutes:

1. Zoom in close enough to see the part that you want to mute.

   Figure 16.35 shows a stretch of relative silence between words that can be muted.

2. Turn off Snap.

3. Open an automation subtrack for the track if one isn't already open.

4. Select Mute from the drop-down menu to select the parameter that you want to automate (**Figure 16.36**).

5. Using the Draw tool, click the top half of the automation subtrack to turn on muting where the silence begins and ends (**Figure 16.37**).

6. Click the bottom half of the automation subtrack at about the same places to finish the muting (**Figure 16.38**).

7. If you need to adjust where the muting starts and ends, use the Object Selection tool to drag the breakpoints.

Viewing and Automating Other Parameters

Figure 16.39 The automation parameters initially available for an audio track.

The examples in this chapter use only a few of the available parameters. Of course, you are not limited to these parameters when creating automation. You can always open more automation subtracks to view additional parameters, but this procedure can get cumbersome and clutter the Project window mightily. As an alternative, you can set any automation subtrack to show any parameter for automation.

To view additional automation parameters:

1. Open an automation subtrack for the track you will be automating.

2. Click the drop-down menu (**Figure 16.39**) to see some of the more common parameters and select the one you want.

3. If the parameter you want is not in this list, select More (**Figure 16.40**).

4. In the Add Parameter window that opens, select the parameter that you want to automate (**Figure 16.41**) and click OK.

    When you return to the Project window, that parameter will be selected for that automation subtrack, and you can edit it as you wish.

Figure 16.40 Select More to see more possible automation destinations.

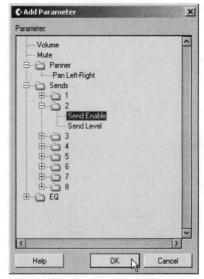

Figure 16.41 Some of the additional parameters, any of which can be viewed on any automation subtrack.

Non-Audio Channel Automation

The examples in this chapter have focused on audio channels, and these will probably be the most commonly automated tracks in a mix. But remember that you can automate any track in the mixer. Here are the other types of automation that you might want to use in a mix:

◆ **MIDI** channels are automated nearly identically to audio tracks. The only differences are the parameters that can be automated and the location of the automation subtracks under the MIDI tracks.

◆ **ReWire** channels are automated exactly like audio channels. You can create automation for them using all of the same tools as for audio channels.

◆ **VST instrument** channels are also automated like audio channels. One thing to remember when working with a VSTi, though, is that it's usually triggered by a MIDI channel. You can automate the level of a VSTi both by writing automation on the MIDI channel that triggers it and by writing automation on the VSTi output. This can sometimes create some confusion because the same result can come from two different places. You could change the volume of a VSTi, for example, by automating the fader for the VSTi output or by automating the fader on the MIDI channel that triggers the VSTi.

◆ **Group** channels use all of the same tools and parameters as audio tracks.

Two Types of Parameters

You probably noticed that Mute automation looks different from Volume automation. This makes sense if you remember that some parameters (mute, effect on/off, bypass) are either on or off, while other parameters (volume, pan, filter cutoff, delay feedback) can vary continuously.

On/off parameters are sometimes a little harder to see and edit manually. A parameter like Mute, since it has only two settings, is shown in the automation subtrack as set either fully to the top or fully to the bottom of the track. If the line is at the bottom of the track, the setting is off, and if it is at the top of the track, it's on.

Another quirk is that because all automation values start with an initial value, you sometimes need to add a breakpoint. In the previous example, the initial value was set to *off*, which is what we wanted. If you wanted to change that value, you would have added a breakpoint and defined it as *on*. The new value would remain in effect unless you added another breakpoint to change it. Remember, if you're editing on/off values, you may need to create a breakpoint to change the initial value established at the start of the track—otherwise it remains in effect.

An Example of Mix Automation

Everyone mixes and writes automation differently, but here are a few more suggestions based on how I generally do it.

I usually start out mixing a song with automation completely turned off. I have an external hardware controller for Cubase, so I start by adjusting the levels and basic EQ, compression, and effects settings so that the mix sounds good to me. If tracks need to go to groups, I set them up early so that all of the necessary mixer channels exist. I rarely automate EQ or compression at any stage in a song, and I often go back and change them throughout the mixing process.

Then I turn on write automation for all of the tracks and get the basics of the mix correct. I change fade and pan settings on the tracks that need modification and make whatever special changes I need to make. I do all of this in one pass; if it's a train wreck, I erase all automation for the track and start over.

Once I have a complete rough take, I turn on read automation for the whole mix and listen to it. Usually, there are obvious places where things aren't right, and in those cases, I usually redo the entire automation for that one track, writing to it while reading the other tracks. I do all of this, of course, with my hardware controller; you might want to try the same thing using the mouse and Cubase mixer.

The last thing I do with the hardware controller is muting. Usually I make a pass or two just writing mutes to any track that needs them, with both read and write automation turned on for all tracks.

With the mix in that state, normally I then switch to the Project window for any final exacting tweaks. I might more carefully control the level of some tracks or add specific automation to a soft synthesizer or automate the effects sends. For those tweaks, I turn off write automation for all tracks and turn on read automation for all tracks.

After I finish working in the Project window, the mix should be finished. Once I start writing automation manually, though, I rarely go back to the mixer or my hardware controller. I find switching back and forth to be confusing, and once I make the break into the Project window and begin manually writing automation, I usually stay there for the duration of the mix.

Using
External Effects

One of the best things about using Cubase
is the wealth of really interesting software
plug-ins—including the very good plug-ins
bundled with the program and a massive
collection of third-party VST plug-ins—that
you can use with Cubase.

That said, you may already own some hardware processing equipment you really like
and want to keep using. Maybe you have a
favorite external digital reverb box, a super
high-quality outboard EQ/compressor, or
an early '80s analog stereo phase shifter that
sounds heavenly. You certainly don't want
to be forced to choose between your digital
recording system and your collection of
favorite (and expensive) external hardware.
Cubase doesn't force you to do so, as long as
you have a few extra outputs on your sound
card and are willing to spend a little time
learning how to get the job done.

In this chapter, you'll learn how to set up
Cubase to use external signal processors as
both send and insert effects. You'll discover
some of the options for monitoring hardware effects as you work with them and also
learn how to include external effects in your
final mix.

Routing External Effects

Using software effects is certainly easier than working with external hardware. If you are using VST or DirectX effects, all of the routing and processing happens right inside the computer, and all of your parameters and settings are saved with the project. Cubase even manages the plug-in latency for you in some circumstances.

Using external effects is a bit more cumbersome than using software, but it's not all that difficult once you understand how the process works. This is the basic procedure:

1. The audio from a channel or send is routed to one of the hardware outputs on your sound card.

2. The signal travels from the sound card output to the input of the effect unit and is processed by the effect.

3. The processed signal is routed back from the output of the external effect unit to an input on your sound card. From there, it can be monitored in (or recorded with) Cubase.

As you can probably guess, you usually need at least four outputs on your sound card to do all of this. The two main outputs are for monitoring your mix, and the second pair can be used to route audio to the external effect. If you use many external effects devices, you'll need to assess the number of I/Os you'll need on your sound card.

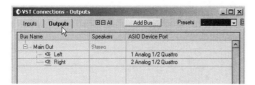

Figure 17.1 Selecting the Outputs tab on the VST Connections panel.

Figure 17.2 This panel is used to create a new VST connections bus.

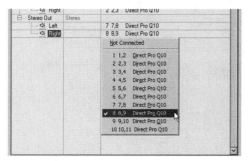

Figure 17.3 Choosing the hardware outputs for the bus.

Figure 17.4 Naming the bus.

Configuring VST Connections

To use an external effect, you'll need to have the correct VST connections active, and you should name them if possible.

To configure VST connections for external effects:

1. From the Devices menu, select VST Connections.

2. On the VST Connections panel that opens, select the Outputs tab (**Figure 17.1**).

3. Click the Add Bus button (also visible in Figure 17.1) to open the Add Bus panel.

4. Select a stereo or mono bus, depending on the kind of effect you're using, and click OK (**Figure 17.2**).

5. On the right side of the VST Connections panel, select the physical outputs for the external effect.

   Figure 17.3 shows outputs 7 and 8 for my sound card being set up as outputs.

6. If a particular effect will be used permanently on a certain channel, you might want to name the VST connection for it (**Figure 17.4**).

CONFIGURING VST CONNECTIONS

Using an External Send

The simplest way to use an external send effect is to use the available send effects on the channel strips to route audio to the VST output bus. The process is the same whether you route your audio to external hardware or to internal send effects or groups. A channel—whether audio, VSTi, or ReWire—can route a signal to any FX channel, any output bus, or any active group channel. Each send on the channel strip can also route to any active VST outputs. To use an external effect, you need to make the VST outputs available using the Devices menu.

Figure 17.5 Select Sends to make send effects visible in the extended view area for the channel.

To create an external send effect:

1. Be sure that your VST connections are configured to route audio correctly to your external effect (see "Configuring VST Connections" earlier in this chapter).

2. On the mixer channel that will be the send source, click the drop-down menu above the input setting and select Sends (**Figure 17.5**) to make send effects visible in the extended mixer.

3. Click one of the effects slots and, from the drop-down menu, select the hardware output for the external effect.

   Figure 17.6 shows Mo FX being selected for a send slot.

4. Click the power button for the send and adjust the blue-green slider to control the amount of the signal from the channel that is fed to the external effect (**Figure 17.7**).

Figure 17.6 Selecting one of the external effects, in this case, one named Mo FX, as the send destination.

Figure 17.7 Adjusting the amount of the signal sent to the external effect.

Figure 17.8 Use this button to show or hide input and output routings in the Cubase mixer.

Figure 17.9 The Output setting.

Figure 17.10 Selecting the external effect that will be an insert effect for the mixer channel.

ReWire and VSTi Effects

Always keep in mind that in Cubase, you can do anything with a ReWire or VSTi channel that you can do with an audio channel. This includes using external effects as both sends and inserts. You can run your favorite Reason synth through a funky old analog delay, route a VSTi synth through an external synth filter, or run your samples triggered in a software sampler through an external reverb unit.

Creating an External Insert Effect

In my experience, when people work with digital systems, they tend to use more external send effects—such as outboard reverb, delay, or modulation units—than external insert effects. The common insert effects such as EQ and compression are usually created with plug-ins or applied to the signal on its way to the computer before it's recorded. Still, there is no reason why you can't run a track through an external insert effect if you want to do so. If you have a special synth filter or a borrowed "magic pixie dust" compressor or EQ that you want to use on a track, it's no more difficult to use this than a send effect. The Mo FX unit used in the previous send effect example also has a great tremolo effect; the following example uses the same effect unit as an insert.

To create an external insert effect:

1. Be sure the VST connections are properly configured and active.

2. At the lower left of the Cubase mixer, in the global section, click the Show Input and Output Settings button (**Figure 17.8**).

3. In the extended mixer, click the output setting, which is located at the top of the channel strip, above the Sends, EQs, and so on (**Figure 17.9**).

4. In the pop-up menu that opens, select the external effect.

   Figure 17.10 shows the Mo FX effect being selected.

Monitoring the Effect Results

The previous two examples show you how to route audio to the proper locations, but you have to be able to hear the result of the external effect. There are several ways to do this, either using external hardware or through Cubase.

◆ You can use an external hardware mixer to mix the effected signal with the master output from Cubase.

◆ If your sound card has a mixer control panel, you often can use this instead of an external hardware mixer.

◆ You can monitor using an input channel in the Cubase mixer.

◆ Depending on the latency of your sound card, you may be able to monitor with Cubase by selecting the inputs on your sound card for a channel that is record enabled.

Although all three monitoring options have their advantages and disadvantages, you should monitor the effect return through Cubase if you can. This approach gives you more options at mixdown, such as a fader to quickly turn the effect return up or down in the mix, and the ability to record the effect return to its own track for archiving or for further mixing. You can also automate a Cubase channel, but then you may not be able to automate an external hardware mixer or the mixer control panel for your sound card.

Figure 17.11 The Inputs panel for VST connections, with some of the inputs named so you can more easily set up monitoring.

Figure 17.12 Using the Track inspector to select an input bus; if you monitor it, you'll hear the effects return.

To monitor an effect return through Cubase:

1. Route whatever channels you want through the external effect.

2. Note which of the inputs on your sound card takes the signal back from the external effect. If necessary, configure VST connections inputs using the VST Connections panel.

   Figure 17.11 shows the inputs on my sound card; note that I've named the effects return on some of the inputs.

3. In the Project window, find an empty track, and be sure to choose a track that is stereo for a stereo effect or mono for a mono effect.

4. In the Track inspector, select the inputs that receive the signal from the external effect (**Figure 17.12**).

5. Record enable the track to monitor it in the mix.

✔ Tip

■ Latency is introduced both on the way out of the computer and on the way back in, so the total latency of the external effect loop will be twice the latency of your sound card. If the latency of your sound card 1.5 ms, you probably won't notice it much. If you have to run at higher latency, though, latency may become a problem, particularly for rhythmic parts like drums and percussion. If latency is an issue, the easiest thing to do is to move the track back in time a little bit in the Project window.

MONITORING THE EFFECT RESULTS

Using Groups for External Effects

In Chapter 13, "Audio Effect Plug-ins," you learned how to use group channels for effects. Groups are convenient because they use one fader to control the levels of multiple tracks, they can apply a single effect to more than one source track, and they can chain multiple effects. The same actions can be applied to groups and external effects. For example, some outboard reverb units sound horrible when too much low-end sound is fed to them; using groups, you can apply a high-pass filter to the low-end sound out of the signal before it is sent to the external reverb. You can also have a delay plug-in as an insert on the group and then feed the delays to an external chorus, reverb, or phase-shifting effect.

To use an external effect via a group channel:

1. Choose a group channel, add any insert effects or EQs to it that you want, and name the group (**Figure 17.13**).

2. Click the lower-left corner of the Cubase mixer to display the Input and Output settings in the extended mixer.

3. Route the group channel to the VST connection that is connected to the external effect (**Figure 17.14**).

Figure 17.13 If a group channel has a good, descriptive name, you can more easily set up send effects to it because the send effects drop-down menu will display it.

Figure 17.14 Choosing the output bus for the group channel.

Figure 17.15 In the channel with the send effect, you can select the group channel as the send destination.

Stereo vs. Mono Effects

One of the few things that I don't like about Cubase is the way it deals with mono channels and effects. The mixer allows effects sends to be either pre-fader or post-fader, but they cannot be post-pan and post-fader. This is a minor limitation unless you happen to perform very complex effect routings, such as sending multiple mono channels to an external stereo effect. You're out of luck if you want to maintain the pan position of the mixer channel at the output; you can choose only the left or the right channel of the hardware outputs on your sound card.

Let's say, for example, that you have three tracks: one each panned left, center, and right. You can't send them to an external stereo effect and keep their pan positions for the effect, because for each track you can select only either the left or right output on the sound card. The only option is to copy the tracks to three new mono tracks, route them to a group, where they'll retain their pan settings, and send the group to the external effect. The routing of the entire channel is post-fader and post-pan. The process is cumbersome, but it works.

4. Find a track to use as a source for the external effect. Select Sends to be viewed in the extended mixer.

5. Choose an empty send effect slot and click it to open the drop-down menu. Select the name of the group from the list (**Figure 17.15**).

6. Adjust the blue-green slider for the send effect to send more or less of the signal to the group and external effect.

7. Repeat steps 3 through 6 for any additional channels you want to send to the group or external effect.

✔ Tip

■ You can even use groups to route multiple tracks through an external effect as an insert if you want to get really nutty.

Pre-Fader and External Effects

External effects, more than software plug-ins, can have problems interfacing with line-level equipment such as a computer and sound card. Some older effects are designed for much lower input levels than current gear, and you may wind up using crazy effects like guitar distortion pedals or vocoder inputs. Because of these potential problems when using external effects, you may particularly want to be able to control the level sent to an effect by making it pre-fader.

Pre-fader send effects allow you to send any amount of the signal to the effect, no matter where the channel fader is set. The fader may be set to zero, with the track not playing in the mix, but a pre-fader send will still route the signal to the effect.

To use an external effect pre-fader:

1. Configure the VST connections to route audio to the external effect.

2. In the Cubase mixer, find the track that you want to send to the external effect pre-fader and select Sends from the drop-down menu to view send effects in the extended view area.

3. Click a send effect slot and select the output that connects to the external effect (**Figure 17.16**).

4. Click the button to make the send a pre-fader effect (**Figure 17.17**). When the button is selected, it turns orange.

5. Adjust the blue-green slider (**Figure 17.18**) to control the amount of the signal that is sent to the effect.

   Because the effect is pre-fader, this slider alone will control the level sent to the effect, regardless of the setting on the main channel fader.

Figure 17.16 Selecting the output bus, just as you would for a post-fader effect.

Figure 17.17 This button makes the send a pre-fader effect. The button turns orange when it is selected.

Figure 17.18 Adjust the amount of the pre-fader sent to the external effect.

PRE-FADER AND EXTERNAL EFFECTS

Mixing with External Effects

There are a couple of serious differences between mixing with external effects (or a combination of external effects and plug-ins) and mixing in a purely software environment. The biggest difference is probably that, when working only with plug-ins, you can bounce, render, and process audio offline, at a time of your choosing. When external effects are introduced, though, all mixing and processing will usually happen in real time.

The process gets most complex when you have to create a final mix. How do you include your external effects, such as delays and reverbs, in the main mix? The answer has a great deal to do with how you are monitoring. If you are monitoring with an external mixer or your sound card mixer control panel, probably the best approach is to record to another computer or hard disk recorder.

If you are monitoring your external effects through Cubase, you have two options. First, you can record the master output to another machine, as you would if you were using an external mixer. Second, you can record all of your effects returns to audio tracks. Then, using the recorded effects returns as audio tracks within Cubase, you can bounce and render mixes in much the same way as you would in a software-only effects setup.

I recommend that you use this last option if you can, recording your effects returns to a track in Cubase. This requires only one pass through the song, makes creating a final mix easy, and gives you an archive of the output of your external effects.

EXPORTING & RENDERING TRACKS

When you work in Cubase, you'll spend most of your time working with audio and MIDI files within the program. Sometimes, though, you will need to create a file that will be played back outside of Cubase: for instance, when you want to create a final stereo mix for mastering, or when you want to generate a file that can be streamed over a Web server.

You may also sometimes want to create a stereo track from a larger group of tracks in the course of a project. Once you have a multitrack drum mix sounding good, for example, it may be easier to work with it as a single stereo file. Or you may want to save the output of a VST instrument or a ReWire track to an audio file for further mixing or manipulation.

All of these situations require the same fundamental processes, as you will see in this chapter. In this chapter, you will learn how to bounce multiple audio events and parts to a single file. You will also learn how to print effects and EQ to a track by rendering a new file with the effects included. You will also learn how to create a final mix of your song, both as an uncompressed, full-bandwidth audio file and using a number of compressed audio file formats.

Bouncing, Exporting, and Rendering

When people talk about the various ways that Cubase can save, combine, and output audio files, they often use multiple terms interchangeably, even though they refer to slightly different processes. This can be quite confusing. This chapter focuses on rendering, but you may also hear people use the terms *bouncing* and *exporting* to refer to the same process. Here are some definitions to help you understand how the processes differ.

◆ **Rendering** is the process of saving a new version of a track or tracks with effects, fades, mixing moves, and other processing included in the rendered file. In other words, the real-time changes in the sound are printed to the new file.

◆ **Bouncing** refers to a technique used with analog tape decks when a project needs more tape tracks than are available. On a four-track system, for example, music recorded on the first three tracks may be mixed onto the empty fourth track. This frees the original three tracks for more recording. Believe it or not, many classic recordings were made using just this process.

◆ **Exporting** a sound or track saves it in a new format, but the piece sounds the same. For instance, you might export WAV files as SoundDesigner II files for use in another program, or you might export a loop or sound to a new format to load it into a hardware sampler.

Most of this chapter focuses on rendering—creating a new file with mix or effects processing included in the saved file—but you will also learn a bit about bouncing and exporting.

Figure 18.1 Selecting all events on a single track.

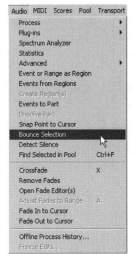

Figure 18.2 Choose from the menu to bounce the selected events to a new file.

Figure 18.3 The result of the bounce; compare this result to the separate events in Figure 18.1.

Bouncing a Track

Bouncing in Cubase terms means something slightly different than bouncing in analog tape recording. In Cubase, bouncing involves taking discrete parts and events on a track and combining them into a single event. A heavily edited vocal line or guitar part, for example, can be bounced to a new file that includes all of the edits. You can use bouncing to make an edited file easier to see in the Project window or to create a file that is easier to import into another program for further editing or processing. The following task shows you how to bounce all of the events in an edited track to a new file and event.

To bounce an audio track:

1. Select the parts and events you want to bounce. You can select them manually or open the context menu for the track in the track list (**Figure 18.1**) and choose Select All Events.

2. With the events and parts selected, open the context menu and select Audio > Bounce Selection, or use the Audio menu and select Bounce Selection (**Figure 18.2**). A status bar shows the progress of the bounce, and a dialog box opens when the file has been created.

3. Choose Replace to place the bounced file on the track and replace the selected audio. **Figure 18.3** shows the result of the bounce.

✔ Tip

■ Notice that the bounce here involves a bit of rendering. The last event in Figure 18.3 includes changes made to the level and fade with the handles, and those are included in a bounce; however, other effects and processing are not included.

Bouncing Multiple Tracks

You may encounter a problem if you record in Cubase but want to mix your song in another program, such as Pro Tools or Digital Performer, or on another system. One way to eliminate the problem is to bounce every track in your project. Doing this chews up hard disk space quickly, but you will finish with a discrete file for each track that is exactly the same length as the original, which then can be imported into another application for mixing.

To bounce more than one track:

1. Set up events and parts with all edits, fades, and crossfades just as you want them.

   Figure 18.4 shows a group of three tracks that will be bounced.

2. From the toolbar or context menu, choose the Range Selection tool.

3. Using the Range Selection tool, select the intended range for the tracks that you want to bounce (**Figure 18.5**).

4. Open the context menu and select Audio > Bounce Selection, or do the same using the Audio menu.

5. In the dialog box that opens, select Replace. The bounced tracks will replace the originals (**Figure 18.6**). Those files can be imported to another platform for mixing.

Figure 18.4 Three tracks before a bounce.

Figure 18.5 The Range Selection tool selecting all of the tracks.

Figure 18.6 After the bounce, each track is continuous and includes the edits and fades from the original events.

Figure 18.7 Setting the channel fader.

Figure 18.8 Setting the left and right locators.

Figure 18.9 The Export Audio Mixdown dialog box: These settings will create a new mono 24-bit file.

Rendering a Track

To render audio, you follow a basic set of instructions, described here and used in the rest of this chapter. Cubase has the ability to spit out an exact digital copy of whatever appears at its master outputs, and the file can include insert effects, send effects, automation, and EQs. The following task shows you all of the steps, including how to print the compression and EQ settings on a track.

To render a single track with effects:

1. Set the EQ and compression as you want for the track and then click the S button to solo the track.

2. Set the channel fader to 0.00 (**Figure 18.7**), or raise or lower the fader to make the rendered file louder or softer.

3. Open the mixer and set the master fader to 0.00 or raise or lower the fader to make the rendered file louder or softer.

4. Set the left and right locators (**Figure 18.8**) at the boundaries of the part of the track that you want to render.

5. From the File menu, select Export > Audio Mixdown.

6. In the Export Audio Mixdown dialog box, set the options you want for the file.

   Figure 18.9 shows the file name set to BassCompFX and specifies creation of a mono, 24-bit, 44.1-kHz WAV file. The Pool and Audio Track buttons are selected, so the rendered file will also be brought back into Cubase on another audio track.

7. After you set all of the options in the dialog box as you wish, click Save.

   A status bar will show the progress of the export process.

Track Rendering Versus Audio Processing

Rendering a single mono or stereo track (as described in this chapter) and processing audio (as described in Chapter 9, "Advanced Audio Editing") are somewhat similar operations. In previous versions of Cubase (and in many other audio programs), the only way to print effects and EQ to a track was to use a render-and-import file operation. In Cubase, you can use either rendering/importing or audio processing, and there are advantages and disadvantages to each method.

Rendering and importing gives you a few options that aren't available with audio processing. For example, consider the application of EQ to a track: you can print VST EQ when rendering, but the only way to apply EQ to a track with audio processing is to use a plug-in. You can also use groups for send effects when rendering, and you can export multiple tracks, or a full mix, to a single file; neither of these operations are possible with audio processing.

However, you can undo, edit, and rearrange audio processing after the fact, whereas if you want to change a rendered file later, you have to make your edits and render the file again. Audio processing is also a little quicker and more intuitive.

My advice is to use rendering for the situations where it's necessary, such as when creating mixes and printing send effects to a track, and to use audio processing the rest of the time. In any case, it's important to learn how to do both well.

Figure 18.10 The selected range shows the offset in an exported file.

Figure 18.11 The bottom, rendered track has been moved manually back to match the timing of the original.

Figure 18.12 With Snap on, the file can be snipped easily.

Figure 18.13 You can also use the Delay parameter in the Track inspector to correct the offset.

Workarounds for Timing Offset

Rendering a track sometimes produces an offset in timing within the exported file. If the timing on your rendered track seems a bit off, one possible cause is that plug-in latency may not be correctly factored in. In addition, some people report that certain combinations of ASIO cards and computer hardware generate this problem.

Figure 18.10 shows a timing offset. The Range Selection tool is highlighting about 25 milliseconds of silence incorrectly inserted into the rendered file, which is on the bottom. The rise in each waveform should happen at the same time. There are two primary ways to work around this problem:

◆ Turn off Snap and manually line up the files (**Figure 18.11**). Then turn Snap back on and use the Scissors tool to snip the beginning of the file (**Figure 18.12**).

◆ Open the main tab in the Track inspector for the rendered track and enter a negative delay setting equal to the offset. **Figure 18.13** shows 27 milliseconds entered for that parameter.

Of course, this offset problem may not occur in your work, so don't worry about it unless it shows up visually or audibly in your projects.

Rendering Multiple Tracks

The same basic rules used to render a single track apply when you need to render more than one track. Set up all of the tracks, with effects if you want them, so that the master output sounds exactly as you wish; then render to a new file. Rendering multiple tracks is useful in many musical contexts. For instance, you may want to create a single stereo file of a multiple-microphone drum part, or if you have multitrack backing vocals that you have edited, tuned, and tweaked to sound just right, you may want to create a single stereo file so you can control all of the backing vocals in the mix with one fader.

Figure 18.14 A group of channels ready for rendering.

To render more than one track:

1. Set each track, including pan, level, and send and insert effects, so the master output sounds as you wish.

2. Solo all of the tracks you want to include in, or mute all tracks you want to exclude from, the rendered file (**Figure 18.14**).

3. Check to see that the master fader is set to 0.00 (**Figure 18.15**), unless you want the overall level of the rendered file to change.

Figure 18.15 Setting the master fader to 0.00.

4. Set the left locator where you want the rendered file to start, and set the right locator where you want the rendered file to end.

5. From the File menu, select Export > Audio Mixdown.

6. In the Export Audio Mixdown dialog box, type a name for the rendered file and set the options you want. In this example, change the Channels setting to Stereo Interleaved to create a single file with two channels of audio (**Figure 18.16**).

7. Click Save to start the file rendering process.

Figure 18.16 Because a stereo drum mix is being exported, you must be sure to create a stereo file.

Figure 18.17 Setting the fader of the ReWire channel to 0.00.

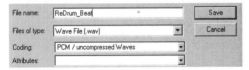

Figure 18.18 Naming the file to be exported.

Figure 18.19 Selecting the correct ReWire outputs.

✔ Tip

■ Look at Figure 18.19 again. Note that the pop-up menu can be used to render any channel in the mixer, including audio and VSTi channels. This can be very, very convenient if you know you need only a snippet or loop as a discrete file.

Rendering ReWire Tracks

Track rendering is also very convenient when you are working with ReWire applications—for instance, when you create a loop in Live, program a beat using the pattern sequencers included with Reason, or trigger a synth sound in another ReWire application. Working with these applications in real time is great, but when a track is ready to be mixed, the easiest approach often is to print everything to an audio file in Cubase. You can still use the method described earlier—solo and render—but you can also use a new feature in SX 2 that lets you choose specific mixer channels for rendering. The following example does just that.

To render ReWire tracks:

1. In the Cubase mixer, set the channel fader for the ReWire channel you want to render to 0.00 (**Figure 18.17**), or to a higher or lower value if you want to raise or lower the output of the rendered file.

2. Set the left and right locators at the beginning and end of the section you want to render.

3. From the File menu, select Export > Audio Mixdown.

4. In the Export Audio Mixdown panel, name the file (**Figure 18.18**).

5. Click the Outputs pop-up menu and select ReWire and then the specific output you want to render (**Figure 18.19**).

6. If you want to change the type of file or sample rate before rendering, do so.

7. Click Save to render the file.

Creating a Final Mix

After all of the recording, editing, and mixing is finished, you need to create a final stereo mix of your song. If you are using external effects or triggering hardware synths and samplers, you will have to record the final mix in real time. If, on the other hand, all of your files are inside Cubase and all of the effects still in use are software plug-ins, you can render the final mix.

To render a final mix:

1. Configure the full mix to play precisely as you want it, including mixer automation, effects, VSTi, and ReWire tracks.

2. Set the left locator a bit before the song begins, and set the right locator a bit after the song ends.

3. From the File menu, select Export > Audio Mixdown (**Figure 18.20**).

4. In the Export Audio Mixdown dialog box that opens, name the file (**Figure 18.21**) and set other parameters as you wish.

   When rendering a final mix, you should choose at least 24 bits for the output file. You should also decide whether you want to import the final mix back into the project (where you can solo it and listen to it), or—if you are sure that you're happy with it—export it as a new, separate file.

5. Check to be sure you're rendering the correct output. You'll probably want the default, which is your main stereo bus, but check the Outputs pop-up to be sure.

6. Click Save to render the mix.

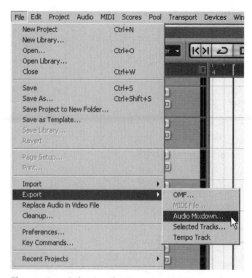

Figure 18.20 Selecting the Export option.

Figure 18.21 Naming the final mix FinalMix01.

Bits, Floats, and Rates

Cubase supports a number of options for exporting files, whether they are individual tracks and loops or full mixes. You can export files with a sample rate of from 8 to 96 kHz and with a bit depth of 8, 16, 24, or 32.

When choosing the sample rate, you need to consider the sample rate of the project itself and the sample rate of the delivery format. If you plan to deliver the mix on CD, for example, at some point the mix will have to become a 16-bit, 44.1-kHz file because that is the only kind of file that an audio CD can use. More often than not, your CD projects will have been recorded at 44.1 kHz, so this will not be an issue. If for some reason your project was recorded at another sample rate, such as 96 kHz, you can export to 44.1 kHz from within Cubase, or you can keep the final mix at 96 kHz and create the 44.1-kHz file later. In general, you should export the stereo mix at the project sample rate. This gives you a file with the highest fidelity possible, and you can use it to create a CD-compatible audio file if you need it.

For bit depth, use 8 bits only in situations where file size is critical. Most situations where you would consider an 8-bit file are better served by one of the compressed file formats described later in this chapter, such as MP3 or Ogg Vorbis.

Use 16-bit files if you are exporting a file to create a CD or to load into a hardware sampler or for any situation where you know you need a 16-bit file.

Cubase can use both 16- and 24-bit files in the same project, and in this case, you should render to a 24-bit file, to preserve as much of the fidelity as possible.

To create an even higher-resolution file, you can use the 32-bit float setting, but not many programs can read these files; use this setting only if you plan to bring the rendered file back into Cubase or another application that you know reads 32-bit float files.

You should consider a number of factors when deciding whether to create 32-bit float files. Internally, Cubase (and nearly all VST plug-ins and instruments) work with 32-bit float audio. When Cubase writes audio to disk or sends audio to the sound card for conversion to analog format, the audio is turned back into a 24- or 16-bit file. Exporting or rendering 32-bit float files keeps absolutely the highest resolution available in the project. However, 32-bit float files are large—twice as large as a 16-bit file, and a third again as large as a 24-bit file—and, as mentioned earlier, fewer programs can open them. Check with your own ears and assess your own equipment to weigh the trade-offs.

Creating a Surround Mix

The previous example created a stereo mix, and although the process for creating a surround mix is similar, there are a few differences. The primary difference is that you need to decide what kind of files you want to export, and how many of them. Most of the time, you'll be importing your surround mix into another application so you can add it to a video, burn it to a DVD audio disc, or compress it for some other release format. Most of those applications will expect that you have exported discrete files: one for each speaker and the subwoofer if one is present. However, Cubase SX 2 and some other applications can also read interleaved files, where one file contains the data from all six channels. If you're going to import the surround mix back into Cubase, you can probably render an interleaved mix, but if you plan to work in another application for final authoring, you'll probably want to export discrete files.

To create a surround mix:

1. After completing all editing on your mix, set the left locator at the beginning and the right locator at the end of the mix.

2. From the File menu, choose Export > Audio Mixdown.

3. In the Export Audio Mixdown panel, open the Outputs menu and select your surround bus (**Figure 18.22**).

4. Open the Channels menu and select Interleaved or Split for your rendered files (**Figure 18.23**).

5. Name the file or files to be created and set the parameters for the type and characteristics of the file, such as its sample rate (**Figure 18.24**).

Figure 18.22 Selecting the surround bus to be exported.

Figure 18.23 This setting will create six discrete audio files: one for each channel in the 5.1 mix.

Figure 18.24 With all settings correct, clicking the Save button will export the surround mix.

Figure 18.25 Choosing MP3 as the output file type.

Figure 18.26 Normally, you should create a final mix in stereo.

Figure 18.27 The options for exporting a stereo MP3 file: the higher the Kbps value, the higher the quality of the audio.

Creating an MP3 Mix

The Web has spawned a group of compressed file formats for audio. A CD-ready, 16-bit, 44.1-kHz stereo file consumes about 10MB of disk space per minute of audio. At some future date, that size will no doubt seem small, but not many people today want to stream 45MB of data from a server to play a four-and-a-half-minute song. MP3 has become the most prominent compressed audio format on the Web because it lets you create files that are fairly small and can sound pretty decent.

Never export your final mix, or even a loop, as an MP3 file. All of the compressed file formats discussed here should be used only for creating files that you put on the Web or distribute in some way other than on a CD. In other words, create your final mix in an uncompressed file format—then create a mix in a compressed format if you like. You use the same methods in Cubase to create an MP3 file that you use to create a WAV or AIFF file, but when you select MP3 (**Figure 18.25**), you have another set of options for the file you will create:

◆ The **Channels** radio buttons let you select stereo or mono output (**Figure 18.26**). In Cubase, you can create higher-resolution files only with this option set to Stereo.

◆ Use the **Attributes** menu to choose a resolution for the MP3 file that you are exporting (**Figure 18.27**). The higher the bit rate, the better the audio quality, and the larger the file created.

◆ The **Quality** setting determines whether the MP3 file is created more quickly or with higher quality. Most of the time, you should set Quality to Highest to get the best-sounding MP3.

◆ If you select the MP3PRO box, the file size will be smaller than that of normal MP3 files, but the sound will be almost as good.

Creating an Ogg Vorbis Mix

MP3 files are by far the most common type of compressed audio files in the world, but not everyone likes everything about them. One potential problem with MP3 files is that the format is patented and subject to license fees in some circumstances. Ogg Vorbis is an open-source, patent-free alternative for compressed audio. If you want more information about Ogg Vorbis files, a good place to start is www.vorbis.com.

The process for creating an Ogg Vorbis file in Cubase is almost exactly the same as for creating an MP3 file. Prepare the mix exactly as you wish, set the locators, choose File > Export > Audio Mixdown, and select Ogg Vorbis File from the drop-down menu (**Figure 18.28**). You then have the following options:

◆ As with MP3 files, you can create either mono or stereo files. You'll almost always want a stereo file when creating a final mix (**Figure 18.29**).

◆ Click the **Quality** drop-down menu to choose among three options (**Figure 18.30**). Normally, you should choose Highest to get the best audio quality, but if you need a smaller file, you can choose Fast or Medium.

Figure 18.28 Choosing Ogg Vorbis as the file type.

Figure 18.29 Selecting Stereo for the Ogg Vorbis file.

Figure 18.30 Ogg Vorbis files have only three quality options.

Figure 18.31 Setting the file type to be exported to RealAudio.

Figure 18.32 With RealAudio files, you can choose the speed of the connection you stream to.

Figure 18.33 RealAudio files also allow you to choose the source audio to be compressed.

Creating a RealAudio Mix—PC Only

Another common Web-centric audio format is RealAudio. This format was created by RealNetworks (www.real.com), and the files have the extension .rm. RealAudio files are attractive primarily because they are very small and thus are easy to stream over a variety of types of network connections. Generally, they are not great-sounding files, so you may not want to choose RealAudio files if you are after the highest fidelity.

You can use Cubase to create RealAudio G2 files (**Figure 18.31**). After you've set the mix, locator, and export parameters, you can choose between two sets of options for creating RealAudio files:

◆ A **G2** file has two sets of options. Use the Coding menu (**Figure 18.32**) to choose the kind of network connection you expect will be used by the person playing back the file. Use the Content menu (**Figure 18.33**) to describe the source material of the mix, to give the compression algorithm an idea of how to compress the file for the best results.

As of this writing, the Real Audio export option is not available for Mac users of Cubase SX 2.

Creating a Windows Media Mix—PC Only

Windows Media files are created in a proprietary format written by Microsoft. They are usually quite small but maintain decent audio quality. They have the file extension .wma. Usually, people create WMA files to stream them over a Windows media or Web server. There is only one drop-down menu for creating a Windows Media mix. Use the **Attributes** menu (**Figure 18.34**) to choose the network connection speed of the computer that will be downloading the file. Choosing a faster network connection speed will create a larger file with higher-quality audio.

You can also use Cubase to create a Windows Media Pro file, an updated version of the WMA specification. The big news here is that you can create a compressed 5.1 mix, with the caveat that only Windows XP machines with new versions of DirectX and the right hardware can play them. Still, it's a start. If you click the Options button, the configuration panel for exporting a WMA Pro file will open (**Figure 18.35**). The default settings shown are a good place to start. If you want more control, there is a lot you can change; check the electronic documentation that comes with Cubase for more information if you are working with compressed surround mixes.

Unfortunately, only the Windows version of Cubase SX 2 offers export options for creating Windows Media files.

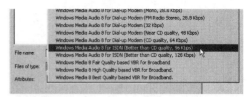

Figure 18.34 The options for creating a Windows Media file.

Figure 18.35 The setup panel for exporting a Windows Media Pro mix.

Streaming Format Considerations

Compressed audio is normally used for streaming over a Web or media server, and the kind of server will usually determine the kind of file you want to create. Some Web servers can stream only RealAudio files, while others can stream only Windows Media files.

To create fairly good-sounding, small files for sharing with friends over the Web or burning to CDs, you should probably choose MP3. Pretty much every computer in the world these days can play back an MP3 file. If you are an open-source advocate, Ogg Vorbis files offer a patent-free alternative to MP3. You should use the other formats only when the particular streaming technology demands it.

19

MASTERING

In the old days, *mastering* referred to the arcane and difficult process of making a master disc from analog tapes. This master disc was sent to a duplication plant, where it was the template for pressing vinyl records. A mastering engineer was the person who prepared tracks to get consistent level and sound and also made sure that the needle wouldn't skip out of the groove on the finished product. It was a one-shot, real-time process, and if the cut master didn't sound right or a fade was too early, another master had to be made.

The digital era changed this. Duplication houses have been taking burned CDs for years now, so in theory, anyone with a CD burner can make a CD master. Mastering engineers tend to be rather smart people, and they've transformed themselves quite effectively from vinyl jockeys to digital gurus. Because anyone can now make a master CD, professional mastering engineers make their money by making your CD sound as good as possible.

The techniques in this chapter will help you understand what goes on in a professional mastering session, and you can use the same techniques to master your own songs. You will learn how to create a mastering project; how to sequence tracks, create fade-ins and fade-outs, and control the level and sound of each song; and how to export the final 16-bit files to burn to a CD.

The Case for Professional Mastering

If you are releasing a CD on a commercial label or plan to print CDs in large quantities to be sold for profit, you should seriously consider hiring a professional mastering engineer. Top mastering engineers have the experience, ears, and gear to make your mixes sound fantastic. They spend their lives listening to full program material and getting it to sound its best, and they are paid handsomely to do so. A good mastering engineer can make a huge difference in the sound of your tracks and can be worth every penny he or she charges.

There are also bad mastering engineers, just as there are bad recording engineers, bad drummers, and bad kissers. You should avoid all of them with equal determination. It's entirely appropriate to ask for a sample from a mastering engineer, and be sure to ask for—and listen to—"before" and "after" tracks before agreeing to a deal.

Even if you decide to have your tracks mastered by a professional, you can still be a more informed and productive client by mastering on your own in Cubase. Think of your work as a rehearsal mastering session. Armed with the information in this chapter about fades, song sequencing, and the sound of tracks, you should have a more productive experience at your mastering sessions.

Figure 19.1 Creating a new folder for the mastering project.

Creating a Mastering Project

The first thing to do when mastering your own music is to get all of the songs in the proper form at the highest quality possible. When you talk to your mastering engineer, ask him or her what types of files work best in the mastering studio. Usually you will be asked to create 24-bit AIFF or WAV files at the sample rate of the project. The mastering engineer will make all of the sonic changes necessary and then create the 16-bit, 44.1-kHz files necessary for burning a CD. Here's how to create those files and how to start your own mastering project.

To start a mastering project:

1. Using the techniques discussed in Chapter 18, "Exporting and Rendering Tracks," create stereo files of all of your songs with at least 24-bit resolution. Render those stereo mixes to a separate, distinct folder.

2. Start Cubase and create a new, empty project by selecting File > New Project and selecting the empty template.

   You will be prompted to select a folder for the project in the Select Directory dialog box.

3. Navigate to the folder where you keep your Cubase projects and click the Create button to make a new folder. Name the folder and click OK to create it (**Figure 19.1**).

4. Click OK again in the Select Directory dialog box to dismiss it.

   You will be returned to the Cubase Project window.

continues on next page

5. In the new, empty project, click the File menu and select Import > Audio File.

6. On the Import Audio dialog box that opens, find and select all of the mixes you want to master (**Figure 19.2**) and click Open to import them.

7. In the Import Options dialog box, make sure Copy Files to Working Directory is checked and click OK (**Figure 19.3**).

8. Save the Cubase project by clicking the File menu and selecting Save.

✔ Tip

■ By using the techniques in this task, you've left your original mixes alone. You're working on copies made in the working directory for the mastering project. Any changes you make will be on those copies, and you can take the originals to the mastering studio by burning a CD of those original files.

Figure 19.2 You can use the Import Audio dialog box to import multiple tracks simultaneously.

Figure 19.3 If you check the Copy Files to Working Directory box, you will leave your original mixes intact and work only on copies.

Figure 19.4 A mastering project with nine songs imported.

Figure 19.5 Each song is on its own track, so it's easy to move the songs around and try different sequences.

Figure 19.6 This menu changes the mode for Snap. Events + Cursor is a particularly good choice when mastering.

Sequencing Songs

If you create a project for mastering as described in the previous task, you will wind up with something that looks like **Figure 19.4**. One of the great advantages of this approach is that you will have each song on its own stereo track in Cubase, and the events created will include the name of the song.

With this approach, you can experiment easily with the sequence of songs for your project. Simply drag the files to change the order. **Figure 19.5** shows three tracks set up so that track 3 plays first, then track 1, and then track 2.

✔ Tip

- When you're sequencing a dozen tracks, your project may last an hour. You will have to be zoomed out very far to view all of these tracks, and snapping edits to the closest bar won't really be effective. Here's a useful trick when you're zoomed out really far in a project: Change the way Snap works. Click the Snap menu and select Events + Cursor (**Figure 19.6**), which will make any object you move snap to the location of the cursor either at the beginning or end of any other event.

Adding Fades

Fades are used in mastering for two main purposes. The first is to fade out the end of a song that doesn't naturally stop at a particular point. Rock songs with long instrumental codas are commonly faded out this way. The second reason to use a fade is to fade one track out while fading the next track in. DJs have long done this live. It's called crossfading, and it's often used in electronic and pop music to create one long piece of music with some or all tracks joined.

Regardless of how you will be using fades, you will be in a much better position at your professional mastering session if you have a good idea of when you want fades to start and stop. The following example locates both fade-in and fade-out points for a track.

To find fade-in and fade-out points:

1. If Event Infoline is not turned on, turn it on by clicking its button on the toolbar (**Figure 19.7**).

2. Click the track in the Project window to select it.

    Figure 19.8 shows a selected song and the Event Infoline information for it. Note the Length, Fade-in, and Fade-out numbers.

3. Use the handles—the blue triangles at the start and end of the event—to set the fade-in and fade-out times.

4. Use the Event Infoline values to determine when fades should start and stop.

    Figure 19.9 shows the track with both a fade-in and a fade-out. Doing a little math, you can see that the fade-in will finish about 20 seconds into the track, and the fade-out will start about 2:35 seconds into the track.

Figure 19.7 The toolbar button for Show Event Infoline.

Figure 19.8 Some of the information displayed on the Event Infoline when an audio event is selected.

Figure 19.9 With a fade-in and fade-out set, the Event Infoline can be used to calculate when fades start and stop.

✔ Tips

- You should write down your guesses on fade-in and fade-out times to report to your mastering engineer. He or she will be very excited to learn that you've even thought about such things, and you'll look like you really know what you're doing. You might wind up deciding to change the fade points, but at least you'll have an idea of where to start.

- If you think this process is kind of irritating and nonmusical, you're right. You can always hire someone else to do all of this.

ADDING FADES

Figure 19.10 The Channel Settings window is great for mastering. You can see all of your effects and edit EQ graphically.

Master or Mix

Whether you're mastering on your own or prepping songs for a professional mastering session, you may find situations where a track sounds more than a little bit off. Problems that didn't seem worth fixing in the mix, such as a bad edit or an instrument that is clearly too loud, can become frighteningly obvious when you're listening carefully at a mastering session. It's often hard to see the big picture when mixing each individual track, and sometimes an obvious problem will crop up in a mix when you're mastering the finished mixes.

This is a great argument for doing at least a first pass at mastering a CD yourself. You can always go back and make a few changes in the final mix if the synth pad is too loud or the acoustic guitars disappear in the chorus. Part of finishing a CD is deciding that it's really done, since you don't want to spend 10 years on one CD, but if mastering reveals a flaw in a mix, you can usually fix it fairly quickly if you know exactly what the problem is.

Applying EQ

One of the main reasons to pay for professional mastering is to gain access to bending-end EQ and compression hardware. A good mastering house may have EQ modules pulled from famous British consoles, modern EQs specifically created for mastering full mixes, and a collection of famous old compressors worth more than a nice house. Your mastering engineer ought to have some really special units available to tailor the sound of your tracks. EQ can be used in a huge variety of ways when mastering, but there are usually two main reasons for using EQ.

First, a song may be generally weak in high-end or low-end sound. This may not be obvious when mixing each individual track, but one or two tracks may stick out sonically in a way that is unpleasant when they are compared as a group.

The second situation where EQ may be necessary is to make small corrective EQ changes. One part of the frequency spectrum may be a bit too pronounced, making one instrument stick out too much. With luck, good ears, and good equipment, a mastering engineer can make the kinds of changes needed.

When working in Cubase, you may want to use the Channel Settings window (**Figure 19.10**) to test some of these actions on a track. If you find that some EQ changes help the sound of a track, write down the settings you use and take them to the mastering session.

Applying Compression

Compression, which controls the level of a signal, was discussed in Chapter 14, "Audio Effect Plug-ins." In that chapter, you learned how to use compression on an individual track, such as a vocal or bass track. Compression on a full mix is a very different concept, because the compressor may be working with a mix that includes dozens of different instruments. Each instrument has its own characteristics, and it is very difficult to set a compressor to work with full program material.

The solution to this problem is to use multiband compression. A multiband compressor divides the frequency spectrum into two, three, four, or more slices. Each slice has its own settings for the typical compression parameters of attack, decay, and release. Multiband compression keeps a strong note in the bass, for example, from triggering a compressor to decrease the level of the whole track.

New to version 2 of Cubase SX is the Multiband Compressor plug-in (**Figure 19.11**). This looks like a fairly simple plug-in, but don't let its looks fool you. It offers two main editors and a few settings:

◆ The Frequency Bands editor (**Figure 19.12**) shows the number of bands being used in the compressor, the high- and low-frequency boundaries of each band, and the level of each band.

◆ The Characteristics editor (**Figure 19.13**) works just like the Threshold and Ratio editor in the VST Dynamics plug-ins. When you click a band in the Frequency Bands editor, the breakpoints for that band can be edited.

Figure 19.11 The Multiband Compressor plug-in, new with version 2 of Cubase SX.

Figure 19.12 This part of the plug-in controls the frequency bands.

Figure 19.13 This editor controls the attack and threshold for each frequency band.

APPLYING COMPRESSION

Figure 19.14 The additional settings for the multiband compressor.

Figure 19.15 A decent starting point for a mastering compressor: three bands using roughly the same characteristics.

Figure 19.16 A third-party VST plug-in: The middle section is a four-band multiband compressor.

◆ The remaining options are at the lower right of the plug-in (**Figure 19.14**). The Mode setting toggles between Classic mode, where the plug-in works like a group of single-band compressors with fixed settings, and Complex mode, where the plug-in tries to adapt the settings in real time to work with what is being compressed. Soft Clip prevents all clipping at the output stage by throttling down peaks that may be too high for the output. Solo plays back only the currently selected band. The Output knob can be used to raise or lower the overall level of the audio after it has been run through the plug-in.

Multiband compressors are very difficult to use well and very easy to abuse. This is one of the reasons mastering engineers get paid well: they have difficult-to-acquire and hard-to-use skills. If you want to try using the plug-in, a reasonable place to start is with settings like the ones in **Figure 19.15**. The example preset starts with three frequency bands. The first band covers the lower three octaves, from 20 Hz up to about 160 Hz. The middle band goes from there up to the upper mid-range at 3.5 kHz, and the high band extends from there up to 20 kHz. Just spending some time soloing these three bands can give you a better idea of the timbral content of your mix.

If you want to get deeper into mastering, you also might want to invest in some specialized mastering plug-ins. **Figure 19.16** shows Dynasone, from Prosoniq software, my personal favorite "soup-to-nuts" mastering plug-in. This plug-in includes a versatile four-band compressor, a limiter, low- and high-frequency enhancement, excellent metering, and very clean sound quality throughout. It also won't force you to skip a car payment to pay for it.

Applying Master Effects

So far, when you've applied effects like EQ and compression, you've used them on individual tracks. These are the most common kinds of effects that you'll apply when mastering, but sometimes you'll want to include an effect for all tracks. The easiest way to do this is to use master effects.

Figure 19.17 Click this button to display the master fader.

Master effects are very much like insert effects on a mixer channel, but instead they apply to the full mix sent to the master fader. You should use a master effect when you want to apply a change to every track on a CD. You may want to put a final bit of gentle compression on all songs, or you may want to use a limiter plug-in to control stray peaks that occur in a song. If you are getting ready for a professional mastering session, write down any master effects that you use and the settings that you think sound the best so you can explain to your mastering engineer what you heard in the effect that improved the songs.

Figure 19.18 Setting the output channel to show inserts.

To apply a master effect:

1. Open the Cubase mixer by selecting Devices > Mixer or by pressing F3.

2. In the Cubase mixer, click the button to show the mixer channels for the outputs configured in VST Connections (**Figure 19.17**).

3. Open the extended mixer and select Inserts to show insert effects (**Figure 19.18**).

4. Add any effects you want on the entire mastering project to the insert slots for the main output.

✔ Tip

■ Master effects slots 7 and 8 are different in one important way from the other slots: They are applied after the master fader. Usually these slots will be used for effects that are involved in file exporting—things like sample-rate conversion or conversion of a 24-bit file to a 16-bit file.

Do-It-Yourself Mastering

The previous sections of this chapter assume that you're taking your songs to a professional engineer for mastering. If that's your plan, you can use this chapter to help create a set of detailed notes that you can take to the mastering session. You will know when tracks should be faded in and faded out, you'll have a good idea about which tracks need EQ to make them fit into the whole CD, and you'll have some ideas about other changes that may need to be made.

While a top-flight mastering engineer will truly make a dramatic difference in the sound of a final CD, there are situations where the best idea is to master your own CD. For example, you may not be able to afford mastering, you may be putting together only a rough CD to use for promotion, or you may be making a CD just to send to other musicians to help them learn material. If you decide to master your own songs, you have a few more steps to complete:

◆ You will need to export each song as a new file, including insert effects such as compression and EQ.

◆ You may need to apply master effects to each song on the CD.

◆ You must create files that can be used by your CD-burning application to make a CD. Usually this means 16-bit, 44.1-kHz AIFF or WAV files.

Most of these processes are described elsewhere in this book, but when exporting mixes, there are a few small tricks to make the process a bit easier. Set up each mix exactly as you wish, including EQ, compression, and level settings, and follow the steps described here.

To create mastered files:

1. In the Project window, click the first track of the CD.

2. Open the contextual menu and select Transport > Locators to Selection (**Figure 19.19**).

   This will set the left and right locators at the beginning and end of the selected event.

3. Click the File menu and select Export > Audio Mixdown (**Figure 19.20**) to render a new file of the track.

4. In the Export Audio Mixdown dialog box that opens, name the track.

   A good approach is to name the tracks with a number so the sequence will be obvious. In **Figure 19.21**, the track has been renamed and begins with a number.

5. Select Stereo Interleaved, 16-bit, 44.1-kHz in the Export Audio Mixdown dialog box, as in Figure 19.21.

6. Uncheck the Import to Pool and Audio Track options, as in Figure 19.16. Normally, you will not want or need to import the final 16-bit songs back into the master project.

7. Click Save to render the new file.

8. Repeat steps 1 through 7 for each track of the CD.

✔ Tip

■ Choosing Stereo Split rather than Stereo Interleave in the Audio Mixdown dialog box will split the stereo into separate left and right mono files.

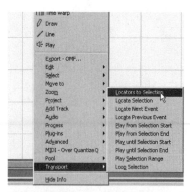

Figure 19.19 This option sets the left and right locators to the boundaries of a selected event.

Figure 19.20 Selecting Audio Mixdown to render a mastered track.

Figure 19.21 Naming the track and setting the parameters for the track to create a 16-bit, 44.1-kHz, stereo file.

A Tale of Two Masters

I don't call myself a mastering engineer because I'm not one. One of the things I do in my studio, though, is what I call CD post-production. I take files or tapes from bands or record labels and make sure the levels are right and the fades are done properly, and I produce a CD with a cue sheet that can be sent to a duplication facility. If asked, I'll also compress and EQ the tracks. The reason I don't call this mastering is because I don't think I'm brilliant at it, I don't have proper mastering gear in my studio, and I just don't like the loaded nature of the term.

I started doing CD post-production when a band I had known and liked for years brought me their newly mastered CD. This band plays very clean, quiet rock—very much in the style of "Candy Says"-era Lou Reed and early R.E.M. They had spent two years, working a few weekends a month and a few full weeks a year, in an all-analog recording studio located in a barn. The band recorded to 2-inch analog tape and mixed with very few effects and no automation on a big, old analog mixing board. The first trip the audio made into the digital domain was when the mixes were recorded to a DAT tape.

Armed with this DAT tape, the group went to a quite expensive mastering house in New Jersey. They came to me after the session because they just didn't think the final CD sounded right, and they wanted my opinion. Listening to the DAT versus the mastered CD was unbelievable. The original DAT mixes had sections so quiet and delicate that you could hear birds chirping outside the barn, and the mastered CD sounded overly compressed, like a Celine Dion record broadcast over AM radio. The mastered CD was loud, for sure, but did a horrible job of representing the sweat and time the band had put into the songs.

The band was pretty much drained of cash from the recording and mastering costs, but they were all friends of mine, so I told them I would give their songs a shot. I took their mixes, loaded them into Cubase, and used a third-party multiband compressor and a little EQ. The songs held together well and had a consistent sonic thumbprint, so it was easy to get a general idea of what small changes to make to get them sounding nice and buffed.

I wouldn't be telling this story if the band didn't print the CD using every one of my mastered mixes. This doesn't mean I'm a super-brilliant mastering engineer—I'm not. What it does mean is that even if a guy has a $40,000 Pro Tools rig in an anechoic chamber in an industrial park, he still may squash your acoustic jazz trio CD until it has the dynamic range of a Metallica record. If you hire a mastering engineer, make sure you are prepared to speak your mind and get the results for which you are paying.

Using UV22 Dithering

There are lots of factors that can make digital audio sound terrible, including clipping, bad converters, and bad levels from the analog source. You can avoid those mistakes by recording with care, but some processes that can cause audible problems in digital audio are unavoidable. One of these is conversion of a 24- or 32-bit file to a 16-bit file. For complex mathematical reasons, this process creates an inevitable amount of low-level audio trash.

You are better off recording at 24 bits in your Cubase projects, but at some point you will need to create 16-bit files that can be burned to a CD. This will create some of that sonic trash, and the way to deal with this is a process called dithering. Dithering puts a tiny amount of noise in the converted file, and this low level of noise masks the sonic junk introduced in converting the 24-bit file to 16 bits.

The minutiae of various dithering algorithms and the particular type of noise used in the dithering process are the kinds of details that generate almost never-ending debate among audio geeks. You're in luck, though, because Cubase includes a very high-quality dithering plug-in called UV22. There are two versions of the plug-in: the UV22 (**Figure 19.22**) and the UV22HR (**Figure 19.23**). Both do the same thing and differ only in that the UV22HR allows you to specify the bit depth of the file whereas the UV22 automatically dithers to 16 bits. Both plug-ins use technology licensed from Apogee, a top audio hardware manufacturer, and both are in the "Other" section of the plug-ins list.

◆ You select the dithering algorithms by clicking the **Normal** or **Low** button. Normal works for nearly all situations; Low introduces the smallest amount of dithering noise.

Figure 19.22 The UV22 dithering plug-in: This version dithers only to 16 bits.

Figure 19.23 The UV22HR plug-in does the same thing as the UV22 but includes options to create other than 16-bit files.

◆ **Autoblack** creates true silence during sections that are so quiet that the dithering noise is more likely to be noticed.

◆ **Bit Resolution** (UV22HR only) sets the output to 8, 16, 20, or 24 bits. This option is available only in the UV22HR plug-in. When exporting, you should be sure that the setting in the UV22HR plug-in matches the resolution you are rendering in the final mix.

GLOSSARY

ASIO: Steinberg developed ASIO as a cross-platform protocol for transferring multiple channels of audio to and from an audio interface at very low latencies. Always use the ASIO driver for your audio interface when working with Cubase.

Audio Event: Events are the smallest building block in Cubase. An audio event is a single audio clip or part of a clip that is displayed in the Project window. More than one event can be contained in an audio part, and much confusion about events arises from this fact. An event is the audio itself, the part is a container in Cubase to hold one or more events. See also, Audio Regions.

Audio Interface: The hardware used to get audio in and out of the computer is called the audio interface. Audio interfaces can use USB or Firewire to connect to the computer, or they can be PCI cards that install inside the machine.

Audio Part: (see *Part*)

Audio Region: An audio region is a part of an audio clip (event). When an audio file is recorded with Cubase, it creates an audio clip to represent that file for editing and processing. Parts of a clip can be designated as

independent audio regions, which can then be easily converted to additional events in the project window, or exported and processed into new discrete audio files. Audio regions are almost always created and edited in the Sample Editor.

Automation: Moves and actions performed in the Cubase mixer can be automated. After writing automation, the mixer can reproduce the moves automatically when the project is played.

Bit Depth: When an analog audio is sampled to create digital audio (see *sample rate*), each sample can be of greater or lesser resolution. Cubase can record 16, 24, or 32-bit samples. The bit depth for an audio file or project is the resolution of the recorded samples—for example, a CD uses 16-bit samples—therefore it has a bit depth of 16.

Breakpoint: When a parameter is displayed graphically, and its setting changes over time, Cubase often will use breakpoints to show a change in direction or value for the parameter. Breakpoints are used extensively for things like setting a fade-in or fade-out curve, or for editing automation data.

CC Data: (see *MIDI Continuous Controller Data*)

Comping is taking multiple passes at the same musical part or phrase and selecting the best parts of each to create a new performance. Cubase has extensive tools for creating comps in the Audio Part editor.

Core Audio is the system-level multimedia toolkit that ships with Mac OS X that includes a driver type and plug-in format. Most Mac Cubase users will use ASIO drivers and VST effects, but other applications (and perhaps Cubase in the future) might use Core Audio.

Crossfade: When two audio parts or events are immediately adjacent to each other or overlap, the transition between them will often sound unpleasant. A crossfade quickly fades one out while fading the other in, smoothing the transition between the parts or events.

Cycle Recording: It's possible to record in Cubase when looping the project over the same section repeatedly. This is called cycle recording, and can be used to create MIDI and audio by combining the results of more than one pass over the same section of the project.

DirectX is the system-level multimedia toolkit that ships with Windows, which includes driver types and a plug-in format. Usually shortened to DX, this kit is used to support system level audio and MIDI transfer. Most Cubase users will rely on ASIO drivers, but many will have some DX plug-ins and perhaps a DX-supported MIDI interface.

Event: Events are the smallest building blocks in Cubase. An event can be a MIDI note or a sound sample or a recorded piece of audio. In the Project window, every event is contained in a part, and parts contain one or many distinct events.

Group Channel: A group in the Cubase mixer is a specialized channel that is used to mix other channels. A group receives audio from the other channels in the mixer, instead of from an audio track, ReWire channel, or VST instrument.

Insert Effect: An insert effect processes the entire signal for a channel. The entire audio signal from a channel is fed into the effect, the audio is modified in some way, and the audio output with the effect is fed to the rest of the mixer channel.

Mixer Channel: Each channel in the mixer controls an audio signal or a MIDI track. The audio signal can be from a VST instrument, a ReWire application, or an audio track in the Project window. MIDI channels control MIDI data from a track in the Project window.

MIDI stands for Musical Instrument Digital Interface. MIDI data most often is note and velocity information from a keyboard or other MIDI instrument. After MIDI has been recorded, the data can be used to trigger samplers, sound modules, and synthesizers.

MIDI Continuous Controller (CC) Data: Not all MIDI data is about notes. MIDI can also be used to control parameters in synthesizers and effects units. For example, it might be advantageous to record changes made to knobs and buttons on the front panel of a synth. In this case, the changes made on the front panel will be recorded as Continuous Controller data. CC data is edited and can be created manually in Cubase using the Project window, the Key editor, or the List editor.

MIDI Interface: The hardware used to move MIDI data in and out of the computer is a MIDI interface. Most current MIDI interfaces connect to the computer via USB.

MIDI Part: (see *Part*)

MIDI Sysex Data: Sysex stands for System Exclusive. The MIDI specification defines certain commonly used parameters to particular CC numbers, and leaves many CC channels undefined to apply as users and manufacturers see fit. Even this flexibility, however, is not always enough, and sysex data fills the gaps where MIDI is deficient. A manufacturer can use sysex to control any parameters they can dream up, essentially allowing proprietary uses of the open MIDI spec. Sysex is often used to back up and restore the entire state of a synth, effect unit, or studio.

Monitoring: Listening to the playback of a project is called monitoring. The best way to monitor in Cubase will depend on how your audio hardware is configured and what you are doing with Cubase.

Multitimbral: A synth (hardware or software) is said to be multitimbral if it can play different sounds when triggered by different MIDI channels. MIDI channel 1 might trigger a synth bass sound, while MIDI channel 10 triggers drums.

Mute: A track, part, event, note, or mixer channel can be muted. Once muted, it is silenced and will not play back in the project.

Part: A part in the Project window can contain MIDI or audio events. Parts are containers for events, and make it easier to work with more than one event.

Plug-in: Plug-ins are used to process audio and MIDI in the Cubase mixer. Cubase includes some plug-ins and additional, third party plug-ins can be added to the program. A plug-in lets you add sonic options to your palette without having to learn a whole new application.

Polyphonic: A synth is called polyphonic if it can play more than one note at a time. Many of the classic analog synths of the '70s were monophonic, meaning they could play only one note at a time.

Project Tempo: Each Cubase project has an assigned tempo, expressed as beats per minute (BPM). The higher the BPM, the faster the tempo of the project. Cubase has a special track, called the tempo track, for creating and editing changes in project tempo.

Punch Recording: Cubase can automatically start and stop recording at any point in a project. The points where Cubase starts and stops recording (called *punching in* and *punching out)* are set in the project window before starting playback, hence the term punch recording.

Quantize: Quantizing modifies the timing of a MIDI note or notes, usually to bring the MIDI notes closer to a tempo grid. Most often quantizing is applied after creating a MIDI part to tighten the timing of the performance.

Record Enable: When the red Record Enable button is pressed, a track is ready to record. When the Record button on the Transport is activated, whether manually or automatically, all tracks with the Record Enable buttons selected will start recording.

ReWire: Steinberg and Propellerheads jointly developed ReWire, a protocol that allows multiple applications to transfer audio, MIDI, and tempo data. ReWire is used to slave one piece of software to another on the same computer.

Semitone: Western music divides each octave into twelve notes that are all pretty much the same distance from each other. A semitone is the distance in pitch from one note to the adjacent note above or below it. An easy way to visualize a semitone is the piano keyboard: each key is a semitone apart from the next key.

Sample Rate: Digital audio is created by taking a specific number of snapshots (or samples) of an analog audio signal over time. The number of times the analog signal is sampled is called the sample rate. Common sample rates supported by Cubase include 44.1 kHz, 48 kHz, 88.2 kHz, and 96 kHz. At 44.1 kHz (the sample rate for CDs) the signal is sampled 44,100 times each second.

Send Effect: A send effect is an effect that runs parallel to the main path of the audio channel. When using a send effect, a copy of the original signal is split off and sent to the effect, leaving the rest of the audio path for the channel untouched. The audio processed by the send effect is mixed back with the non-effects signal, usually at the master fader.

Solo: When the Solo button is clicked, only that track will be played back. More than one track can be solroed to hear only a few tracks.

Sysex: (see *MIDI Sysex Data*)

Template: A Cubase template is a project that can be opened with the File > New command. You can create customized projects for your various needs, and save them as templates.

Tempo Track: The tempo track is an audible, but usually invisible, track in every Cubase project. The tempo of the project will be governed by the tempo track if the Master button on the transport is clicked on. The tempo track can be graphically edited in the Tempo Track editor.

Track: Cubase tracks are where MIDI and audio data are placed in the Project window. Think of each track like a clothesline: audio and MIDI parts and events are hung on the clothesline as they are recorded, and are rearranged when audio and MIDI are edited.

Transient: The initial part of a sound, particularly on an instrument that is plucked or struck, is called the transient. The transient is the short, loud, initial onset of the sound.

Velocity: Every MIDI note comes with data to represent how hard the MIDI controller was struck. This parameter is called velocity, and usually controls the overall output that results from the MIDI note.

VSTi: VSTi is short for VST (virtual) instrument, and is the general term for software-based sound generators. Most VSTis are synthesizers or samplers that generate sounds when triggered by MIDI.

Word Length: The sample taken when creating digital audio (see *sample rate*) can be of varying resolution. Often the samples are referred to as "words" and the resolution of the sample is called the word length. A project might be recorded with a sample rate of 96 kHz with a word length of 24 bits.

REMIXING "BLUE GLOVE"

Demian Shoemaker and Suzanne McClean of *"Emma's Mini."*

http://magnatune.com/extra/cubase

When we were putting together the second edition of this book, my editor contacted the people at Magnatune (www.magnatune.com), an innovative new record label, about allowing me to remix one of their artists' songs and then post the files on their site so that you can follow along. It's thanks to Magnatune that you can hear not only the before and after versions of "Blue Glove," but you can even download the Cubase SX 2 project file and audio that I used to make my remix. The archive will be about 20 MB to download, so it's not exactly small, but if you go to http://www.magnatune.com/extra/cubase, you can hear not only the remix, but also the building blocks that created it.

The artists who were kind enough to give me one of their songs to remix, Emma's Mini, describe themselves as "electronic pop with a rock edge." I don't think there's much rock edge left in my version, but I do think it's a useful example of what can be done with a track in Cubase. Nearly all of the effects are the stock effects included with SX 2—I did use a few freeware plug-ins that I'll describe as I'm going along, and I also did a little compression on some tracks using the Universal Audio UAD-1 plug-ins that I own. All synth parts are from the included synths.

Emma's Mini recorded the song with an integrated hard disc recorder—not in Cubase. Demian Shoemaker, one half of Emma's Mini, transferred all of the audio files to a computer running Cubase, and sent me a CD of the whole project. I wound up using only a little of the audio they sent me. Because the original track was not made in Cubase, the web site only has the project file and source audio files for my remix. Still, it's not hard to hear the differences between the versions by listening to the before and after MP3s.

The song

The original "Blue Glove" is driven mainly by the female vocal, a strong picked bass line, a four on the floor beat, and some fairly heavy guitars. Of the original tracks, I kept only the vocals. I also decided that just to challenge myself, I wouldn't put any guitars back on the track. Guitar is the only instrument I play well enough that people will pay me for that skill on occasion, so to make myself work harder with Cubase, I didn't use guitars. The track clicks along nicely at 113 bpm, which is a bit out of my comfort zone but fits the song very well. I usually work at very slow tempos, and if a track gets above 130 bpm, I start to think in half time, but as much as I like my dub tracks, working at 56.5 bpm (half of 113) is way too slow for me.

Because of the no-guitars rule, I had to do a little rearranging of the song. The lyrics of the verse go right up to the last beat, and the original has a four-bar descending guitar figure that introduces the chorus. Because I had to chop out that guitar part (shortening the song while doing so), I had to rearrange the chorus a bit. Also, I had to do a few things to get everyone ready for the chorus since there is no pause in the lyrics before the chorus starts.

The other major change is the solo section that in the original was a guitar solo. Of course, this didn't sit well with the zero-guitar rule, but I had a few options. I could have done a big, swirly, synth thing, kind of like a trance tune, or I could have played a different solo. However, I chose to keep only a few parts going and to rearrange the beat for a rhythmic breakdown instead.

Beyond that, the song is pretty standard, with intro, verse, chorus, verse two, chorus, solo, chorus out.

The parts

The song opens with one of the most prominent parts of the song: the electric piano part. Because Cubase has no built-in electric piano, I had to use a different source—in this case, a sample patch in Reason. I loaded a Rhodes Suitcase piano from a commercial Reason ReFill called Dirty 'Ol Relics and

played a simple descending E-minor to C-major figure. I routed the sound via ReWire to a stereo group in Cubase, but rendered the audio and put it on an audio track in SX 2 for you to hear. It's still routed to the Epiano group, so you can turn the effects on and off to hear what's been done to the dry sound. The sound goes through a delay, then a phase shifter, and then a filter. The delay is one of the few third-party effects in the mix; it's a freeware effect from Voxengo (www.voxengo.com) called TempoDelay. Grab it from the Web site if you are a PC user; if you're a Mac user, open the first insert slot on the Epiano, add a Double Delay effect, and open the effects preset called PianoDelay. It will get you pretty close to what was in the mix.

The rhythmic part of the mix consists of a group of drum and percussion parts from a couple of sources. The main beat was programmed using the ReDrum module in Reason; I rendered it and put it on its own track for you to hear. It's a simple beat that, if slowed down, would sound more hip-hop than anything else. The percussion parts are a very prominent shaker that goes through the whole song, a conga loop, and a tabla loop. All three of those parts are from commercial loop CDs, and I edited them and time stretched them in Live. Because of this, they are rendered as a single stereo so I can stay on the right side of the law.

The bass line was played by me and recorded through my sound card. The bass is so ancient and lo-fi I'm not willing to admit it here, but I tracked it through a SansAmp Bass DI. The verse line is looped, mostly to keep the size of the file download reasonable—if I had my way, the bass would have been one of the live tracks, providing a little variation from the heavy looping. The chorus bass line is actually the verse bass line edited. The batteries in my SansAmp ran out, so just to have something to work with, I edited together a bass line. After a while, I got used to it and kind of liked it, so I left it as is.

The verse vocal was treated pretty heavily with a Step Filter plug-in, VST Dynamics (acting only as a limiter to catch peaks), and an effects send to a delay. The original vocal certainly sounded great, but I decided the filtered sound made it pop out a little more. I think because the frequency range is a bit limited, it makes the ear seek out the vocal a little more in the mix.

The chorus vocal consists of two parts. One is a part of a line from the harmony vocal that I cut out to be a discrete part. That short line goes through the SX vocoder in external mode, meaning that one channel has the carrier and the other the speech. In this case, the speech is the vocal itself, and the carrier is an a1 VST instrument being triggered by a MIDI track in Cubase. The MIDI track is called VocodeCarrier; you can experiment with other vocoder settings and carrier tracks for fun. To use the vocoder as I used it here, the tracks need to be panned hard left and right and sent to a group. I named the group Vocode, and after the vocoder insert, the signal goes through a DoubleDelay plug-in and a single band of low-pass EQ, just to get rid of a little of the screech.

The other parts in the song are an arpeggio driving another a1 synth, a pattern-sequenced line driving yet another a1, and various other little snippets of sound played here and there.

The arrangement

The structure of the song is the classic pop song pattern: intro, verse, chorus, verse two, chorus, bridge (solo or something), chorus out. A short description of each section follows. One point to keep in mind is that we have been trained over the years to hear music in

chunks of 4, 8, 16, and 32. Thus, I often do something—change the drum beat, filter a part, and so on—to reinforce the changes that take place in a song at those points.

Because this is an electronic-oriented song, I started the intro with a comparatively non-rhythmic part, to make life a little easier for the DJ trying to fade it in. The first heavy dose of the tempo is the shaker part, which starts at bar 10 in the SX 2 arrangement. Four bars later, the very quiet arpeggio starts at the same time as the drum beat. The only resonant filter plug-in with Cubase is the Step Filter, so to make my life easier, I just set the filter cutoff and resonance flat and used mix automation to control the cutoff point of the filter. Automation also turns off the plug-in just as the first verse starts.

The first verse is the one part of the song where the electric piano drops out, and where the bass line first comes in. I think this helps the vocal pull the ear a little more. The conga part also starts here.

The electric piano makes a (hopefully triumphant) return in the first chorus. The chord changes are different in the chorus, but use the same two E-minor and C-major chords. Because the harmony is so simple, I was able to move the main lyric (the one that isn't vocoded) ahead in time, putting the vocoded part first. Something you may want to try when playing with the mix is moving the vocal parts around in the chorus and changing the vocoder to see if you can find a better sound than I did.

The second verse is almost identical to the first one, save that the Rhodes is back in the mix. I thought there had been enough popping up of new parts and sounds, so decided to give the listener a break and return to familiar ground. This is also the one section of the song where pretty much everything is going on at once.

The second chorus is, once again, fairly close to the first chorus. The tabla part comes in for the first time here; I faded it in so that it's at its highest level about halfway through the chorus. Also, just to keep things a little interesting, I used automation to change some settings on the main vocal filter and bumped up the feedback on the delay as well.

The bridge, breakdown, or solo section is after the second chorus. In the original, there was a guitar solo, but in my version I decided to make the changes rhythmic. Some of my favorite electronic music makers in the world are a bunch of fabulously creative drum'n'bass DJs and producers. Some of them have started doing really creative stuff with heavily edited, very computerish beats next to their dance floor crushers. I'm new to working that way but decided in this song to try my hand at it. I gave myself the first bar of the rendered file and decided to edit and process that loop for as much rhythmic variety as possible. None of the drum'n'bass guys need to worry, I think, but it's interesting in a sample mix like this to try to make the most of the editing tools. You'll notice a lot of crossfades, processed snippets, and other editing tricks if you look closely at this section. I like the play between the tabla, shaker, and edited beat in this section.

The chorus-out section is used to fade out some of the individual tracks, ending with only the shaker and the vocal. Again, ending the song with these parts would make it easy to mix this song with another track, and a tempo change could even be added in a DJ set using the final delayed vocoder.

Your mix

You can do whatever you want to this mix, of course, but here are a few suggestions that might be helpful, and that also point out what I think are the strengths and weaknesses of this mix.

First, I've taken a song with a fairly uplifting message (free yourself!) and given it a slightly spacey, moody, minor-chord feel. Is that really appropriate for the tune? Is there a better way to build the arrangement and parts to match that message?

Next, did I choose the right basic beat for the song? Would a four-on-the-floor beat sound better? There isn't an open hi-hat in the whole tune, so are there ways to improve the beats?

Look at the arrangement; by cutting out the guitar figure that introduces the chorus, did I crowd things too much in the mix? To be honest, I think I did, so I made some changes in the verses to signal to the listener that the chorus is on the way maybe a little sooner than expected. Also in the chorus, is the electric piano too similar to the verse? Again, I think it might be, and if I were to work more on this song, that would be a place I would check.

Big, big thanks to Emma's Mini (and to John Buckman at magnatune.com) for letting me use their song for this exercise. Check out their other tunes at www.magnatune.com when you have the time.

REMIXING "BLUE GLOVE"

INDEX

A

INDEX

INDEX